WHOSE KNOWLEDGE COUNTS IN GOVERNMENT LITERACY POLICIES?

D1553109

"Finally! A book that offers smart thinking about federal literacy education policies by the professionals who know literacy best. . . . This book connects the dots between current literacy policies, who is writing those policies, and what ultimately happens when the policies are implemented in school classrooms. These international scholars provide glimpses of parallel events happening around the world, beg us to question why knowledge about literacy research is being ignored, and challenge us to consider who really gains when 'science' is valued over knowledge."

—Renita Schmidt, The University of Iowa, USA

Accountability, in the form of standardized test scores, is built into government literacy policies around the world, with severe consequences for public schools and districts that fail to meet ever-increasing performance levels. The key question this book addresses is whose knowledge is considered in framing government literacy policies? Distinguished by its global focus on the issue of marginalizing knowledge, it raises awareness of the degree to which expertise is being ignored on a worldwide level and pseudo-science is becoming the basis for literacy policies and laws.

The authors, all leading researchers from the USA, UK, Scotland, France, and Germany, have a wide range of views but share in common a deep concern about the lack of respect for knowledge among policy makers. Each comes to the common subject of this volume from the vantage point of his or her major interests. In some cases that means an exposition of what should be the best knowledge utilized in an aspect of literacy education policy. Others deal more directly with how political decisions are impacting literacy policy. Still others lay out the history of events in their own country. Collectively they offer a critical analysis of the condition of literacy education past and present and suggest alternative courses of action for the future.

Kenneth S. Goodman is Professor Emeritus, Language, Reading and Culture, University of Arizona, USA.

Robert C. Calfee is Professor Emeritus, Stanford University School of Education, USA.

Yetta M. Goodman is Professor Emerita, Language, Reading and Culture, University of Arizona, USA.

WHOSE KNOWLEDGE COUNTS IN GOVERNMENT LITERACY POLICIES?

Why Expertise Matters

Edited by
Kenneth S. Goodman, Robert C. Calfee
and Yetta M. Goodman

Routledge
Taylor & Francis Group

NEW YORK AND LONDON

KH

First published 2014
by Routledge
711 Third Avenue, New York, NY 10017

Simultaneously published in the UK
by Routledge
2 Park Square, Milton Park, Abingdon, Oxon OX14 4RN

Routledge is an imprint of the Taylor & Francis Group, an informa business

© 2014 Taylor & Francis

Library of Congress Cataloging-in-Publication Data

Whose knowledge counts in government literacy policies? : why expertise
matters / edited by Kenneth S. Goodman, Robert C. Calfee, and Yetta M.
Goodman.
     pages cm
     Includes bibliographical references and index.
1. Literacy—Government policy.   2. Expertise—Political
aspects.   3. Decision making.   I. Goodman, Kenneth S., editor of
compilation.   II. Calfee, Robert C., editor of compilation.   III. Goodman,
Yetta M., 1931– editor of compilation.
    LC149.W38   2014
    302.2'244—dc23   2013009875

ISBN: 978-0-415-85800-7 (hbk)
ISBN: 978-0-415-85801-4 (pbk)
ISBN: 978-0-203-79684-9 (ebk)

Typeset in Bembo
by Apex CoVantage, LLC

9/8/15

DEDICATION

This book is dedicated to all Reading Hall of Fame members and others whose contributions advance our understanding of literacy development, instruction, and the impact of socio-political contexts on our work. Yetta and Ken Goodman and Robert Calfee, editors of this volume, deserve specific recognition for their vision and efforts through the years and in the creation of this important collection. We thank them for gathering this outstanding set of papers. They challenge readers to address the political and policy issues surrounding the implementation of "research" findings. By providing valuable international and historical perspectives they deepen our understanding of literacy research and implementation and make our responsibility to respond clear.

This book is also dedicated to all the children whose literacy is the goal of our efforts.

Donna Ogle, National Louis University
President, The Reading Hall of Fame

CONTENTS

FIGURES

TABLES

FOREWORD

This collection of essays highlights the political determination of school knowledge in the field of literacy instruction. As the essays in this volume indicate, this is a global phenomenon resulting from a variety of political forces, including multinational corporations, the World Bank, and USAID. These organizations, as discussed in this volume, promote the same agenda in developing nations in Africa, Asia, and Latin America.

The most recent example in the United States of linking literacy instruction to the needs of multinational corporations is the Common Core State Standards issued in 2010 by the National Governors Association. The political and economic purposes of the Common Core State Standards are clearly given in its mission statement:

> The Common Core State Standards provide a consistent, clear understanding of what students are expected to learn, so teachers and parents know what they need to do to help them. The standards are designed to be robust and relevant to the real world, reflecting the knowledge and skills that our young people need for success in college and careers. *With American students fully prepared for the future, our communities will be best positioned to compete successfully in the global economy.*
>
> (Common Core State Standards, 2013, emphasis added)

Since the 1983 report, *A Nation at Risk: The Imperative for Educational Reform,* declared that public schools were causing the United States to fall behind in global economic competition, there has been a steady drum beat from politicians that school work should result in improving America's global economic prowess (National Commission on Excellence in Education, 1983). The Common Core

State Standards are another step, with important implications for literacy instruction, in this process of aligning schools with the employment needs of multinational corporations. The literacy components of the Common Core State Standards exemplify the overall theme of this book, namely that political and economic education goals increasingly determine the content of literacy instruction.

The effect of aligning literacy instruction with the needs of global economic competition is exemplified by statements made by David Coleman, an architect of the Common Core State Standards and President of the College Board. Coleman argues that in preparing for corporate work students should write fewer personal and opinion pieces. Coleman asserts that in the working world a person would not say: "Johnson, I need a market analysis by Friday, but before that I need a compelling account of your childhood" (Lewin, 2012). Reflecting on the Common Core State Standards, David Liben, a former New York City teacher and now a senior literacy specialist with Student Achievement Partners, told the teachers, that the Common Core "virtually eliminate[s] text-to-self connections" (Gewertz, 2012). Liben directed teachers to eliminate from basal readers any questions dealing with how students feel about a reading along with any questions asking about the meaning of the reading in the students' lives. "In college and careers, no one cares how you feel," Mr Liben said. "Imagine being asked to write a memo on why your company's stock price has plummeted: 'Analyze why and tell me how you feel about it'" (Gewertz, 2012).

Besides focusing on students' abilities to write corporate reports and documents, the Common Core State Standards, despite its global economic goals, stresses the teaching of Americanism. Introducing students to global and multicultural literature is reduced to myths and stories. The Standards state:

> In English language arts, the Common Core State Standards require certain critical content for all students, including: Classic myths and stories from around the world; America's Founding Documents; Foundational American literature: and Shakespeare.
>
> (Common Core State Standards, 2013)

Why include Shakespeare in these reading requirements? Certainly, America's Founding Documents and Foundational American literature can be seen as requirements that boost American nationalism. Shakespeare is certainly a favorite of many English teachers, but there is no proof, as far as I know, that studying Shakespeare will give an economic edge to American workers. The answer may be related to twentieth century arguments against the teaching of multicultural literature in favor of literature that strengthens Anglo-American culture. The argument that United States' institutions are founded on Anglo-American culture, and, therefore, that culture should be strengthened through school instruction, was most clearly made by historian Arthur M. Schlesinger, Jr. in *The Disuniting of America: Reflections on a Multicultural Society* (Schlesinger, 1998). Conservative arguments, like those of Schlesinger, were used in the twentieth century to stop the spread of multicultural literature in schools.

In conclusion, this book exemplifies the continuing political use of literacy instruction. The volume also highlights the global scope of this phenomenon. The Common Core State Standards in literacy illustrates the central theme of this volume by its call to teach, what for a better word I will call, "corporate-speak", and Anglo-American nationalism.

Joel Spring

References

Common Core State Standards. (2013, January 29). *Myths vs. Facts*. Retrieved January 29, 2013, from Common Core State Standards Initiative: www.corestandards.org/about-the-standards/myths-vs-facts

Common Core State Standards. (2013). *Common Core State Standards Initiative*. Retrieved January 29, 2013, from Mission Statement: www.corestandards.org/

Gewertz, C. (2012, May 9). *Teachers Reflect Standards in Basals*. Retrieved January 29, 2013, from Education Week: www.edweek.org/ew/articles/2012/04/26/30basal.h31.html?qs=Gewertz

Lewin, T. (2012, May 16). *Backer of Common Core School Curriculum is Chosen to Lead College Board*. Retrieved January 29, 2013, from New York Times: www.nytimes.com/2012/05/16/education/david-coleman-to-lead-college-board.html?_r=0

National Commission on Excellence in Education. (1983). *A Nation at Risk: The Imperative for Educational Reform*. Washington, DC: U.S. Department of Education.

Schlesinger Jr., Arthur M. (1998). *The Disuniting of America: Reflections on a Multicultural Society: Revised and Enlarged*. New York: W.W. Norton & Company.

ACKNOWLEDGMENTS

The editors are grateful for the support of the members and officers of the Reading Hall of Fame. Their shared concern for our responsibility to speak out for scholarship, wisdom, and fairness in literacy policy making is what inspired this book. While the Reading Hall of Fame encouraged this book, the opinions are those of the separate authors. We also wish to recognize countless teachers, teacher educators, and researchers who maintain their integrity and their professionalism on behalf of the students whose literacy they have devoted their careers to, often at great personal risk. Marie Ruiz and Kelly Allen supported editorial and technical preparation of the manuscript. Special thanks to Naomi Silverman, of Routledge, who encouraged and facilitated the book.

1

INTRODUCTION—KNOWLEDGE, EVIDENCE, AND FAITH

How the Federal Government Used Science to Take Over Public Schools

Robert C. Calfee

In January 2002, President George W. Bush signed the *No Child Left Behind Act* (*NCLB*; PL 107–110), instituting a major federal encroachment on public education in the United States. Prior to *NCLB*, schools operated largely under State control. Neither education nor schools are mentioned in the Constitution, and the Tenth Amendment provides that "The powers not delegated to the United States by the Constitution . . . are reserved to the States respectively, or to the people" (Guthrie, 2013). Most states in turn passed control to local districts.

The Office of Education was established in 1867 to collect information about public schools. With the passage in 1965 of the Elementary and Secondary Act, the federal government assumed significant responsibility for dealing with inequities in public education. In 1979, the Department of Education was established as a cabinet-level unit of the government, in recognition of the increasing priority of education on the national agenda. With the reauthorization of ESEA in 2002 as *NCLB*, the federal government instituted programs of standardized testing and school-level accountability that now significantly influence "what counts"—what is taught, how it is taught, and how it is assessed. The greatest impact of *NCLB* has been on reading instruction in the elementary grades. Based on recommendations of the *National Reading Panel* (*NRP*; NICHD, 2000), the federal *Reading First* program (*RF*) led to widespread adoption of *NRP* recommendations by elementary schools and teachers. Those who had doubts, and there were more than a few, were assured that the practices were supported by *scientific evidence*.

This book looks into this story in the United States, and into similar stories elsewhere around the world. The focus is on literacy, but the implications are far reaching, and go to the core of the intersections of science and politics, of knowledge and power, and of the balance between federal and local control, as these affect the education of young children. The United States has for generations relied on practical experience, professional knowledge, and local control in deciding how students should be taught to read. Recent changes in the locus of control in the United States warrant attention, as do similar events in other countries. As the "flat world" takes shape (Darling-Hammond, 2010), it will be important to "get it right" in educating coming generations, and literacy is clearly at the top of this agenda.

Faith and Science

The *National Reading Panel* (*NRP*) was established in 1997 by Congress to "convene a national panel to assess the status of research-based knowledge, including the effectiveness of various approaches to teaching children to read . . . [and], if warranted, to recommend a plan for additional research regarding early reading" (NICHD, 2000, p. 1.1). The assignment appears straightforward, but two words required significant interpretation: "reading" and "research." Educated people know how to read, and most have something to say about the topic. Likewise, they know about research, although they may be less certain about this knowledge. Under *NRP*, "reading" was very specifically defined, as was "scientific evidence." "Reading" was portrayed as a set of basic skills, to be trained during the early school years by direct instruction. "Scientific evidence" was restricted to findings from *randomized controlled experiments* (*RCTs*), excluding much of the available evidence. *NCLB* and *Reading First* (*RF*) then took shape according to *NRP* pronouncements.

One might argue that such restrictions are the price of progress. Literacy encompasses an enormous array of topics, from reading a word to reading a page, and beyond. Focusing on the earliest stages of reading seems sensible as a beginning. And everyone knows that experiments are "real science." We learned the model in high school. One group of participants receives a special treatment, the other undergoes "business as usual"; pre- and post-test measures are taken, and the question is whether the experimental group shows more improvement than the control group. If so, then it is *evident* that the treatment has caused an effect. We have clear *evidence* that provides sound basis for action.

The devil resides in the details. From one perspective, the *NRP* project was enormously successful. The Report proclaimed clear courses of action for the nation's schools based on "scientific research." It defined what should count as indicators of reading achievement. It defined what should count as the research literature from 1970 to 2000. It defined "What Works" for the federal clearing house on educational products. It defined the classroom materials, practices, and outcomes that counted in awarding federal funds. It defined what should count as reading and reading instruction. And it has continued to direct public policy regarding reading instruction in the early grades for more than a decade, with little sign of respite.

The evolution of *NRP* illustrates the dangers of federalization, issues reminiscent of Eisenhower's warnings about the military–industrial complex. One concern centers on the individuals chosen to formulate the "problem" and decide how to investigate it. *NRP* Panel members were capable scholars who shared a concern about the wellbeing of the nation's students. They all believed that the time was right for federal action. They held a common conception of reading as a basic skill to be mastered in the primary grades through direct instruction (with one notable exception). Finally, they shared a common faith—the belief that experimental studies provide the most trustworthy guide for action. Nonetheless, and for whatever reasons, they decided at the outset to explore a very limited portion of the research terrain (the Report indicates that the database contained at least 100,000 studies; fewer than 1,000 were incorporated in the analysis—less than 1 percent).

The *NRP/NCLB/RF* story also demonstrates the power of an individual to shape policy and practice. The chief architect of these programs was Reid Lyon, a psychologist who joined the National Institute of Child Health and Human Development (NICHD) in 1992, becoming Chief of the Unit in 1996 (Lyon, 2006). For the next decade, Lyon created a research program that engaged a wide-ranging group of investigators in studies became centerpieces for the *NRP* Report (NICHD, 2003). Lyon played a major role in the formulation of the Education Sciences Reform Act of 2002, which proclaimed controlled experiments to be the only trustworthy source of evidence in educational research. He was convinced that phonological awareness (PA) and phonics were the essential foundations for reading acquisition (Lyon, 2006); the *NRP* Report devoted 170 pages to phoneme awareness and phonics, versus 99 pages to vocabulary and comprehension. From the Panel's perspective, they were simply identifying studies that met the criteria of scientific rigor (controlled experiments), which in turn reflected NICHD funding patterns established under Lyon's tenure. Lyon served as education advisor to George W. Bush from 2001 until 2005, and estimated the NICHD research investment during his tenure as Chief of NICHD at around $60 million annually (2006), a relatively modest amount (around $600 million over ten years), but one that has leveraged billions since then in federal outlays to the public schools.

The Panel Report set forth several recommendations for practice and for practitioners; these were generally quite prescriptive, with relatively little room for professional judgment (NICHD, 2000):

- "The findings [on phoneme awareness] show that teaching children to manipulate phonemes in words was *highly effective* across all literacy domains and outcomes." (p. 2.3, emphasis added)

- "Can phoneme awareness [PA] be taught? *Yes*. The results clearly showed that PA instruction is effective in teaching children to attend to and manipulate speech sounds in words" (p. 2.5).
- "Does phonemic awareness instruction assist children in learning to read? *Yes*. ... teaching children to manipulate the sounds in language helps them learn to read. ... If so, which students benefit? Across various conditions of teaching, testing, and participant characteristics, effect sizes were all significantly greater than chance and ranged from large to small, with the majority in the moderate range. Effects ... lasted well beyond the end of training" (p. 2.5).
- Does PA training help children from low-SES backgrounds? One might think that this question would have received special notice, given recurring concerns about the achievement gap. In fact, the question is not posed in the Report, but does appear in a statement at the end of one of the sections: "The effects of PA training on reading outcomes were also influenced by SES, with mid-to-high SES associated with larger effect sizes [.84] than low SES [.45]" (p. 2.4). That is, PA training did *not* help low SES students as much as high SES students.
- "Does systematic phonics instruction help children learn to read more effectively than nonsystematic phonics or no phonics? ... Findings provided solid support for the conclusion that systematic phonics instruction makes a bigger contribution to children's growth in reading than alternative programs" (p. 2.92).
- "Are some types of phonics instruction more effective than others? ... systematic phonics programs are all significantly more effective than non-phonics programs; however, they do not appear to differ significantly from each other ... " (p. 2.93).
- "Is phonics instruction beneficial for children who are having difficulty to read? ... Phonics instruction produced substantial growth among younger at-risk children ..., but failed to exert a significant impact on the performance of low-achieving readers in 2nd through 6th grade" (p. 2.94).
- "Does phonics instruction improve children's reading comprehension? ... Systematic phonics produced significantly greater growth ... in younger children's reading comprehension ... [but] the effects on text comprehension in readers above first grade were mixed ..., with significant gains for disabled readers ..., but not for the older group in general ... " (p. 2.95). For younger students, "comprehension" typically calls for understanding phrases, sentences, or simple stories.

In the normal course of events, the *NRP* Report would have garnered headlines, and recommendations would have gradually filtered down through states and districts to schools and teachers. The primary response would have been revisions to commercial reading materials. Along the way, voices of experience and scholarship would have augmented the shape of implementation activities. In this instance, however, the federal government immediately implemented *Reading First* (*RF*), a $1 billion program introduced during 2002/2003 as part of the *NCLB* legislation.

RF conducted workshops and summer institutes to train teachers to use instructional materials incorporating the five curriculum components featured in the *NRP* Report: PA, phonics, vocabulary, fluency, and comprehension. Implementation of *RF* was a condition for receipt of federal funding under *NCLB*, and so districts serving at-risk students were effectively mandated to participate in *RF*.

The *RF* legislation also funded an extensive evaluation of the program. Data were collected in the 2004–2005 and 2005–2006 school years, with reports emerging two years later (Gamse, et al., 2008a; 2008b). In a sense, this project amounted to an enormous controlled experiment evaluating the validity of the Lyon model. Almost 4,800 elementary schools participated in *RF*; the evaluation included a total of 12,000 *RF* students and 13,000 control students. An original plan called for administration of individually-administered tests for all five components, but this proved impractical because of the cost. Reading comprehension was assessed at the end of first, second, and third grade, as were (1) time on the five components; (2) the amount of highly explicit instruction; (3) the amount of "high quality student practice"; and (4) the percentage of students engaged with print.

Abt Associates conducted the evaluation, which met the criteria for a controlled experiment. Note that these two papers were issued as technical reports; they did not go through the peer-review process required of articles selected for the *NRP* Report. The results, reported in April and November 2008, were unequivocal:

(1) "*Reading First* produced *positive and statistically significant impacts* on the *practices* called for by the program . . ., professional development in scientifically-based reading instruction, support from full-time reading coaches, amount of reading instruction, and support for struggling readers";

(2) "*Reading First* produced *positive and statistically significant impacts* on the *amount of time* spent on the five essential components of reading instruction promoted by the program"; and

(3) "*Reading First did not produce a statistically significant impact* on *student reading comprehension test scores.*"

(Gamse, et al., 2008b, p. v, emphasis added)

The findings were clear cut but rather discouraging: (1) time spent on the program components increased—teachers did what they were told to do; (2) program impact on reading comprehension was negligible; and (3) there was no trend for comprehension performance to increase over the grades as the teachers gained more experience with the program. As a one-shot effort to reprogram primary-grade teachers in the United States, *RF* clearly succeeded. It produced substantial changes in the primary-grade basals used in the early years of schooling. Phoneme awareness training is now established as a significant component of reading instruction in kindergarten and first grade, and is likely to remain in place for years to come, even though the evidence suggests that, as now implemented, it requires substantial instructional time but provides little benefit.

The Report concludes, "Findings based on exploratory analyses do not provide consistent or systematic insight into the pattern of observed impacts" (Gamse, et al., 2008a, p. xvii). An enormous investment of time and money had demonstrated the ineffectiveness of ideas and practices that many had challenged from the beginning—*but nothing useful was learned from the exercise*. In this age of educational accountability, one might have expected serious repercussions, significant apologies, and a thorough reexamination of what led to the debacle. Nothing of the sort happened, and in the Common Core Standards released in 2010 (NGA/CCSSO, 2010), the Lyon model occupies a significant place in the Foundation Skills section of early reading.

Those of Other Faiths

Many researchers and scholars, including the authors of this book, disagreed with many of the assumptions and beliefs that undergirded the NICHD programs — assumptions and beliefs about both the nature of literacy and the nature of scientific research (e.g., Shannon, 2007). The bottom line, however, was that we were unable at the time to make a convincing case to either the public or the Congress. Our counterargument was grounded in a different view of reading, which will be laid out in the chapters that follow, but since "everyone" knows about reading, this facet of the debate received little attention. Instead, the spotlight was on "research," specifically on controlled experiments as the gold standard. There are many forms of scientific inquiry, most fundamentally the technique of *observation*, of close examination of the phenomena under investigation, of "kidwatching" in the case of reading (Goodman, 1985; Owocki & Goodman, 2002). For those steering the ship, however, these areas of research simply did not count. They were too soft, too subjective, too qualitative.

It is clearly important not to be soft about science; those who conduct investigations on messy problems using messy methods (educators) must work hard to gain respect from colleagues in more established domains (medical doctors, but cf. Bach, 2012). Within the social and behavioral sciences, educational researchers are often viewed with disdain by experimental psychologists and economists. By establishing controlled experiments as the gold standard, Congress sought to help educators (and the Department of Education) to get their act together. Educational researchers were encouraged to emulate the medical model, where controlled experiments provide the foundation for the public's trust in medical practice. In fact, this image of medical research is misleading. Not until the 1970s did controlled experiments became widespread in the health field. More to the point, the entry of such studies into the development and approval of medical treatments has in no way diminished the physician's role:

> To enter mainstream use, any treatment typically needs to clear a high bar. It will be subject to randomized trials, statistical significance tests, the peer

review process of academic journals, and the scrutiny of government regulators. Yet once a treatment enters the mainstream—once we know *whether* it works in certain situations [and whether it causes harm in other situations]—science is largely left behind. The next questions—*when* to use it and on *which* patients—become matters of judgment, not measurement. These decisions are . . . left to a doctor's informed intuition.

(Leonhardt, 2009)

The identification of controlled experiments as the gold standard for reading research—indeed, for *all* educational research—was subjected to careful scrutiny shortly after the release of the *NRP* Report. In 2002, the National Academy of Science released *Scientific research in education* (*SRE*; Shavelson & Towne, 2002), which presented a broad framework for the conduct of empirical and conceptual research, placing controlled experiments within a context of other techniques, and giving particular attention to the challenges of conducting *well-controlled* experiments in social settings (Prideaux, 2002). The Report laid out a framework for the conduct of empirical investigations, with particular attention to ways of strengthening federal support for educational research (Shavelson & Towne, 2002). The *SRE* Report was weighted toward STEM research, and no one on the *SRE* Panel was particularly knowledgeable about literacy research. The *NRP* and *SRE* reports have yet to be connected in any substantial way.

From the beginning, the *NRP* project was also challenged about its limited view of reading and of reading instruction, and the disregard of practitioner experiences and voices. Many concerns sprang from ideological and epistemological differences about learning and development; others arose because of commercial implications. The Panel recommendations clearly favored some instructional materials and professional development programs over others, and federal funds required that the recommendations be incorporated in the materials and programs. As will be noted below, "science" was also missing in the work of the Panel, which looked at significance levels but not at the understandings that might be captured from the studies.

The concerns ran deeply through the reading research community, and continue to reverberate to the present. Michael Pressley, an experimental cognitive psychologist, could certainly not be described as a soft scientist. The Panel cited his work in the section on comprehension, but none of his empirical studies passed muster for inclusion in their review. In December 2005, shortly before his untimely passing, Pressley reflected on the *NRP/NCLB/RF* program in a lengthy and balanced article in *Education Week* (Pressley, 2005). His points merit attention today as the Unites States moves forward with implementation of the Common Core Standards (NGA/CCSSO, 2010; Rothman, 2011), nominally a state level undertaking, but with substantial involvement of the federal government and the business community. Pressley presented his case as an "extension of concerns about federal reading efforts that have accumulated over the past six years":

- "As soon as the [Panel] report appeared, there were outcries that the Panel had been prematurely selective in its coverage of topics . . ., and in the methodologies it was willing to accept."
- "[Since then], skepticism about the effectiveness of the Reading First program has been growing . . ., [and] the best data available [none available in peer-reviewed journals] show small gains after a year or two of Reading First . . ."
- "A broader problem with evaluations [including Reading First] is that the focus is on whether a program 'works,' rather than how or why it works. Science probes more deeply than the 'what works' question, for only by understanding how and why an intervention works can we adapt it to new populations and settings . . ."
- "Real progress has been made in understanding how to create balanced programs that provide differentiated instruction depending on learners' needs . . ., but balanced instruction seems an anathema to many of those who identify with the phonological, sound-, and word-level models of Reading First."

Pressley emphasized the importance of "understanding why and how something works." Scientific experiments are designed around hypotheses, ideas, models, and processes. Empirical experiments serve a purpose, but they provide little in the way of understanding, and so are of limited value in answering questions about the generalizability of the findings. There was no "science" in the *NRP* Report. Over the past half century, an enormous amount of science has been invested in learning about the reading process and the development of reading (e.g., Barr, et al., 1991; Kamil, et al., 2000; Kamil, et al., 2011; Pearson, et al., 1984). The Panel briefly surveyed some of this work, but made no attempt to evaluate the conceptual quality of the studies that they selected for review. As a consequence, when *RF* was taken into the field, it took shape as a set of prescribed activities that were dutifully put into place by practitioners who were following orders, often under protest (Manzo, 2005). Scientific research can be complex and time consuming—and expensive. In a centralized system, leaders are impatient—they need results, simple results, and right away. With *RF*, the federal powers proceeded to implement the program immediately, with no time for the localized beta tests that are part of most new ventures in business and industry.

Deciding What Should Count: Three Challenges to Reading Researchers

The *RF* story is a reminder that developing and evaluating early reading programs is quite complex. Difficulties arose in this instance partly as a result of federalization; programs moved ahead helter skelter without a solid foundation in either literacy or science. Literacy research is also really quite difficult under the best of circumstances. The reasons for this situation are manifold, but one issue is the lack of a disciplinary foundation. Ask for advice about mathematics, science, history, and even literature, and you can call upon university departments with certified experts. The same is not true of literacy; the field lacks a coherent disciplinary core, and so is vulnerable to the emergence of a virtually unlimited variety of claims, afflictions, and remedies. The issue is not a lack of disciplinary expertise, to the contrary. The domain is rich with expertise, but like the Tower of Babel, the inhabitants speak different languages and communication can be a challenge.

In this section, I suggest three specific matters that bear on the *NRP/NCLB/ RF* episode. (1) *Definitions*—the reading wars continue to cloud the arena and muddy the water, creating uncertainty about the most appropriate formulation of research questions. (2) *Development*—for reading, the learning goal is inherently influenced by large variations in time and space, where the goals are sustained growth and transfer over many years. (3) *Indicators*—partly reflecting definitional issues, reading research is plagued with the lack of valid assessments, and frequently resort to hollow instruments such as multiple-choice tests and DIBELS (cf. Chapter 2). These three topics offer lenses for reflecting on *NRP/NCLB/RF*.

Definitions

The contrast between learning to read and reading to learn (Chall, 1983; 1995) may have been on the minds of Panel members, although the phrase does not appear in the Report. As noted earlier, Lyon's definition of reading was simple: *Phoneme Awareness* → *Phonics* → *Reading* (Lyon, 2006). This definition is consistent with the Panel's operational definition of reading, as can be seen in the coverage of the various topics: Phoneme awareness, 98 pp.; Phonics, 81 pp.; Vocabulary and Comprehension, 99 pp. The implicit assumption is that the early stages of reading instruction should focus on learning to translate print to spoken language.

The Panel dedicated considerable space to PA (the coverage began in the late 1970s, leaving unmentioned earlier discussions of the concept; cf., Calfee & Norman, 1999). The focus was on a variety of tasks involving phoneme identification and manipulation. Early notions of linking awareness and articulation (e.g., McGuiness, 1997, p. 31ff) received little attention. The question was whether programs that taught phoneme identification and manipulation increased student performance on similar tasks, and the answer was "yes." Students learned what they were taught. The Panel also assessed the impact of such training on "learning to read," generally assessed by standardized tests, along with a variety of experimenter-developed instruments, and again found a positive effect on "reading." These effects were actually on word reading, not text/passage comprehension, and on immediate post-tests, and the impact of PA training diminished with time (NICHD, 2000, p. 2.63ff).

A different image of literacy focuses on the end point and maps backward. Here is the definition from the framers of the Common Core Standards:

> The Standards lay out a vision of what it means to be a literate person in the twenty-first century. Indeed, the skills and understandings students are expected to demonstrate have wide applicability outside the classroom or workplace. Students who meet the Standards readily undertake the close, attentive reading that is at the heart of understanding and enjoying complex works of literature. They habitually perform the critical reading necessary to pick carefully through the staggering amount of information available today in print and digitally. They actively seek the wide, deep, and thoughtful engagement with high-quality literary and informational texts that builds knowledge, enlarges experience, and broadens worldviews. They reflexively demonstrate the cogent reasoning and use of evidence that is essential to both private deliberation and responsible citizenship in a democratic republic. In short, students who meet the Standards develop the skills in reading, writing, speaking, and listening that are the foundation for any creative and purposeful expression in language (NGA/CCSSO, 2010, p. 4).

This view of literacy emphasizes the idea of gaining meaning from texts, an idea that resonates with parental practices in story reading. They immerse their children in a variety of books, including ABC books, along with fairy tales and Richard Scary favorites. Reading to learn and learning to read take shape as synergistic, iterative processes. The discussions of *balanced reading/literacy* that appeared during the late 1990s captured the notion of literacy as a constellation of interacting elements—words, phrases and sentences, paragraphs and texts—all working together to promote communication (Pressley, 2005). The *NRP* Report, if built upon a balanced view of literacy, might have taken a very different path, with very different recommendations.

Development

Learning to read takes place across a span of many years. The portrayal of reading laid out by the framers of the Common Core Standards may appear daunting at first glance, especially if one accepts the idea that all children are to achieve the Standards. By the same token, school is the centerpiece of a student's life for 13 years. The key to realizing the Standards is backward mapping. From kindergarten on, the development of comprehension, composition, and communication competencies is on the agenda in developmentally appropriate fashion. The *NRP* actually took note of this matter at the end of the section on Phonics:

> Phonics should be integrated with other reading instruction to create a balanced reading program . . . [It] should not become the dominant component in a reading program, neither in the amount of time devoted to it nor in the significance attached. It is important to evaluate children's reading competence in many ways, not only their phonics skills but also their interest in books and their ability to understand information that is read to them (NICHD, 2000, p. 2.97).

Embedded in a paragraph at the end of the Phonics section, however, this advice never made it to the headlines, or to *RF*.

There are challenges, for both research and practice, in dealing with developments that span years and contexts. Knowledge of the ABCs in kindergarten is highly correlated with later school success, including performance on reading tests. So should we rush to teach the alphabet to preschoolers? It turns out that correlation is not causality in this instance; teaching the ABCs does no harm, but neither does it help over the long run. What about phoneme awareness and phonics, the driving forces in the Lyon model?

The studies reviewed by *NRP* show that students can learn to do PA tasks and can decode short, simple words. But what is the payoff over the long term and over the broader range of capacities envisioned in the Standards? Most educational experiments last no more than two or three years at the outside. Following students is difficult, especially those from poor families; they move around a lot. Assessing reading is costly, and usually entails simple tasks similar to those in the original training.

One can find longitudinal studies, but these are seldom part of controlled experiments, and so none is found in the *NRP* review. However, an interesting snapshot is available from a study conducted by the Oregon Direct Instruction (DI) team after the Follow Through experiments conducted as part of Johnson's War on Poverty from 1967 to 1995 (Kennedy, 1978). The DI program far outperformed competitors in this massive horse race; at-risk students who spent three years in an intensive program that emphasized phonics (and an early version of phoneme awareness) performed at or near national norms on standardized reading tests by the end of third grade. Despite the spectacular performance from DI, however, there was no rush to install the DI program throughout the nation, much to the disappointment of the Oregon team.

Convinced of the benefits of their program, the team tracked down Follow Through students who had participated in DI activities from first through third grade, and tested them in fifth and sixth grade, using the same instruments employed during Follow Through (Becker & Gersten, 1982; it did not appear in the Panel Report). The end of elementary school is a critical transition; when students enter middle school, they need to be well on the way to "reading" as envisioned by the Standards. One can imagine three outcomes from this follow-up of Follow Through. DI might promote reading skills that were self-sustaining, and that promoted learning to learn, even for students from at-risk backgrounds. In this instance, the students would perform above the norm. A second possibility is that the students retained what they had learned, and were able to maintain their relative standings. The third possibility is that training on basic skills, while useful for handling primary level tests, provided little transfer to the more demanding tasks that emerged during the late elementary grades and beyond, in which case their relative achievement would decline to levels more typical of at-risk students.

The follow-up report (Becker & Gersten, 1982) put a positive tone on the findings: "Results indicated consistently strong, significant effects on reading/decoding scores . . ., but without a continuing program [of DI instruction], most students demonstrated losses when compared to the standardization sample on achievement tests" (p. 75). The percentile scores were very close for the Follow Through (FT) and Control (CN) groups (Table 5, p. 84: Grade 5, FT = 21.0, CN = 20.4; Grade 6, FT = 28.2, CN = 25.0). The students did not lose what they had been taught, as shown by their scores on word-level tasks. But they had not learned how to handle the more difficult reading activities that confronted them when they left the primary grades. The writers concluded that "without effective instruction which continues to build on these [basic] skills in the intermediate grades, children are likely to lose ground" (p. 89). The suggestion seems to be that students required additional instruction following the DI model. An alternative suggestion is that students might have benefited from the primary grades onward from instruction designed to promote the capacities identified by the authors as essential in the later grades: reading comprehension, expressive writing, independent study skills, and so on—the elements typical of a balanced program.

Indicators

How should "reading" be assessed? Controlled experiments are expansive and expensive, and so researchers generally rely on multiple-choice selected-response standardized tests. They are relatively cheap, and they do not take much time. They are reliable, in the sense that if a sample of students is administered two or more tests from different publishers, the scores tend to be highly correlated. There are many ways of testing reading, of course. A relatively new entry is DIBELS, in which a student is given a list of items (letters, words, pictures) and asked to read the list as quickly as possible (Good & Kaminski, 2011). Under some conditions, DIBELS scores are correlated with other standardized scores, which might suggest that the instruments all measure the same thing. Which raises the issue of validity—to what extent can one judge an individual's level of achievement in a particular domain based on a particular indicator? The most trustworthy assessment of a student's reading competence is arguably a performance task. Sit the youngster at a table or before a tablet PC with a collection of books, and ask him or her to select some books, do "some reading," and talk about what he or she makes of it. Assessment of this sort ("sitting beside" a child), is time consuming and subjective, and no studies incorporating this approach made it through the *NRP* criteria, even though others made recommendations along these lines.

The Standards have called for major changes in the assessment of literacy—of reading and writing. They call for students to learn to read and write in areas that really matter—literature, but also science, social studies, and technical subjects. Two assessment consortia, SBAC and PARCC (Herman & Linn, 2013), were established in 2011 with the promise of a new era in educational assessment, in which student accomplishments will be gauged by projects rather than pencils, by pursuing a new and different answer rather than marking the one right answer. Halfway through these development projects, the early promises seem to be waning, jeopardized by costs in time and money. If implementation of the Standards is driven by summative assessments, and if summative assessments continue to be driven by considerations of time and money, then the prospects for significant changes in literacy instruction will be limited. The Standards promote a vision of language and literacy of enormous importance, which will require adoption of indicators that are trustworthy reflections of that vision.

History of the Book

The story of this book begins at the 2010 convention of the American Educational Research Association, at a symposium, *Leveraging what we know: A literacy agenda for the 21st Century* (Gutierrez, 2010). Chaired by Kris Gutierrez of the University of Colorado, the audience heard from 11 speakers spanning a broad spectrum of experiences and perspectives. The announced purpose of the session was to explore the road ahead, but for many in the audience the equally important contributions were the retrospectives on earlier accomplishments.

A few weeks later, at the International Reading Association meeting in Chicago, Hall of Famer Karen Wixon also connected the audience with earlier times (Wixon, 2010):

> *Michigan's "new" definition of reading, 1983:* Reading is the process of constructing meaning through the dynamic interaction among the reader's existing knowledge, the information suggested by the written language, and the context of the reading situation.
> *Michigan English Language arts Framework, 1995:* The English language arts encompass both process and content—**how** people communicate as well as **what** they communicate.

Wixon's powerpoint slides featured these statements, along with newspaper articles reporting the rejection of all of these ideas by the Michigan Board of Education.

Following Wixon's presentations, two of the editors of the present book (Ken and Bob) met to reminisce and ruminate. The 1970s and 1980s had been times of great promise and excitement, so unlike the doldrums of *NCLB*, of standardized tests and accountability. What might be done to restore and reenergize earlier accomplishments? We decided that (1) we should explore the federalization of literacy practice in schools and literacy research in universities; and (2) we should try to provoke action by the professional organizations of which we were members, starting with the Reading Hall of Fame (RHOF). In July 2010, we presented a framework to RHOF members for sponsorship of several literacy conferences in 2011. Sessions were subsequently held at the American Education Research Association in April, at the European Reading Conference in May, at Mons, Belgium in July, and at the National Council of Teachers of English in November. The European participation emerged during discussions with several RHOF colleagues, who resonated to the issues laid out in our framework. "The same thing is happening to us—we need to compare notes!"

Our framework was originally titled *Reading 2011: Know where you are coming from—it's not enough to know where you are going*. A continuing theme of the RHOF is the importance of a historical perspective, and our framework has tried to capture the halcyon days of the 1970s and 1980s. Time is dynamic, of course, and along the way, new events have altered the course of the project, as have some recollections from earlier times. Looking ahead, after the Chicago IRA meetings, the Common Core State Standards were released, offering hope that the *NCLB* tide might be shifting. As this chapter nears completion, however, federal policies continue to emphasize standardized testing and punitive accountability measures. Looking back, this chapter was originally framed to span the past quarter-century, but then I came across *Toward a literate society* by Carroll and Chall (1975), Lyndon Johnson's "War on Poverty," the *Right to Read* program, and the Cooperative Reading Experiments (Bond & Dykstra, 1967). It was suddenly déjà vu all over again:

> [The nation] should ensure that every person arriving at adulthood will be able to read and understand the whole spectrum of printed materials that one is likely to encounter in daily life . . ., an individual cannot participate in modern society unless he can read, and by this we mean reading at a rather high level.
>
> (Carroll & Chall, 1975, pp. 8, 9)

"Daily life" is much different today than it was in the 1970s, but the fundamental aspirations are the same.

The chapters in the present book cover a lot of territory in time and space. The reader will need to supply connective tissue along the way; the Editor's Notes at the opening of every chapter should help with this task. The reality is that this is an enormous story, ranging over science and practice, politics and policies, and the endless sweep of a giant pendulum. Along the way, the world has broadened and flattened, posing new challenges and opportunities to every newborn who enters the world. A critical task for every democratic society is to ensure that all children reach their full potential for thriving in the new world, including the capacity to think, to solve problems, and to communicate—the new literacy.

The chapters in the first part of this book deal with broad issues of *what* knowledge should matter in determining government literacy policies. The government is often inclined to search for information to support a predetermined position rather than developing a position around sound evidence. The *NRP/ NCLB/RF* episode exemplifies selective science, rather than sound science. The chapters in the second part, written by recognized authorities in aspects of literacy education and research, focus on pragmatic issues. They exemplify the kind of knowledge that should be influencing literacy policies and curricula. Taken together, the collection provides snapshots of a work in progress. We know a lot about reading, about what works and what doesn't. We have much more to discover, but our schools and teachers would be much more effective and confident if decision makers made better use of the full spectrum of validated knowledge that exists—the knowledge that *should* count.

References

Bach, P.B. (2012). The trouble with "doctor knows best." *New York Times*, June 4, 2012. p. D5.

Barr, R., Kamil, M.L., Mosenthal, P.B., & Pearson, P.D. (Eds.) (1991). *Handbook of reading research, Vol. II*. New York: Longman.

Becker, W.C., & Gersten, R. (1982). A follow-up of Follow Through: The later effects of the Direct Instruction Model on children in fifth and sixth grades. *American Educational Research Journal, 19*, 75–92.

Bond, G.L., & Dykstra, R. (1967). The cooperative research program in first-grade reading instruction. *Reading Research Quarterly, 2*, 5–142.

Calfee, R.C., & Norman, K.A. (1999). Psychological perspectives on the early reading wars: The case of phonological awareness. *Teachers College Record, 100*, 242–274.

Carroll, J., & Chall, J. (1975). *Toward a literate society*. New York: McGraw-Hill.

Chall, J. (1983). *Stages of reading development*. New York: McGraw-Hill.

Chall, J.S. (1995). *Stages of reading development*. New York: Harcourt College Publishers.

Darling-Hammond, L. (2010). *The flat world and education*. New York: Teachers College Press.

ETS. (2010). *Center for K–12 assessment and performance management*. Austin, TX: Author. Retrieved April 22, 2012, from www.k12center.org

Gamse, B.C., Bloom, H.S., Kemple, J.J., & Jacob, R.T. (2008a). *Reading first impact study: Interim report* (NCEE 2008–4016). Washington, DC: National Center for Education Evaluation and Regional Assistance, Institute of Education Sciences, U.S. Department of Education.

Gamse, B.C., Jacob, R.T., Horst, M., Boulay, B., & Unlu, F. (2008b). *Reading first impact study: Final report executive summary* (NCEE 2008–4038). Washington, DC: National Center for Education Evaluation and Regional Assistance, Institute of Education Sciences, U.S. Department of Education.

Good, R.II. III, & Kaminski, R.A. (2011). *DIBELS next assessment manual*. Retrieved from www.dibels.org

Goodman, Y. (1985). Kidwatching: Observing children in the classroom. In A. Jaggar & M.T. Smith-Burke (Eds.), *Observing the language learner* (pp. 9–18). Newark, DE: International Reading Association.

Guthrie, J.G. (2013). *State educational systems—the legal basis for state control of education, school organization models, and the school district consolidation movement*. Retrieved from http://education.stateuniversity.com/pages/2448/State-Educational-Systems.html

Gutierrez, K.D. (2010). *Leveraging what we know: A literacy agenda for the 21st Century*. Symposium presented at Annual Meeting of American Educational Research Association, Denver, CO.

Herman, J., & Linn, R. (2013). *On the road to deeper learning: The status of Smarter Balanced and PARCC assessment consortia, CRESST Report 823*. Los Angeles, CA: Center for Research on Evaluation, Standards, and Student Testing.

Kamil, M.L., Mosenthal, P., Pearson, P.D., & Barr, R. (Eds.) (2000). *Handbook of reading research, Vol III*. Mahwah, NJ: Lawrence Erlbaum Associates.

Kamil, M.L., Pearson, P.D., Moje., E.B., & Afflerbach, P.D. (2011). *Handbook of reading research, Vol. IV*. New York: Routledge.

Kennedy, M. (1978). Findings from the Follow Through planned variation study. *Educational Researcher, 7*, 3–11.

Leonhardt, D. (2009). Making health care better. *New York Times*, November 3, 2009, p. MM31.

Lyon, G.R. (2006). *From the laboratory to Congress; From the White House to the classroom: The NICHD reading research program and the birth of evidence-based research*. University Park, TX: Southern Methodist University.

McGuiness, D. (1997). *Why our children can't read and what to do about it*. New York: Free Press.

Manzo, K.K. (2005). States pressed to refashion Reading First grant designs. *Education Week, 25*, 1.

NGA/CCSSO (2010). *The Common Core Standards for English Language Arts and Literacy in History/Social Studies, Science, and Technical Subjects*. Washington, DC: National Governors' Association; Council of Chief State School Officers.

NICHD (2000). *Report of the National Reading Panel. Teaching children to read: An evidence-based synthesis of the scientific research literature on reading and its implications of reading instruction*. (NIH Publication 00–4754). Washington, DC: National Institute of Child and Human Development.

NICHD (2003). *The NICHD Reading Program: Three decades of research to understand how children learn to read, and why some children have difficulties doing so, and what can be done to prevent and remediate reading failure*. Washington, DC: National Institute of Child and Human Development.

Owocki, G., & Goodman, Y. (2002). *Kidwatching: Documenting literacy development*. Westport, CT: Heinemann.

Pearson, P.D., Mosenthal, P.B., Kamil, M.L., & Barr, R. (Eds.) (1984). *Handbook of reading research*. New York: Longman.

Pressley, M. (December 14, 2005). The rocky road of Reading First: Another chapter in the long history of complaints about federal reading efforts. *Education Week, 25*, 24–25.

Prideaux, D. (2002). Researching the outcomes of educational interventions: A matter of design. *British Medical Journal, 324*, 126–127.

Public Law 107–110, The *No Child Left Behind* Act of 2001. (Enacted). (PL 107–110, 2001).

Rothman, R. (2011). *Something in common: The Common Core Standards and the next chapter in American education*. Cambridge, MA: Harvard Education Press.

Shannon, P. (2007). *Reading against democracy: The broken promises of reading instruction*. Portsmouth, NH: Heinemann.

Shavelson, R.J., & Towne, L. (2002). *Scientific research in education*. Washington, DC: National Academies Press.

Wixon, K.K. (2010). *An interactive view of reading (dis)ability revisited*. Paper presented at the Annual Convention of the International Reading Association, Chicago, IL.

PART 1

The Political Realties

2

WHOSE KNOWLEDGE COUNTS?

The Pedagogy of the Absurd

Kenneth S. Goodman

Editor's Note: Democracy is vulnerable to those with money and power to use the institutions of democracy for their own selfish ends. Movement Conservatism is at the base of what seems like a spontaneous distrust of professional educators everywhere. It uses an attack on the teaching of reading as a means of making universal education a failed goal. Like many events in the world's history—even the Holocaust—though terrible it is also absurd. An example of this absurdity is DIBELS, a program mandated in many of the states which has taken over the primary curriculum in many schools. Even more absurd is the expansion on DIBELS to EGRA, sponsored by USAID and the World Bank for developing nations in Africa, Latin America, and Asia.

KSG

Knowledge and Its Use

The issue in literacy education is not what knowledge exists but rather what knowledge is worth paying attention to. In the time of Galileo and Copernicus the only knowledge worth attending to was not the holy books but the official dogma of the church in interpreting the Holy Scriptures. Copernicus waited until he was dying to publish. Galileo published his last work in secret because the science and its theoretical explanation challenged that dogma. And regardless of its truth, knowledge that challenged the dogma was heresy.

What is happening in the field of literacy has to be put in a similar political context. I live in a state where the Secretary of State was required by law to see a birth certificate before putting President Obama on the ballot in 2012, where it's legal to carry a gun without a license, and skin complexion is cause for suspicion of arrest. In the context of 21st century America, all that we have learned about literacy through our research and the theory we have built from it are less valued than the concepts of literacy that serve the political and economic purposes of those who have the power to control the decision making of federal, state, and local politicians. And the reason those concepts are valued has nothing to do with literacy.

For a dozen years through Republican and Democratic administrations, the law of the land in American education is No Child Left Behind (NCLB). For half of those years there has been widespread agreement that it needs to be changed. But Congress has been unable or unwilling to change it. And nothing I see in the proposals to amend or replace that law values knowledge. The definitions and mandates enacted or proposed as law are part of the Pedagogy of the Absurd. Absurdity is legally framed as scientifically based reading research. Sound research becomes anti-science by law. Nonsense becomes knowledge and knowledge becomes nonsense.

Diane Ravitch, once a staunch supporter of NCLB, now says, "Under NCLB, the federal government was dictating ineffectual remedies, which had no track record of success. Neither Congress nor the U.S. Department of Education knows how to fix low-performing schools" (Ravitch, 2011, p. 101).

Truth and Heresy

In the 21st century, multinational corporations have policies that are bent on reducing government influence on how they conduct their business, produce their products, treat their customers and employees, and how much their profits are taxed. From this perspective, the only knowledge worth attending to is that which benefits the bottom line of multinational corporations. With their money and the brains of amoral think tanks, they can subvert the political process and frame bad as good and good as dangerous. It should not surprise us that the attack on anything public—including education—in the name of privatization and deregulation is international. The world's economy is increasingly controlled by multinational corporations.

The pursuit of profit is the driving force. In their view, every aspect of modern economy that has been considered a public (governmental) responsibility—prisons, mail, roads, bridges, and education—should be operated for profit. Universal compulsory free public education is expensive and from the moral perspective of multinational corporations, privatizing education creates both a source of potential profits in privatized schools and publishing and elimination of the tax burden of supporting universal public education. After all, modern technology has eliminated the need for large numbers of low- or semi-skilled workers. Modern industry needs highly skilled technicians but they can be produced through a system that educates only an elite few. And privatizing education gives control of access and content of education to business interests.

However, unlike the robber barons of the past, who didn't hide their greed or refrain from confrontation, today's power elite have working for them neo-conservative think tanks of very bright people who can, for a few million dollars, co-opt the law makers and even the very groups they seek to control. They cleverly cast their campaigns to limit the costs of education as reform. And they feed on the lack of success of poor people to marginalize those who have the knowledge to solve the problems of education. Thus they can in fact get people to vote against their own best interests.

In the pursuit of their goals they are free to conceal their agenda, framing bad as good, greed as job-creation, and reaction as reform. The result is both tragic and absurd at the same time. The Holocaust was a terrible tragedy, but the highly organized killing of millions of Jews and others was also absurd. In the Italian movie *Life is Beautiful* (1997, directed by Benigni) the situation of the death camp is so absurd that a father convinces his young son that the absurdity of their suffering can't be real, that they are playing a game.

Education decision making, in both the developed and developing parts of the world, is in this condition of comic tragedy that I call the "Pedagogy of the Absurd". There are those who are convinced that if we could only make those with power understand what we know, they would change their opposition. But it is precisely because they know that knowledge exists that could equalize access to literacy and success in education that they frame good ideas as bad and science as the anti-science. They know that framing the key question in literacy education as "which phonics is best?" is absurd. In fact, considering how smart those who speak for the think tanks are, they have to know that what they are mandating doesn't work. They want public education to fail. They know they are promoting absurd solutions, just as they know that the earth is warming, and regulation could have avoided the housing meltdown.

What We Know That Doesn't Count

In the last half century we have come to understand much about reading and writing, how they develop, and how teaching facilitates literacy development. We've gained an appreciation of the universal ability among all humans to think symbolically and to invent language as it is needed. Research on the nature of written language has advanced to the point where we are able to use knowledge from several disciplines to understand how literacy works, how written language relates to oral and other language forms such as American Sign Language, and how the explosion of digital forms of communication are extending the overlap of oral and written language. Theory and research in literacy have been supporting each other. While there are still major differences among researchers, the issues that should be the ones being debated are not the ones politicians and the press are highlighting.

In my own research with my students and colleagues, we used miscue analysis in combination with eye movement research to examine reading as it happens. In Europe, research on the uses and functions of literacy has helped us to put literacy development in the context of its use rather than seeing literacy as a set of autonomous skills. There is broad agreement that comprehension is what literacy education must always be about.

Progress in Curriculum and Pedagogy

Our understanding about the importance of comprehension leads to less focus on didactic materials and more on use of real comprehensible literature both fiction and non-fiction. In the period of the 1980s–1990s this led to a boom in the publication and sales of children's and young adult literature. The simple insight that the more predictable a book or story is for a particular reader the easier it will be to read led to a whole new genre of predictable books.

It is no coincidence that teaching and teacher education are under attack. In both developed and developing nations, there have been major strides toward the professionalization of teachers. Some of the most advanced educational policies can be found in developing nations. As they seek to move beyond the colonial heritage, they have produced more professional teachers and better materials. Their problem, however, is the lack of funds for teacher education and staff development. Pressure from the World Bank has caused many to cut back on their support of schools and social services.

Professional teachers understand literacy and its development and know-how to support learners in becoming literate. And that is dangerous to those who would control the democratic processes for profit.

Why Literacy?

Free universal public education is not an easy institution to attack. It is seen in the United States and in fact the world as the key to economic and political democracy. So the attack has aimed to paint universal public education as a failed institution: It cannot even teach children how to read. That's why literacy is the focal point in attacking universal education. And it is those with the knowledge to make literacy universal who are the target of the campaign.

Movement Conservatism

The attack on literacy education is by no means spontaneous. It is part of a movement conservatism campaign. Two things need to be understood about movement conservatism. The first is that its real goal is always framed as something quite different. The Reading Excellence Act (1997) and Reading First/No Child Left Behind (2001) are framed as reforms to assure that every child will read, but their actual goal is to make public education look like a failed social experiment and to privatize education. The second is that it is not a conspiracy. In a conspiracy, the participants conspire to achieve a purpose they share. Movement conservatism uses many groups with their own agendas to do the work of the campaign. There are many interconnections among these groups through people and funding. But only one group has the connections, power, know-how, and money to carry out the campaign. It is a powerful web of neo-conservative think tanks that Joel Spring (1997) describes in his book, *Political Agendas for Education*. He quotes James Smith in *The Idea Brokers*: "In the early 1970's, executives in a handful of traditionally conservative foundations redefined their programs with the aim of shaping the public policy agenda and constructing a network of conservative institutions and scholars" (p.180).

The campaign seeks to shape the agenda, to shift it away from the real issues—poverty, health, access—to distrust of schools and teachers and their unions. A crisis in literacy is manufactured and those with the best knowledge are blamed for the crisis (Berliner & Biddle, 1995). Then simple sounding solutions are promoted ostensibly as quick cures but in fact to assure failure. Those in charge of the campaign enlist the support of groups who believe in what they are doing but those running the campaign know better. Very bright people are paid well to plan the campaign strategies over the long term to achieve the goals of multinational corporations. They are funded by seemingly non-profit foundations, which have the appearance of the older philanthropic foundations such as Carnegie or Ford. They channel money from the corporations to the think tanks. Within the think tanks, task forces are in charge of the campaign. With the money and connections the system provides, a small group can tightly control a very significant campaign. Their corporate clients control much of the media and that also adds to the effectiveness of the campaigns.

In the United States, we have documented that it is no coincidence that the same issues, tactics, and phrases seemed to pop up in every state—neither should it surprise us that developments in all parts of the world have the same refrains and issues—even when they are a poor fit for local reality (Goodman, et al., 2004).

The think tanks are at the center of the seemingly coincidental eruptions everywhere: They have perfected a campaign model, which is suitable for a local election or a national or international campaign. Through this campaign strategy they can, at modest cost, accomplish major successes for the profit producers.

The literacy campaign manufactured the literacy crisis, declared the reading wars, which are framed as two opposing forces at war over literacy education. Whole language is a teacher-led pedagogy having success with students whose schools traditionally failed. Its influence was exaggerated (perhaps 20 percent of classrooms in the United States were using some version at its peak). And whole language was then blamed for the crisis in literacy. Its adversary was the one true method of teaching reading: Systematic phonics.

According to Richard Feulner, head of the Heritage Foundation, a conservative movement uses the four M's: **Mission**, **Money**, **Management**, and **Marketing** (Kuttner, 2002). Here is my reconstruction of how these work in this campaign.

Mission and Management

The mission of the campaign to privatize education is part of a more general conservative movement Kuttner calls a long term "alliance between organized business, ideological conservatism, advocacy research and the Republican party." But he quotes Christopher DeMuth of American Enterprise Institute: "All fundamental changes are bi-partisan." Senator Ted Kennedy in the Senate and Representative George Miller in the House, both liberal Democrats supported both Reading Excellence and Reading First. The Manhattan Institute, according to Kuttner, is "Especially nimble at co-opting liberals."

The small group of neo-conservatives who are managing this campaign know it has nothing to do with reading. Their mission is to control school curriculum and destroy public education. Their strategy is to frame the campaign as reform of a failing educational system. They chose to attack reading methodology and write into law a simplistic phonics model as a key to making public education appear to be failing. They are responsible for the emphasis on testing, the labeling of schools, and the punishments, which are designed to lead to their privatization.

Marketing

The campaign exploits the willingness of the press to print negative stories about the public schools. They build on the public confusion between science and technology particularly promoting mass high stakes tests and rehashed phonics as the new research based simple sure-cure for what ails the schools.

The Manhattan Institute specializes in targeting opinion elites, according to Kuttner (2002). In the campaign that produced NCLB (2001) and similar state laws, legislators and school board members were literally bombarded with opinion pieces, "research" reports and summaries, and other propaganda designed to keep the message in front of them and give the impression of widespread public support.

The campaign conducts its operations patiently over a long period. But it can mount massive media efforts to achieve an immediate goal. A striking example of the power of movement conservatism took place as Barack Obama was being elected President in 2008. I found remarkable documentation in the coverage of *Education Week*. Linda Darling-Hammond, a prominent and knowledgeable educator, had been principal education advisor to Obama during the campaign. It was widely expected that she would either become Secretary of Education or his White House advisor on education.

The following sequence of articles shows the power of this *Education Week* campaign:

November 30, 2008: A few weeks after the election, Susan Graham (2008) reported: "There are rumors that Dr. Linda Darling-Hammond, President Elect Obama's education transition team leader, is a serious contender for the Cabinet seat herself."

January, 2009: Guest blogger Stephen Sawchuk (2009) reported a gala reception in her honor:

> The drinks flowed, the sushi rolled, and the head of President-elect Obama's education-policy review team, Linda Darling-Hammond, sparkled in an elegant bronze silk gown for a reception held in her honor tonight at a swank downtown Washington hotel.
>
> Speaking in her honor were representatives of McGraw-Hill and the National Urban Alliance for Effective Education, which helped sponsor the event; Dan Domenech, the executive director of the American Association of School Administrators, and New York City schools Chancellor Joel I. Klein.

There is irony in the list of sponsors and speakers: McGraw-Hill has been a major supporter of NCLB and publishes tests and reading programs that have been widely promoted by the campaign.

December 12, 2008: Movement Conservatism campaign had already swung powerfully into action.

Alyson Klein (2009) reported:

> Last Friday, both *The Washington Post* and *The New York Times* ran editorials or op-eds criticizing Stanford education professor Linda Darling-Hammond as a possible choice for a high-level position in the Obama administration, such as Secretary of Education or even Deputy Secretary. And today there was another editorial in the *Los Angeles Times* that blasted Darling-Hammond.

Who has the power to get the same editorial message published in three of the nation's most influential newspapers on the same weekend? Klein was moved to comment: "It looks like Darling-Hammond's detractors have some high-level contacts in the opinion writing world, while Darling-Hammond's supporters are good petitioners." Petitions were in fact signed by many prominent educators in support of Darling-Hammond. A letter to the editor of support for her appeared in *The Post* and the *NY Times* published her own letter, which Klein quoted:

> Since I entered teaching, I have fought to change the status quo that routinely delivers dysfunctional schools and low-quality teaching to students of color in low-income communities. I have challenged inequalities in

financing. I have helped develop new school models through both district-led innovations and charters. And I have worked to create higher standards for both students and teachers, along with assessments that measure critical thinking and performance.

But she had been painted by the campaign as a tool of the teacher unions and an enemy of "reform," their code word for the attack on public education. And the campaign had won. The new administration backed away from the high placed challenge.

February 19, 2009: Klein wrote:

> Linda Darling-Hammond, who was widely rumored for a top job in the U.S. Department of Education, told me today that she is going to stay in California and support President Barack Obama's agenda in her role as an education professor and researcher at Stanford.

Money

The campaign has no shortage of available funding from wealthy right wing "non-profit" foundations who convinced the Internal Revenue Service that their support of these political campaigns is charitable and not political. The $70 million or so a year that these neo-conservative think tanks cost their bene-factors, Kuttner (2002) says, is "chump change" considering what they deliver in return.

In democracies, public opinion is very important because decisions are made on the basis of popular voting or the vote of elected representatives who in theory pay close attention to the views of their constituents. But it is possible that the processes of democracy can be manipulated by clever people with sufficient resources. Movement conservatism is designed to take advantage of the very processes they seek to subvert.

The long campaign paid off. The US Congress rewrote the Elementary and Secondary Education Act—which originated during the civil rights period to use federal money to equalize educational opportunity. It became No Child Left Behind (NCLB) with Reading First, a major part of NCLB explicitly outlawing all aspects of whole language and mandating phonics—code named Scientifically Based Reading Research.

The campaign got the National Science Foundation to house a National Reading Panel (2000) funded by the National Institutes of Health. The panel included prominent academics and researchers who could be counted on to conclude that phonics was the sure way to teach reading. When the lengthy report that the handpicked panel produced seemed to be a bit equivocal, a glossy 35-page condensed version, written by the PR firm Widemeyer Baker, was released prior to the full report. At the same time, the same firm was also representing McGraw-Hill and its reading programs (Garan, 2004, p. 99).

Imposing DIBELS

Most important, the task of enforcing the literacy agenda of Reading First was given to a group centered at the University of Oregon that represented an extreme form of phonics linked to a primitive form of behaviorism and a methodology of direct instruction. They dominated committees that reviewed state proposals for funding under NCLB. States were required to use programs developed by the reviewers and in particular one screening test, DIBELS (Dynamic Indicators of Basic Early Literacy Skill).

DIBELS is on the surface a series of sub-tests each of which takes one minute to administer. In most sub-tests, the child has three seconds to respond to each item. Scoring is always quantitative. In no sub-test is there any judgment of the quality of the comprehension. The final test is the reading of a short text, which has more a chain of events than a story. The score on that is the number of words read correctly in one minute (wrong words are not counted).

One sub-test is a test of the ability to sound out nonsense digraphs and trigraphs. The premise of this test is that the best test of phonics is in non-words where meaning doesn't get in the way of the phonics. Elsewhere I have done a complete analysis of DIBELS, which is the ultimate absurdity in the campaign. There is widespread agreement among reading authorities and psychometricians that this is a very bad test (Goodman, 2006). But it is more than a test. It becomes the whole curriculum. The test is administered three times a year minimally. Those who fail are taught the "skills of the test" and then retested as often as weekly, until they reach an arbitrary score. This is not just a timed test: It also is so focused on speed and accuracy that any concern for meaning is totally lost in trying to say as many words as possible in a minute.

The inspector general of the US Department of Education found gross conflict of interest in that the authors of this test were sitting on the committees judging states applications for NCLB funds and were making the adoption of DIBELS a condition of the approval of the state's funding (Manzo, 2007). When a government report documented that, over six years, the phonics-based program had produced no significant changes (IES, 2008), Representative George Miller (2008), Chair of the US House Education and Labor committee responded:

> From day one of the creation of the Reading First program, it has been corrupted by the Bush administration—plagued by severe mismanagement, poor implementation, and gross conflicts of interest. Despite these serious issues, I had, nevertheless, hoped that the program would produce better results than these. Billions of taxpayer dollars have been spent administering this program over the years . . . Because of the corruption in the Reading First program, districts and schools were steered towards certain reading programs and products that may not have provided the most effective instruction for students. That may explain why we are seeing

these results. . . . We all share the goal of helping all children learn to read. But this report, coupled with the scandals revealed last year, shows that we need to seriously re-examine this program and figure out how to make it work better for students. Our nation's schoolchildren and taxpayers deserve a program that is both properly managed and successful in boosting the reading skills of students.

But the campaign had succeeded through NCLB in establishing legal definitions of reading, reading research, and reading assessment turning science on its head. And American five-year-olds became school failures in kindergarten. Legal action was never taken against those who profited from conflicts of interest. DIBELS is still mandated for several million American children each year.

DIBELS: Suffer Little Children

Here are the beliefs on which DIBELS operates in contradiction to the best knowledge:

- Reading development is mastering a single, universal sequence of component skills.
- That belief is implicit in the choices the authors make of what to test in each sub-test, how the tests are sequenced, and how each component is tested.
- Each test, therefore, is a necessary prerequisite to the following test and to competent reading.
- Thus, failure to achieve an arbitrary benchmark score in a single sub-test is failure in the whole program.
- A one-minute test score is reified as if it really tests what the name suggests it does.

So a test that counts words read correctly in one minute is treated as actually measuring oral reading fluency.

How DIBELS Treats Children

- In DIBELS, there is an assumption that literacy is only developed through direct instruction of component skills.
- It assumes that all children become literate in the same way regardless of experience or culture.
- It tests what they can't do—not what they can do.
- It requires children to adjust to the school rather than adjusting school to the learner.
- It ignores the culture and values of the community.

How DIBELS Treats Teachers

- It treats teachers as interchangeable cogs in a delivery system.
- It treats teachers as untrustworthy technicians who cannot make qualitative judgments.
- It does not permit teachers to use professional judgments to adjust to the learners.
- It assumes that local teachers and administrators have no useful knowledge to contribute.

It demands fidelity to the program through use of Timed Tests:

- Timed tests are inappropriate for most of the skills being tested. Floor and ceiling effects are exaggerated. Some aspects are either/or. They are not scalable, eg. letter knowledge.
- Timed tests disadvantage learners with little experience or motivation for such tasks.
- Children aged five, six, or seven have difficulty responding to items in three seconds.
- Children already reading lose time trying to make sense of nonsense. Children who learn to play the game of ignoring meaning and responding quickly will be overrated.

DIBELS is the ultimate absurdity in this campaign. And now comes absurdity built on absurdity.

From DIBELS to EGRA

USAID, the US agency responsible for aiding education in developing nations decided, with the World Bank, to fast track literacy as a major effort in Africa, Asia, and Latin America.

USAID set its goal: Improved *reading skills* for 100 million children in primary grades by 2015 (Gove & Wetterberg, 2011). I discuss this from the perspective of Africa because the literacy situations in Asia, Latin America, and Africa are very different.

Why would these agencies commit themselves to such a short goal to solve so pervasive a problem as literacy in the undeveloped nations of the world? Their reasoning is simple. If children can't read it should be easy to teach them and solve that problem. We'll fund teams to come in with an effective technology and teach them. Setting a target date of five years from the beginning of the program shows how simple these decision makers think the situation is. Or perhaps they think it is necessary because there is a literacy crisis among third-world people. Inevitably, setting such a deadline for such a major goal causes those carrying the initiative out to look for quick cures and short cuts. And only those who promise such quick cures need apply.

Let's consider what the best knowledge suggests about how to bring literacy to African children. Any literacy campaign has to start with the reality: How is literacy a factor in the lives of the children who will be the students? What are the facilities available? Who will do the teaching? What will the students read? For what purposes in their current lives?

1. We need to know what the need for literacy is in the lives of African children.
   a. What do their parents and other neighbors need literacy for?
   b. Will literacy help them to be better members of their community or will it be seen as a threat to the culture and community?
   c. How do the elders view literacy for girls as compared to boys?
   d. Who reads and what is there to read in their communities?
2. What education for literacy is available?
   a. Is there a school?
   b. Who stays in school and who leaves?
3. What language requirements are there?
4. What is the history of success in the current situation?
5. Is there literacy instruction in the home languages?
   a. Does the school have qualified teachers?
   b. Are there literacy resources (books, paper etc.)?
6. How can the program build on the existing literacy needs of the child, the child's family, or the community?
   a. What will we ask the child to read or write?
   b. How can we keep the learners in school to continue learning?
   c. Can we make books with the children?

Only after such questions are asked can we consider the next questions:

1. What language skills can we build on?
2. How can we assure professional teachers?
3. How will we produce the materials for the students to read?
4. Where will the children be taught?
5. How can we use the facilities available?

Literacy isn't an autonomous skill that can be taught outside of its value and use to the learner. But that is what USAID and the World Bank assumed. They treated literacy as a skill to be learned which then would be useful to those who became literate. USAID awarded a contract to RTI, a research institute that applies for grants and then hires the staff to do the study. RTI was to develop and administer a test in these former colonies to use in assessing the reading abilities of their students.

No consideration was given to assessing the need for or functions of literacy in the villages or towns the children come from. But why write a new test when there is a test already out there that is easy to use and that gives definite scores that represent degrees of reading ability?

So DIBELS becomes EGRA (early grade reading assessment) (Gove & Wetterberg, 2011). In record time, tests are created in the major colonial languages: English, French, and Spanish, and in several of the native languages. DIBELS shows little linguistic sophistication in its construction and the rapidly produced versions of EGRA do not show that they went beyond DIBELS in that regard.

The fact is that there are many groups with many approaches, some naïve and some quite sophisticated, working to bring literacy to African people. Some are more successful than others but no one who knows the complexity of literacy education in this very diverse continent would ever suggest that literacy for all (or even most) could be achieved through a technology in five years (Hoffman, 2012).

But when the World Bank comes calling and seems to offer money and help, no African Department of Education is likely to say no. So the programs were approved by politicians who assigned civil servants to work with the EGRA teams. In fact it probably never occurred to the RTI group that there might be local expertise. James Hoffman, in his critique of the EGRA campaign, classes EGRA among many failed aid programs that come in from the outside with a pre-made program with no preparation or involvement of local informed educators (Hoffman, 2012).

EGRA in Senegal and Gambia

In Senegal, where the home language is French for only 2 percent of the pupils, they were tested in French. On a test of letter names, almost 40 percent could name fewer than 20 letters on a page of letters in a minute. Sixty percent could not sound out more than nine pseudo words in one minute. But one-third read more than 20 words correctly in a 47 word text (Sprenger-Charolles, 2008b). Contrary to DIBELS/EGRA theory, real words are easier to read than nonsense.

In Gambia, where the testing was in English, 80 percent of first graders could read no real words and 91 percent read no pseudo words. For third graders 59 percent read no real words and 76 percent read no pseudo words (Sprenger-Charolles, 2008a). Consider this absurdity: 46 percent of third graders in Gambia could not read a single word of a connected text.

The Gambia Education Minister announced that it was shocking that 46 percent of third grade students could not correctly read a single word of connected text although these poor results were consistent with the national assessment tests. We should ask: If that's so, what did they need EGRA for?

Still the Gambia Minister of Education said EGRA was useful because results created awareness of the scale of the problem. He sees EGRA as very easy to understand. Teachers can use it for diagnostic, instructional, monitoring, and re-medial purposes in classrooms.

But what is the nature of the problem of low literacy in Gambia (or any-where)? EGRA gives no useful information about that. The net result of the use of this absurd test is that children will not stay in school. In Africa, as in most developing nations, children who are not succeeding drop out or are kept out of school by their families.

DIBELS/EGRA and the Pedagogy of the Absurd

In the developers' own words, this was the result of the EGRA campaign:

> Early grade reading assessments . . . have been applied in numerous coun-tries around the world. Between 2005 and March 2011, assessments were completed or are in progress in 42 countries and 74 languages.
>
> Overwhelmingly these assessments have revealed that alarming numbers of children do not know how to read a single word in a simple paragraph by the end of grade 2 or grade 3. And these zero score percentages . . . do not account for the students who scored slightly above zero in oral reading fluency but for all purposes are functionally illiterate (Gove & Wetterberg, 2011, p. 35).

It does not seem to occur to the authors that this is absurd. Could it be that it is the test that is at fault and not the children? Shouldn't someone have pointed at the naked emperor and asked: Where are his clothes? If it wasn't so tragic, we could laugh at the absurdity:

- We have a test based on an extreme view of reading.
- It's composed of skills, which can be tested in one minute with three seconds for each response.
- We administer it to kids in a language other than their home language.
- They show little or no ability to perform on the test.
- So we'll teach them the "skills" the test tests: Letter naming, counting pho-nemes, sounding out nonsense.
- Then we'll retest them and claim progress because they are likely to learn to perform better on the test.

Aren't there dedicated local educators and insightful outsiders who could have suggested much more positive and practical ways of spending money to improve literacy among the world's children? How many children could have the food and health care needed to make them ready for schooling? How many books could have been produced? How many teachers could have been educated? How many adults could have been helped to acquire functional literacy to serve the literacy needs of their children and their communities? And how much useful research could have been produced by those who have the knowledge needed to do it?

DIBELS/EGRA is an absurd set of silly little one-minute tests that never gets close to measuring making sense of print. It is absurd to spend large sums of money to find out what any local educator knew without the test. It is absurd to claim that improving scores by teaching the test is actually teaching reading. It is absurd that scores on these silly tests are used to judge schools, teachers, and children. It is absurd for the United States and the World Bank to ignore the best knowledge in promoting a widely discredited test and technology.

Building knowledge is what research is all about. But knowledge cannot make a difference in and of itself. Educational decision making is political. Ironically, the de facto black list of ideas and those that advocate them has made the research community realize that we have more in common than we thought. Though we differ on minor and major aspects of literacy, we were moving toward some broad agreement on what literacy is, how it is learned, and how best to support learners in becoming literate.

As literacy researchers, we have an obligation to stand up and work for respect for knowledge and truth. If we want the knowledge we produce to be valued, if we want science to be valued over nonsense, if we care about what is done to teachers and kids in the name of science then we have to become political. As individuals and through our professional organizations, we have to recognize the nature of what is happening to governmental literacy decision making.

Our organizations have let themselves be co-opted. The International Reading Association co-sponsored a conference promoting EGRA. National Council of Teachers of English (NCTE) is supporting the common core in exchange for a seat at the table. The American Educational Research Association has taken no stand on how knowledge is being ignored in government policies.

In Europe and the other English speaking countries, unions and professional organizations have taken stronger stands than similar groups in the United States. At the same time, there are many courageous professional, informed teachers, teacher educators, and administrators who are not afraid to put the best knowledge to work. They need our support.

I have no doubt that over time wisdom prevails over nonsense, truth over falsehood. Good research drives out bad. Together we can recognize our responsibility to work collaboratively to make knowledge count. It is even possible that this small book will serve as a rallying cry for those who have been marginalized to fight back.

References

Berliner, D., & Biddle, B. (1995). *Manufactured crisis: Myths, fraud & the attack on public schools.* Reading, MA: Addison-Wesley.

Garan, E. (2004). *In defense of our children: When politics, profit and education collide.* Portsmouth, NH: Heinemann.

Goodman, K. (2006). *The truth about Dibels: What it is and what it does.* Portsmouth, NH: Heinemann.

Goodman, K., Shannon, P., Goodman, Y., & Rapoport, R. (2004). *Save our schools.* Oakland CA: RDR Books.

Gove, A., & Wetterberg, A. (2011). *The Early Grade Reading Assessment: Applications and interventions to improve basic literacy.* Research Triangle Park, NC: RTI Press. Retrieved from www.rti.org/pubs/bk-0007-1109-wetterberg.pdf

Graham, S. (2008). Why not Darling-Hammond? *Education Week*, November 30.

Hoffman, J. (2012). Why EGRA—a clone of DIBELS—will fail to improve literacy in Africa. *Research in the Teaching of English*, 46:4, 340–357.

Institute for Educational Science (2008, May) Preliminary Report. Retrieved from http://ies.ed.gov/ncee/pdf/20084016.pdf

Klein, A. (2009). Linda Darling-Hammond to stay in California. *Education Week*, February 19.

Kuttner, R. (2002) Philanthropy and Movements. *American Prospect*, July. Retrieved from www.prospect.org/cs/articles?article=philanthropy_and_movements

Manzo, K. (2007). Evaluation indicates limited effects under early reading first program. *Education Week*, June 13.

Miller, G. (2008). Rep. Geroge Miller, Chair of the House education and Labor committee. Responding to IES report on reading first, May 1.

National Reading Panel. (2000). Retrieved from http://lincs.ed.gov/communications/NRP

No Child Left Behind. (2001). Retrieved from www2.ed.gov/nclb/overview/intro/execsumm.html

Ravitch, D. (2011). *Death and life of the great American school system: How testing and choice are undermining education.* New York: Basic Books.

Reading Excellent Act. (1997). Retrieved from www.govtrack.us/congress/bills/105/hr2614

Sawchuk, S. (2009) A celebration for Linda Darling-Hammond. *Education Week*, January 18. Politics K-16. Retrieved from www.edweek.org/ew/section/blogs/index.html

Sprenger-Charolles, L. (2008a). *The Gambia Early Grade Reading Assessment (EGRA): Report for the World Bank.* Research Triangle Park, NC: RTI.

Sprenger-Charolles, L. (2008b). *The Senegal Early Grade Reading Assessment (EGRA): Report for the World Bank.* Research Triangle Park, NC: RTI.

Spring, J. (1997). *Political Agendas for Education: From the Religious Right to the Green Party.* New York: Routledge.

3

RE-READING POVERTY; REORIENTING EDUCATIONAL POLICY

Patrick Shannon

Editor's Note: At a World Reading Conference in Edinburgh a few years ago, I asked an official of the World Bank if there are enough resources in the world to assure every child nutrition, health, and education. He said "of course. It's a matter of priorities." In this chapter, Patrick Shannon shows that poverty is the result of policies that are determined by those in our society who blame the poor for their own condition. He provides ample evidence that increased poverty is a major factor in diminished success in schools. This is a prime example of governmental policies that ignore the widely available knowledge of experts and instead substitute the self-serving dogma of those with money and power. So decisions are made that diminish resources for schools that serve the poor, reduce their curriculum to basics, and then blame professionals for the inevitable failure of their policies.

KSG

During an interview with members of the National Council of Teachers of English, Secretary of Education Arne Duncan (2011) explained the logic behind his push to reauthorize the Elementary and Secondary Education Act (ESEA), refocusing on the lowest performing 5 percent of America's public schools. Speaking of his time as Chief Executive Officer of Chicago Public Schools, he declared, "What became clear to me was kids were poor because their families were poor, and families were poor because the quality of education in that community hadn't changed at all" (p. 1). Implied in this statement is Duncan's assumption that if the quality of schools would change, then poverty would end in the United States. The schools, he reasons, are responsible for poverty. This echoes the sentiment that Commissioner of Education Francis Keppel expressed when the ESEA was first passed in 1965. Keppel paraphrased Archimedes, substituting public education as the lever and federal assistance for the fulcrum in order to move children out of poverty (the world). Unmentioned in Duncan's echo, however, are the scope and tenacity of the federal assistance that accompanied the original ESEA legislation in the short-lived War on Poverty.

Duncan frames the opportunity to learn entirely within the public school building, positioning schools as the driving force behind individual, regional, and national prosperity. He argues that schools could provide the conditions of education that would enable all citizens to acquire the knowledge, skills, and dispositions to make them productive workers in a global information economy. The Obama Administration's *Race to the Top* is his fulcrum to save the United States and each individual citizen from falling behind their global competitors. Highly educated workers, Duncan believes, would attract businesses and services to a region, raising the living standards of locals, fueling their aspirations for their children, and providing the requisite dispositions to enable the United States to "win the future." He concludes that all that is necessary to start this economic juggernaut is for schools to change. If schools fail to change, however, they will drag the United States to third world status.

In this chapter, I describe briefly the growing conditions of poverty in the United States and place them within the context of other developed countries, document consequences of poverty on individuals' learning and their acquisition of other forms of social capital, explore current American ideological positions on the relationship between poverty and education, and propose some actions educators might take, joining with others in order to wage a new War on Poverty.

Poverty is Real

According to the Census Bureau (Tavernise, 2011), nearly one in six Americans officially lives in poverty. That's over 49.1 million people! It's the highest number in the 52 years that the Bureau has published this statistic. The official poverty line was established in a 1963 Department of Agriculture report, when Mollie Orshansky determined that a typical family of four could prepare three minimally adequate meals per day on exactly $2.736. The President's Council of Economic Advisors established the poverty line through two multiplication problems ($2.736 x 365 days = $998.34 for food annually; and because at that time, the average family spent one-third of its income on food, the Council multiplied the annual food budget by three, establishing $2,995.92 as the threshold of the poverty line). The formula remains unchanged to this day, and the $22,314 threshold in 2010 is simply adjusted for inflation. A new Census Bureau metric (called the supplemental measure) divides Americans into four categories of family income based on the multiples of the poverty line (Tritch, 2011):

Poor (below the poverty line)	16.1 percent of the population
Low income (one to two times the poverty line)	31.8 percent

| Middle income (two to four times) | 24.8 percent |
| Well off (over four times) | 17.3 percent |

Being poor is not distributed equally among Americans. Using Census Bureau terms, 12.1 percent of Asians, 27.4 percent of Blacks, 26.6 percent of Hispanics, and 9.9 percent of non-Hispanic Whites live below the poverty line. The South and the West have greater percentages of poor than the Midwest and the Northeast. The young are more likely to be poor (22.5 percent under 18) than the elderly (9 percent over 65). Women are poorer than men, receiving 77 percent of men's incomes for equivalent work. Combinations of these characteristics influence the likelihood of individuals being poor. For example, 12 percent of White children are impoverished, but the poverty rates for Black and Hispanic children approach 40 percent. Thirty-one percent of custodial single mothers (Bureau term) live in poverty, and 14 percent of single fathers.

According to the Brookings Institution (Kneebone & Garr, 2010), poverty is increasing more rapidly in the suburbs than in either cities or rural areas. Note that few of these figures include the likely negative consequences of continuing high unemployment (near 9 percent nationally, but nearly 40 percent for African American males in urban areas), high home foreclosure rates (more than 2 million in process), and high rates of consumer debt (household debt peaked at $12.5 trillion in 2008).

Poverty threatens people's abilities to meet basic human needs. Despite a dramatic decline in food prices as a percent of income since 1963 and government food support programs, only 85 percent of Americans feel secure about their daily food supply (Coleman-Jensen, et al., 2011). Nine percent report concern for their abilities to feed themselves and/or their families at least once a month, and an additional 6 percent describe such insecurity weekly. Only 59 percent of these individuals are eligible or participate in government food support programs. The Census Bureau documents an increase in the percentage of Americans with health insurance; a federal bill enables families to carry their children on their policies until age 26, and there has been a 31 percent increase in Americans relying on Medicare, Medicaid, and military assistance programs. Still, a million more Americans were without health insurance in 2010 than the previous year. According to the Joint Center for Housing Studies (2010), 16 percent of American homeowners and 25 percent of renters spend more than half their income on housing. An additional 33 percent of the owners and 50 percent of the renters allot between 30 and 50 percent of their incomes to secure a place to live. In order to meet these needs and to begin to "get ahead," Duncan's phrase during his interview, the Wider Opportunities for Women report (2011) estimates that a single worker would require an income of $30,012 a year—three times the poverty line for an individual—at an hourly rate of twice the minimum wage. A family of four would require $67,920. Such income requirements reach well into the newly designated middle-income group, suggesting that more than 50 percent of Americans are unable to get ahead of their bills.

It does not have to be this way. There is nothing natural about the poverty line or the distribution of incomes in America (Chang, 2010). Poverty rates vary across developed nations. In 2007 (the latest year for reliable data, and before the Great Recession), the United States ranked 17th on poverty rates among 21 developed nations (according to the United Nations Human Poverty Index, 2011), and 18th for child poverty (UNICEF, 2007). On both scales, the United States trailed Scandinavian countries, Western Europe (except Ireland and Portugal), Canada, Australia, and Japan. The United States was 17th in children's material well-being (calculated on family income, parent employed, and reported deprivation). The United States ranked last (21st of 21) of the developed nations on health and safety scales (measured by infant mortality rates, birth weight, and immunization). The United States earned its highest ranking (12th) for education (rated by academic achievement, attendance, and graduation rates). These comparisons demonstrate that other nations choose not to tolerate high rates of poverty, and take steps to ensure adequate food, income, housing, and health care through government actions.

Poverty Has Consequences For Students

In *Poverty and potential* (2009), David Berliner outlines out-of-school factors that negatively affect poor students' opportunities to learn. He acknowledges the physical and academic conditions of schools and quality of teaching are factors in students' achievement, but argues that the likely conditions of poverty limit students' learning and achievement as well. He argues vehemently and persuasively against Duncan's assumptions, and his *Race to the Top* solution for school reform.

- One in four people living in poverty does not have medical insurance, leading to poor prenatal care, low birth weight, untreated common illnesses, and undiagnosed vision and dental problems. These chronic issues lead to greater number of absences from school, attendance while still ill, and lower capacities to concentrate on school work.
- When students attend school hungry, their bodies conserve the limited amounts of food energy available, saving it for vital bodily functions, and then, for physical growth. The lowest biological priority is social interaction and learning. Weekends without adequate nutrition can leave students unable to attend, irritable, and slower in cognitive functioning.
- Exposure to mercury, lead, pesticides, and other controlled chemicals in their environments suppresses children's intelligence, behavioral inhibitions, and immune systems. Despite efforts to protect citizens from pollutants, poor Americans are more likely to experience prolonged exposure through inadequate housing, proximity to industrial or agricultural sites, and lack of oversight.
- Coping with poverty and its consequences increases the stress levels within and among impoverished families. Chronic stress is associated with secretion

of the hormone cortisol, which hinders memory, problem solving and judgment, and causes deteriorated immune response and elevated blood pressure.

In his book *Intelligence and how to get it*, psychologist Richard Nisbett (2009) reports that human genes respond to the quality of the human environment. At the top of the socio-economic status scale, nearly 75 percent of the variation in intelligence results from genetic influences, but in poverty, less than 20 percent of the variation in intelligence is caused by genetic endowment. Poor people's environments account for 80 percent of the variation because inadequate environments suppress gene expression. Although these findings have many implications, they show, clearly, arguments that intelligence is fixed and hereditary are wrong; rather, genetic contributions vary according to richness of the environment in an almost perfect correlation. Securing adequate food, housing, health care, and income, and relieving chronic anxiety about coping with poverty have direct effects on people's intelligence, learning, and achievement (Wilkerson & Pickett, 2009).

Anthony Bryk, et al. (2010) are explicit and detailed in their accounts about the effects of poverty on learning to read. Studying 474 elementary schools in the Chicago Public System (before Duncan became its CEO), this research team identified five essential supports that determine whether or not the schools improved significantly during the eight years of community control over neighborhood schools (1988–1995). Schools strong on the essentials (professional capacity, school learning climate, parent, school and community ties, instructional guidelines, and building leadership) were ten times more likely to improve significantly in reading achievement compared with schools weak in some or all of these essential supports. However, they concluded that improvement took hold rarely in schools that served the truly disadvantaged, "where palpable human needs walked through the doors daily" (p. 196). Schools changing to include the five essential supports were insufficient in the very communities that Duncan described in his NCTE interview. Rather, Bryk, et al. suspect that to educate these students (they estimate 40,000 children in Chicago alone) would require concerted efforts to bring food, shelter, health care, income, and physical security to their lives before school reforms could impact the learning of poor children. They call for research to test their hypothesis, and an end to "school only approaches" for closing the achievement gap.

Policy

If educational policy-making were a rational act, then state and federal legislators would use this strong biological, psychological, and sociological evidence to design policies to provide material support for adequate food, shelter, income, and health care for all Americans. These policies would ensure all students an equal capacity to develop fully, raising the likelihood that endowments, and not environments, would influence variability among learners. After providing just opportunities for all students to learn, in-school conditions could begin to close the learning gaps across the income categories. This scenario assumes that policy-makers use the "best" evidence in order to arrive at the "right" conclusion. Policies, however, are not always, or even often, the result of an objective weighing of the facts. Rather, policy-making is more the "authoritative allocation of values" (Ball, 1990, p. 3) held by the most powerful participants in the deliberations. To understand the positions of Duncan and others on educational policy concerning the relationship(s) between poverty and schooling, follow *the values.*

Although most Americans associate poverty with a lack of income, political values color representations of poverty and its causes (Shannon, 1998). Conservatives construe poverty as a personal matter resulting from an individual's lack of ability, initiative, or moral character. Traditional conservatives represent poverty as the result of individual's lack of intelligence or talent, leading to a natural ordering by income.

A classic expression of this position is Richard Herrnstein's and Charles Murray's *The bell curve* (1994), in which the authors declared, "For many people, there is nothing they can learn that will repay the cost of the teaching" (p. 526). People live in poverty because they cannot learn to perform jobs for which employers are willing to pay a living wage. As a result, government intervention at any level would artificially inflate the social, political, and economic contributions of these individuals, diminishing society's ability to function effectively and efficiently, undermining meritocracy and creating unreasonable expectations. Conservatives argue that we (and the poor) should therefore accept the natural consequences of human differences.

Neoconservatives conclude that people are poor because they have not made "good" choices to take responsibility for themselves and their families. Free societies require citizens to develop affirmative behaviors—fairness, self-control, duty, and empathy—in order to function effectively. They create institutions to insure that children and immigrants are socialized toward such values. Individuals lacking these social values do not fit into the prevailing social order, and therefore, suffer the social, economic, and political consequences. William Bennett (1994; 1996) and others (Payne, 2005) explain that the poor must develop useful social and moral capital before they can expect to develop economic and political capital. Governmental attempts to ameliorate the consequences of poverty, unless they attend to values and dispositions, create and maintain cultures of dependence that prolong social and individual problems.

Liberals tend to locate the causes of poverty outside the individual (intelligence or moral character) and inside the opportunities available to acquire the skills necessary to make enough income "to get ahead." Neoliberals argue that continued poverty is a result of institutional failure to provide all citizens with sufficient social capital to enable them to compete in the global economy. This is Duncan's position, and it has informed the core of American educational policy for 30 years, since the A Nation at Risk report (Gardner, 1983). In varying degrees, from Bush's "thousand points of light" to Obama's *Race to the Top*, neoliberals have sought ways to make schools work for everyone, including the poor. These policies began with volunteerism as the answer, and now seek market solutions to lead to the creative destruction of current school forms and a rise of presumptive variations on schooling to accommodate individual needs (Hess, 2010), for example, charter schools.

Traditional liberals understand poverty as an aberration of a just, developed democracy, in which past racial, class, and gender inequalities have been allowed to persist. Rather than reflecting personal problems or singular institutional failure, poverty is the result of systemic, institutional discrimination. Liberals point toward the uneven distribution of poverty within the United States' population as a rationale for targeted programs to reverse poverty among specific groups. Beginning with the War on Poverty and Civil Rights legislation in the 1960s, traditional liberals have sought policies that address the multiple consequences of poverty. During the Johnson Administration, Congress passed laws to help the poor with income, food, housing, medical care, and jobs programs. Although never fully funded, when coupled with the ESEA and Project Head Start, liberal programs reduced poverty rates and narrowed the achievement gap between poor/low income and middle income/well off American students (Berliner, 2009).

What happened to these initiatives? Almost before the ink was dry on that legislation, Congress (liberals included) began to divert funding in order to conduct the Vietnam War. Beginning in the early 1970s, conservatives started to build a movement to enhance their values in government policies, creating think tanks, legal foundations, and political organizations to articulate and distribute their positions for public consumption (Hacker & Pierson, 2010). Working through the US Chamber of Commerce, they assembled a task force of 40 business executives to coordinate movement activities and to increase its accessibility to federal and state legislatures. The origins of the Business Roundtable, the American Legislative Exchange Council, the Heritage Foundation, the Cato Institute, the Manhattan Institute, and Americans for Prosperity can be traced to this group—all designed to uproot liberalism in the United States. The movement has been remarkably successful on at least three fronts: defining politics as an expression of self-interest, representing government (taxes and regulation) as intrusion on individual freedoms, and redistributing wealth toward the very well off (the top 10, 1 and 0.1 percents). As a result, the American social safety nets are under constant threat.

A Way Forward

If poverty is real and increasing in the United States; if it has biological, psychological, and social effects on people that limit their abilities to take up the affordances of classroom opportunities to learn; and if coordinated efforts inside and outside of schools can ameliorate both the extent of poverty and its effect on learning, then anyone committed to public schooling must acknowledge that poverty is a social issue, not just a problem for individuals. These facts argue for a liberal response. Traditional conservatives are wrong to be so pessimistic about the prospects of the poor, because changes in the conditions of poverty increase chances for full genetic expression. Neoconservative claims that social capital is low among some of the poor is understandable (if unacceptable) given the cynicism behind alternating neglect and the miracle reform programs that wash over them annually with little sustained progress (Payne, 2008). Duncan and the neoliberals have it backwards; policies can change the conditions of poverty to enable all students to take advantage of the changes in schools. We know this to be true because coordinated efforts that link education and social policies work in other countries, and they worked in the United States when given a chance.

To address the educational needs of 22 percent of school-aged children, educators must attend to social policies affording access to food, housing, health care, and income security. Currently the odds seem stacked against such policies: Congress cut food support for families in order to fund healthier lunches for all school children, and then declared pizza a vegetable. In order to extend unemployment benefits for the nearly 9 percent of Americans out of work, President Obama accepted an extension of tax cuts for corporations and the rich.

Over strong objections, the US Supreme Court has ruled that Obama's proposed extension of health insurance to more Americans is constitutional. Every modest liberal step forward is met with resistance from various groups in the 40-year conservative movement, including the "bleed the beast" strategy to deny governments' sufficient tax income to run the social programs properly. Federal and state budget deficits weaken the knees of even sympathetic legislators, and they find it easier to loosen or even cut the ties of the safety net rather than to tighten and strengthen them.

Although it will be a difficult struggle, educators must join with others to make legislators listen, and then act accordingly. We cannot rely on the "right" elected official(s) to do this work for us. We must organize ourselves and join organizations in order to demonstrate our understandings that poverty is a social issue, that its existence is a poor public allocation of values and resources, and that its effects limit the possible influences of changes in schools for many among the poor. Based on those understandings, we must demand changes in social policies that provide the poor with equal opportunities to develop and learn to their full capacities. We must prepare and form coalitions with other groups to wage a new War on Poverty, lending our expertise on how reading and writing all texts (of all types—symbolic and embodied) can redirect the allocation of values away from self-interest in which people exist for the economy's benefit and toward a more just society in which the economy exists for people's well-being (Shannon, 2011).

This means that:

- Living wage struggles are educational struggles;
- Pollution problems are educational problems;
- Health care policies are educational policies;
- Fair housing acts are educational acts; and
- Nutritional issues are educational issues.

There can be no separations among social, economic, and political reform and educational reform. The children and families are poor in Chicago (and all around the United States) because we permit them to be poor. We can change that.

References

Ball, S. (1990). *Politics and policy making in education: Explorations in policy sociology.* New York: Routledge.

Bennett, W. (1994). *The book of virtues: A treasury of great moral stories.* New York: Simon & Schuster.

Bennett, W. (1996). *Body count: Moral poverty and how to win America's war against crime and drugs.* New York: Simon & Schuster.

Berliner, D. (2009). *Poverty and potential: Out of school factors and school success.* Boulder, CO: Education Public Interest Center.

Bryk, A., Sebring, P., Allensworth, E., Luppescu, S., & Easton, J. (2010). *Organizing schools for improvement: Lessons from Chicago.* Chicago, IL: University of Chicago Press.

Chang, H. (2010). *23 things they don't tell you about capitalism.* New York: Bloomsbury.

Coleman-Jensen, A., Nord, M., Andrews, M., & Carlsen, S. (2011). *Household food security in the United States 2010.* Washington DC: US Department of Agriculture.

Duncan, A. (2011). A conversation with Arne Duncan. *National Council of English Teachers Council Chronicle, 3,* 1, 4–5.

Gardner, D. (1983) A Nation at Risk: The imperative for educational reform. Washington DC: Superintendent of Documents.

Hacker, J., & Pierson, P. (2010). *Winner-take-all politics: How Washington made the rich richer—and turned its back on the middle class.* New York: Simon & Schuster.

Herrnstein, A., & Murray, C. (1994). *The bell curve.* New York: Free Press.

Hess, F. (2010). *The same thing over and over: How school reformers get stuck in yesterday's ideas.* Cambridge, MA: Harvard University.

Joint Center for Housing Studies. (2010). *The state of the nation's housing.* Cambridge, MA: Harvard University.

Kneebone, E., & Garr, E. (2010). *The suburbanization of poverty: Trends in metropolitan American—2000–2008.* Washington, DC: The Brookings Institute.

Nisbett, R. (2009). *Intelligence and how to get it: Why schools and cultures count.* New York: Norton.

Payne, C. (2008). *So much reform; so little change: The persistence of failure in urban schools.* Cambridge, MA: Harvard University.

Payne, R. (2005). *A framework for understanding poverty*. Highlands, TX: Aha Process Inc.

Shannon, P. (1998). *Reading poverty*. Portsmouth, NH: Heinemann.

Shannon, P. (2011). *Reading wide awake: Politics, pedagogies & possibilities*. New York: Teachers College Press.

Tavernise, S. (2011). Soaring poverty casts spotlight on "lost decade." *New York Times*, September 13, A 1.

Tritch, T. (2011). Reading between the poverty lines. *New York Times*, November 20, SR10.

UNICEF. (2007). *Child poverty in perspective*. Report Card 7. Florence, Italy.

United Nations Human Poverty Index. (2011). Retrieved from http://en.wikipedia.org/wiki/Human_Poverty_Index

Wider Opportunities for Women. (2011). *Living below the line: Economic security and American's families*. Washington, DC: Wider Opportunities for Women.

Wilkerson, R., & Pickett, J. (2009). *The spirit level: Why greater equality makes societies stronger*. New York: Bloomsbury.

4

NEOLIBERAL AND NEOCONSERVATIVE LITERACY EDUCATION POLICIES IN CONTEMPORARY FRANCE

Jacques Fijalkow

Editor's Note: In this chapter, the French experience in literacy is laid out in detail, revealing a remarkable similarity to the same period in the English-speaking world and other European countries. What begins as a professional concern for literacy becomes a manufactured crisis over illiteracy, and a means of attacking education and teacher education. Those with knowledge are marginalized and pseudo-science is elevated.

KSG

To understand "Whose Knowledge Counts in Governmental Literacy Education Policies?" from a French perspective, we must first briefly describe the national context and the key features of the French school system:

1) France has a highly centralized state system. Programs are decided in Paris and imposed throughout the country by means of an impressive array of training and control policies.
2) The French system is based on success in core studies (specifically mathematics and French). Students who do poorly in these subjects are directed to vocational programs.

Success in school is closely tied to the parents' occupation. The latest PISA results show France is one of the countries in which this indicator carries the greatest weight. The educational policies increasingly implemented over the last 30 years reflect the prevailing neoliberal and neoconservative policies. What does this situation mean for literacy education?

Neoliberal and Neoconservative Policies

Neoliberalism embraces five ideological ideas:

1) Freedom is more important than equality.
2) Competition is considered a better way to solve problems than cooperation.
3) It is necessary to reduce the role of the state by giving preference to the private sector over the public one.
4) Social institutions should be considered as businesses.
5) Social problems must be treated as individual cases rather than as the individual expression of collective problems.

Neoconservatism is built around three concepts:

1) The belief that the past is better than the present.
2) Things that come from the past must continue, despite any criticism they may receive.
3) Traditional solutions should replace recently introduced changes.

Recent changes might be called a counter-revolution or a restoration. These changes can be seen on three levels, from the most extensive to the narrowest: Changes on the level of public service (New Public Management), changes on the educational level, and changes on the literacy level.

On the Public Service Level

Since 2007 (the beginning of Nicolas Sarkozy's right-wing presidency), all public services—the financial responsibilities of the state—are in the process of being systematically dismantled. This includes education, but also health, transportation, postal services, energy, housing, etc. Education is thus not an isolated case, but one among many. Public spending over the last several years has been systematically reduced, eliminating one position out of every two vacated due to retirement. This applies to teachers as well as to hospital staff, post office employees, railway employees, etc.

On the Educational Level

According to official figures, while all government departments have lost jobs over the last three years, the Ministry of Education has lost more positions than all of the other ministries combined.

Other changes at the educational level include:

- Fragmentation of the school population: On the one hand, creation of specific structures for children with learning difficulties and, on the other, creation of institutes of excellence for the elite.

- Promotion of an individual elite (the "talented").
- Pseudo-democratization: Setting up access to "*les grandes écoles*" (elitist higher education institutions) for children from disadvantaged areas.
- Replacement of collective means of helping children with learning difficulties by individual assistance.
- Evaluation for purposes of accountability, based on a business model rather than on a public service model.

On the Literacy Level

It is necessary to understand what has happened over the last 30 years in France. It is not an exaggeration to speak of the three wars on literacy.

The First Reading War: Illiteracy

Historical Background

Illiteracy surfaced quite recently in public debate as a new issue, a "discovery." The revelation had an impact comparable to that of the reappearance of an illness such as the plague. People were surprised and worried.

In 1980, a humanitarian association, *Aide à toute détresse Quart-Monde* (*ATD Quart-Monde*), pointed out that extreme poverty goes hand-in-hand with grave deficiencies in children's schooling, particularly in terms of mastery of written language. This announcement supported by the *Association française pour la lecture* (*AFL*, French Association for Reading), led to the creation in 1984, under the government of Socialist Pierre Mauroy, of an inter-ministerial structure, the *Groupe permanent contre l'illettrisme* (*GPLI*). The Group was headed by a politician, François Bayrou, later to become Minister of National Education under a Socialist government. Next, the International Adult Literacy Survey of 1994 revealed such poor results for France that the French Ministry of Education decided to withdraw from the international task force, to ensure that the French "scores" would not be published (OECD, 1997). In 1996, French President Jacques Chirac blamed the crisis in literacy on the "global method" of teaching reading. Several years after the international survey, it was decided to conduct a made-in-France reading assessment. A national institution,[1] specialized in collecting and analyzing social and economic statistical data, but not in educational matters, was hired to conduct this new survey (INSEE, 2004).

Three battle grounds can be identified in this first reading war: The first pertaining to definitions; the second to the number of illiterates in France; and the third over the reasons for the existence of a problem of this kind in France today.

The Battle of Definitions

The first difficulty in this fight is trying to discern what is being discussed. Strictly speaking, illiteracy is currently defined as a level of competence in written language that is insufficient to successfully deal with the demands of life in modern society. The population in question is native French speakers who attended school in France. Immigrants with little or no schooling and whose native language is not French are not included. Thus defined, illiteracy is merely a new name for what UNESCO has long called "functional illiteracy" (*analphabétisme fonctionnel*).

The point to underline is that, unlike the absolute notion of not knowing how to read at all—"pure" illiteracy (*analphabétisme*)—functional illiteracy is a relatively new notion for the French, varying in relation to the level of competency in written language necessary to successfully manage everyday life. This means that a person may be deemed literate at one socio-economic level, but become illiterate if he or she moves up the socio-economic scale. Or, a given person may be deemed illiterate in one place but not in another.

Furthermore, the word "illiteracy" can work like a semantic trap. To clearly understand it, the term should be "de-semanticized" from its formerly and currently accepted meaning of not knowing how to read at all (*analphabétisme*) and "re-semanticized" in the sense of functional illiteracy. The belief that illiteracy is increasing is reinforced when it is presented in language evoking traditional illiteracy (*analphabétisme*). The feeling of illiteracy then becomes a national catastrophe.

Illiteracy defined in this way makes inroads into public life, not in the realm of school children but of adults, not that of emerging literacy but of professional training and employment. The public immediately wants to know how it can be that illiteracy has emerged in a great, modern country like France?

The Battle of Numbers

The scope of illiteracy became political, with illiteracy statistics most likely reflecting as much or more about who reports them and in what context as they do about what is being reported on.

The survey carried out by the National Institute of Statistics and Economic Studies (INSEE, 1994) found that 9 percent of the population could be considered functionally illiterate, a lower percentage than the unpublished results of the international survey that same year. National pride was saved, and French authorities heaved a sigh of relief. It should be noted, however, that this is the same figure reported at the very beginning of this whole story, ten years before, in a report made by the GPLI (Espérandieu, et al. 1984).

Discussion

An explanation particularly appreciated by the media is that of "forgetting." Illiterates are people who have "forgotten" how to read: They no longer know how to read because they did not practice the skill after leaving school. To our knowledge, no study exists showing that people forget how to read. If there is a question of deficiency, it would seem more likely to be on the part of those questioning rather than those in question.

Other explanations have been put forward. For example, Roger Fauroux, former minister in a conservative government and author of an official report entitled *Pour l'école* (For schools, 1996a), claimed that the main cause of illiteracy is in the family's "abandoning" working mothers and absent grandparents result in a lack of family support for school children (1996b, p. 9). None of these accusations was based on any objective research.

In the same souce, Fauroux invokes as a secondary cause, so called "modern teaching methods" (p. 9). The criticism of these methods harks back to the classic argument in favor of the traditional model of schooling: "We have neglected the fundamental nature of learning: effort, emulation, reward" (p. 9). Further on, the author continues to attribute the responsibility for these changes to educational sciences and to the French teacher-training institutes (*Instituts universitaires de formation de maîtres, IUFM*), which were created by a government of the opposing political bent.

These explanations of illiteracy consisted in a characteristically conservative spirit, of successively questioning real or supposed contemporary transformations of both family and school. The fight against illiteracy became a war machine aimed at schools. The consequence of such discourse was obvious: If schools perform poorly on such a fundamental task as teaching students how to read and write, then the institution must be changed. This is exactly what happened over the following years with the return to power of a neoliberal and neoconservative government.

The accusations and affirmations were completely unfounded: Our studies of teaching practices in first grade (Fijalkow & Fijalkow, 1994; Fijalkow, 2003) showed that, in fact, "modern methods" had made few inroads into the classroom. Moreover, nothing proved that, if such were the case, it led to increased illiteracy. Progressive educators support the opposite hypothesis: For them, the traditional methods are at fault, since they do not get the message across to children, especially those from underprivileged backgrounds, that school does make sense. Proponents of the view of increased illiteracy are to be seen, then, as conservatives using this argument to challenge real or imaginary changes, whether in the familial or educational context.

But is illiteracy really a growing problem in French society? We know that the illiteracy rate in France is currently around 10 percent. This figure corresponds, from teachers' experiences, to the period before compulsory education was extended to age 16, at which point two to three students per class in their final year at age 12 or 13 were recognized as having difficulties with literacy. So the facts put forth are not new. What is new is today's political and journalistic exploitation of these cases of long-standing school failure. The "dunces" of old are the "illiterates" of today: Change the name, change the connotation. But there is no guarantee that the individuals concerned come out ahead.

To clearly position this discussion on illiteracy, we need to look at the difference between myth and marketplace. The myth is that this is a new problem and is increasing. In the marketplace, the mobilization around this new public of "illiterates" by reading primer publishers and speech therapists—stakeholders eager to play an active profit-oriented role in diagnosis and therapy—provides an interesting context. Marketplace interests add to a baseline of ideological, pedagogical, and political conservatism.

So, back to the question—whose knowledge counts in governmental literacy education policies? We can see from this first war on reading that the people whose knowledge counts for the governmental literacy education policy in France are:

1. A humanitarian association (*ATD Quart-Monde*) who alerted public opinion to the persistence of a poor and under-educated population.
2. The conjunction of journalists and politicians from across the spectrum who distorted the information, leading people to believe in a new, rapidly evolving reality, and raising questions as to the effectiveness of teaching practices in schools.
3. French reading evaluators believed by the public, rather than international experts.
4. Economists or statisticians believed by the public, rather than experts in education.

In the view of educational authorities, there is no single body of knowledge in literacy education: Anyone able to read and write at a reasonable level can construct a tool for evaluating literacy.

The Second Reading War: Dyslexia

Historical Background

In earlier times, not all children were obliged to learn to read. Today, when a child has reading problems, different kinds of specialist can be called upon but a century ago, in the professional context of the times, people turned to medical doctors. These specialists had discovered that brain injury could result in speech disorders. One case was thus equated to the other, and physicians put forward the hypothesis that children having difficulties with written language suffered some form of brain injury, akin to adults afflicted with speech disorders. The reasoning was acceptable and the hypothesis is legitimate. The fact is that this hypothesis has never been validated, neither directly by clear identification of a brain lesion in children, nor indirectly by more sophisticated means, as shown by a careful review of the literature (Fijalkow, 1984/1996).

But the debate became heated; on the one side, avid proponents of an organic origin for poor reading; on the other, partisans of an environmental origin. The former included members of the medical profession (doctors, speech therapists, cognitive psychologists); the latter hailed from the ranks of clinical psychologists and educators. This second group of specialists, having put forward other explanatory factors—primarily social, clinical, and pedagogical—found it difficult to speak of "dyslexia" for all poor readers. The question of what should be specifically termed "dyslexia" thus became central to the discussion.

Proponents of neurological causality in certain cases of reading disorders can now benefit from new data, thanks to the tremendous technological progress made in brain imaging. Nevertheless, the observation that the brains of children labeled as "dyslexic" present different images than those of control readers does not make it possible to ascertain whether these differences existed before learning to read, resulted from the activity of learning to read, or were merely the trace, on the cerebral level, of observable differences in reading behavior. As the International Dyslexia Association (2012) recently stated: There is "a persistent which-came-first-the-chicken-or-the-egg question about dyslexia."

A conference on *La dyslexie en question* (Dyslexia in question), held in 1972 by the *Centre de recherches de l'éducation spécialisée et de l'adaptation scolaire* (Center for research in special education, CRESAS), presented two sides to the reluctant-reader question: On one hand, some of these children had a problem they called "dyslexia," whereas on the other, the explanation could be found in the family and/or the school environment.

Mauvais lecteurs, pourquoi? (Poor readers, why?, Fijalkow, 1984/1996) offered an overview of the international literature on the hypothetical reasons why some students struggle to learn to read and write, and concluded that there is no single reason and that interdisciplinary research is necessary. Subsequently, and for many years, the phrase *"mauvais lecteurs"* (poor readers) was commonly used to speak about these students instead of the previously used term "dyslexics."

About 30 years after the 1972 conference, this position was again questioned. On March 21, 2001, an "Action plan for children afflicted with specific speech disorders" was presented to the Minister of National Education, of Health and the State Secretary for the Elderly. The text targeted 4 to 5 percent of school children, 1 percent of whom displayed severe problems (Veber & Ringard, 2001, p. 5)—figures that the authors of the report characterized as "a matter of State" (p. 7). This text resulted from intensive lobbying during the years preceding its publication: In those times, it was difficult to escape the mass of articles, films, documents in diverse media showing how the school system was deaf and dumb in the face of so many children unable to learn to read. The documents linked suffering children with an insensitive school system.

Organicists, after first speaking of "dyslexia" in relation to the case of any child having difficulty learning to read, finally relied on a definition stating that "dyslexia" can only be invoked if no other factors are likely to explain the observed difficulties. The reference definition, given by the World Federation of Neurology in 1968 continues to hold force (International Statistical Classification of Diseases and Related Health Problems 10th Revision (ICD-10) Version for 2010; DSM-IV): "Disorder observed in learning to read despite conventional instruction, normal intelligence, and socio-cultural opportunities. It results from fundamental cognitive inaptitude often of genetic origin" (Critchley, 1970, p. 44).

The definition is thus primarily by elimination: identifying a child as dyslexic, in practical and rigorous terms, can only be done by a subtractive approach.

In addition to this established definition, there is also the popular notion that dyslexia is the result of inverting letters. Although a large body of research has made it possible to put this belief into perspective and to thus challenge the determinist position, the notion persists in common thinking—an interesting example of the longevity of a misconceived idea.

The Battle of Numbers

How many children with reading difficulties can be considered dyslexic? People interested in this question, but not understanding what it is all about, will clearly want to know the risk. If the number of cases is limited, then the risk is minimal, but if dyslexia appears to be a widespread phenomenon, then the risk is high. From this perspective, the "how many" question harks back to the "what" question. Absent of a clear definition, dyslexia is a sort of "UMO," or unidentified media-hype object. Recent research from England (Russell, et al., forthcoming) eloquently attests to the difficulty of objectively identifying a child as "dyslexic." The authors presented the case of a six-year-old child to three separate psychologists, asking each specialist to diagnose the child's condition. All three agreed that there were specific learning issues, questions of intellectual competence and that it was necessary to help the child. One diagnosed the child as dyslexic, the second as dyspraxic, and the third as borderline Asperger's syndrome (autism).

The State of Affairs

From a scholarly perspective, despite the vast amount of research and the repeated redrafting of the organicist hypothesis, we are still unable to affirm that children's reading difficulties can be attributed to a single well-defined etiology. Lacking indisputable empirical data, we are left with a mere position of principle. An American team of researchers in neurology (Taylor, et al., 1979) undertook a systematic comparison of two samples of children with reading problems: One sample rigorously fulfilled the aforementioned criteria, whereas the other sample, while experiencing reading problems, did not meet the criteria. Results showed that most tasks did not differentiate between the two groups; there were no characteristics specific to the children labeled "dyslexic."

Respecting scientific rigor, we should, then, perhaps stop using a term that seems to pertain to no specific reality. And yet, in spite of this research, implemented with exceptional rigor, supported by the most prestigious American authorities, and published in a highly respected journal, the discourse remains unchanged: research groups interested by these questions have invariably continued to speak of "dyslexia."

Discussion

If, on both the scientific and professional levels, ideas endure when facts are wanting, dyslexia, in the eyes of an exacting observer, appears not to be a scientific concept but an ideological construct whose amazing longevity reposes on the power of a medical lobby. The latter is backed up by cognitive psychologists who suffer from a lack of social recognition and who defend the existence of dyslexia through a climate of fear and respect adroitly maintained by the media.

Coming back to our question—whose knowledge counts in governmental literacy education policies? We have seen that there were opponents to the governmental plan, mainly researchers and practitioners working in clinical psychology and in education, but that their voices were ignored. Their articles, conferences, and petitions were totally ineffective. After the politicians chose to recognize that some children have neurological problems that hinder their learning to read and write, the number of children diagnosed as "dyslexics" grew tremendously over the next ten years; consequently, support structures are now lacking. There is no further debate on the existence or even the prevalence of dyslexia. This war has completely ended.

Nevertheless, about ten years after the change of orientation taken by the French government, cries of alarm began to be heard concerning probable cases of "overdiagnosis" of children merely showing learning lags and wrongly diagnosed as "dyslexic" (Guilbaud-Witaszek, 2011; Junier, 2011). Clearly, the people whose knowledge counts in governmental education policies on this issue are medical authorities, effectively supported by parents who are convinced that neurological reasons explain their children's reading difficulties. Speech therapists have unsurprisingly replaced the specialized teachers who had been working with these children at school. They also now consult with reluctant readers in their private offices and even, at times, in the schools.

The Third Reading War: The Question of the "Global Method"

Historical Background

The global method, which first appeared in the early 20th century, is linked to the name of the Belgian physician and pedagogue Ovide Decroly, who championed this approach in combating traditional teaching methods in general, including reading. His pedagogical proposals, welcomed enthusiastically by some, provoked strong opposition in others.

The beginning of this third reading war can be attributed to a book, *L'échec scolaire, doué ou non-doué* (School failure, gifted children or not), published in 1974 by the *Groupe français d'éducation nouvelle* (GFEN, French Group for New Education). The work emphasized the sociological characteristics of students failing in school in general and in learning to read in particular. A few years later, on the basis of this book, innovators (teacher trainers, school inspectors) sensitive to the sociological elements relating to failing students, challenged the pedagogically dominant practices, which based the teaching of reading on decoding. It was the beginning of a long and hard war against phonics and in favor of meaning.

At the same time, a similar war in the primary and teacher training sectors was being fought at the university level. The battle ground here was the model of reading: bottom-up or top-down. Yet another battle pitted researchers who considered that prediction is an important part of reading against those who denied that the reading process could be a "psycholinguistic guessing game" (Goodman, 1976).

The debate picked up again in the 1970s when Jean Foucambert and the *Association française pour la lecture* (*AFL*) once again challenged the then current methods for teaching reading and, harking back to Decroly, advocated an "ideo-visual" approach. Proponents of this proposal were waging a new battle—"the battle for meaning."

In mid-December, 2005, to general surprise, the Minister of National Education raised the question of reading instruction in France in terms of alternatives: global or syllabic. His decision to prohibit any "global" method in favor of imposing a syllabic method was quickly followed by several other initiatives underscoring his determination to direct and control the teaching of reading. This position, signifying the return of "b-a-ba," was met with strong reactions and became the "battle of the code." Mistakenly believing that accent on meaning was the dominant teaching orientation, the minister's will was clearly to impose decoding over the latter approach.

How did this third war on reading manage to reach such a state of affairs? Among the measures implemented by the minister leading his troops in the battle of code *vs.* meaning, the following are landmarks:

- Convoking school publishers to harmonize their primers and publications with ministerial orientations.
- Convoking representatives of the Association of French Mayors. This was a case of *a posteriori* verification of the choice of teaching materials, since French municipalities purchase school books for the elementary school level. City governments were asked to buy—or not buy—certain titles. Controlling the choice of teaching materials at the purchasing level thus completed the action taken in the preceding measure.
- A ministerial press conference, followed by the publication of a circular pertinent to teaching reading, January 3, 2006. Attentive observers noticed, however, something which was to be repeatedly confirmed over the next three months: The gap that existed between the minister's words and educational programs that his ministry actually published. Whether this was to be attributed to the difference between political and technical discourse, to possible divergences between the minister's intentions and the expression

of same by ghostwriters,[2] or simply to a display of amateurishness, matters little. Under rule of law in a democratic state such as France, it is the written word alone that counts, and these texts moved towards increased flexibility compared to the intentions initially stated which, in their essence, remained unchanged. The interesting fact from our point of view is that a third tactic was apparent—the legal process—which reflected the will of the minister to control the teaching of reading. Rewriting the 2002 programs boiled down to making the law conform to the minister's decisions—decisions that, retrospectively, can be seen as marked with the seal of authoritarianism.

- Yet again on the legal level, the January circular was followed by a decree presented to the *Conseil Supérieur de l'Education* (CSE, a consultative body) on March 6, 2006, but never discussed, since representatives of unions and parents' associations refused to collaborate.
- Modifications of this decree were immediately prepared by the ministry and a session of the CSE was called for March 14, but again unions' and parents' representatives refused to attend.
- The CSE of March 22 expressed an unfavorable opinion of the ministry's decree, but the latter chose to override the consultative body and opted to implement the decree at the start of the new school year.

So the legal route was at the same time both in synch with the ministerial intentions previously announced, and a difficult path to follow, given the necessary consultation and cooperation with the CSE.

Other measures were also implemented:

- The decision to postpone training sessions on reading led by researchers, targeting future state educational inspectors (*Inspecteurs de l'Education nationale, IEN*). Reinforcing the impact of this measure were zealous initiatives on the part of regional school superintendents; the *recteur* in Montpellier asked the *IEN* under his command to no longer authorize the use of certain primers, and his counterpart in Clermont-Ferrand refused to allow the production of a DVD following a conference given by two researchers at the local teacher training institute (*IUFM*). The outcry resulting from such actions was followed by embarrassed denials, but the state of mind was apparent: the will of the ministry to control thought by prohibiting dissemination of ideas that might not conform to official dogma or mandates.
- The commissioning of a survey among the general public, and parents in particular, on the question of methods of teaching reading. This survey established that, on a massive level, the general French population, and specifically parents, were opposed to the global method. Where man-in-the-street interviews would have sufficed, the ministry preferred a steamroller. Pressure thus came from the *vox populis*: Reporting to a large consensus aims to democratically legitimize actions undertaken.

- The organization in Paris on March 9, 2006, by the Office of primary education (*Direction de l'enseignement scolaire, DESCO*) of a national seminar for *IUFM* directors, *IEN*, and primary school teacher trainers to present theoretical work from researchers. This initiative reflected the desire to control key actors in national education, particularly the *IEN*, who had expressed strong reticence about accepting the ministerial decisions. The seminar came across as a manifestation of intimidation, but missed the mark, thanks to the reaction of researchers. Among those summoned for the purpose of scientifically legitimizing the ministerial decisions, some researchers chose to abstain; among those present, the majority spoke unfavorably to the minister's position; others, known for their political opposition to the minister's policy on reading and thus not invited to this meeting, held a parallel press conference with the unions and parents' associations. So the seminar, which was meant to legitimize the minister's positions and to rein in National Education, had exactly the opposite effect.

The minister's strong and determined positions and the measures to implement them sparked strong opposition on the part of unions, parents' associations, and researchers. Just as the ministry took different angles of attack, so did the opposition. Some examples follow:

- The publication (December, 2005) signed by a group of university professors and *IUFM* teacher trainers ("*Sauvons la lecture*", Save reading). The document was published on-line by Le Monde to enable maximal coverage and collected around 3,500 supporting signatures by March 2006, many with caustic commentary.
- An on-line petition appearing at the same time, on the part of teachers' unions, pedagogical movements, and a few researchers ("*Assez de polémiques, des réponses sérieuses*," Enough polemics, serious answers, *Le Monde de l'éducation* (2006a)).
- The respectful, but negative, reaction addressed to the minister from the secretary of the union representing the state educational inspectors (Patrick Roumagnac, *IEN-UNSA*).
- The publication of texts from various pedagogical movements.
- Public conferences in Clermont-Ferrand, Toulouse, Montpellier, with the participation of university professors and *IUFM* teacher trainers hostile to the new orientations.
- The publication of "*Lecture: le point de vue de scientifiques*" (Reading: the point of view of researchers), by academics who had not signed the first two texts, published in *Le Monde de l'éducation* (2006b) (the educational supplement of *Le Monde*).
- The publication of "*D'autres methods que le b-a-ba*" (Other methods than b-a-ba) in *Le Monde* by first-grade teachers, addressed to the minister.

- The publications by academics and *IUFM* teacher trainers presenting diverse positions such as *Le Café pédagogique* or *Education et devenir* (Education and future), appeared on sites often visited by teachers, and offered a forum for debate outside of the traditional media.

In trying to put this ministerial initiative into perspective, it was clear that such action met with great surprise. No professional with genuine knowledge of learning to read at school would ever have couched the problem in terms of the "global or syllabic method." That the Minister of National Education did so was simply stupefying. Four reasons explain this strong reaction:

- The first pertains to the vocabulary employed: the expressions used had been out of date for a long time.
- The second and more fundamental reason has to do with the simplistic nature of the proposal: any reading professional knows that classroom teaching practices cannot be reduced to two alternatives. Fijalkow (2003), in a study of teaching practices in first grade carried out shortly before the ministerial initiative, demonstrated this multiplicity.
- The third reason is found in the major regression in teaching practices demanded by the minister: Presenting as an ideal primer a publication (*Léo et Léa*) modeled on the archetypal beginning reader *La Méthode Boscher* (first edition, 1905) set the teaching of reading back a century.
- The fourth reason was the general astonishment at seeing a minister so vigorously involved in a question which, to non-initiates, seemed a technical rather than a political issue.

In truth, the simplistic, regressive and ideological nature of Education Minister Gilles de Robien's initiative showed the extent to which the measures were technically and scientifically unfounded. To clearly understand what has transpired since December 2005, the first thing to realize is that the "reading" that the minister speaks of is not reading in the sense that teachers, teacher trainers or researchers understand it, but the ideology of reading: the conceptions of reading independent of pedagogical or scientific facts. The debate is one of ideas, having nothing to do with facts, but rather with the values and partisan interests of those defending the ideas. The reality is not a question of global or syllabic methods. What is important is mobilizing one faction of public opinion against another. The minister's discourse turns the field of reading into an ideological battlefield; reading becomes a political object.

To understand the situation created by the education minister we move beyond the question of "learning-to-read methods," which took center stage in 2006, to embrace the wider context that the anglophone literature calls "the Reading Wars." The minister's stance is neither an isolated fact nor a new one. He was aligning France with a political movement with the following premises:

Difficulties in learning to read are due to modern methods, in this case the "global method." There is degradation in the level of reading expertise in France, or the development of "illiteracy."

This battle over the "methods of reading" was parallel to the war between Whole Language and Phonics. The battle in France mirrored the one taking place in English-speaking countries, initiated by a few advisors to the French ministry. But the terrain for this latest battle in France had already been prepared by the two previous reading wars on illiteracy and dyslexia.

Some months later, the minister ordered a linguist to write two new reports in succession, respectively on the teaching of grammar and of vocabulary. The ministry subsequently changed the official position to return to traditional methods, thus ending the third war on reading. After these decisions were made, teaching of French language skills in the elementary schools returned to what it had been 50 years before.

This total success of de Robien's offensive meant that there was no longer any possible "risk" of seeing a more balanced view of reading in official programs as of 2008. The tidal wave that had washed over schools the preceding years, along with the primers that carried the message, resulted in a sort of *Pax Romana* in the teaching of reading, since no other conception dared take a stand.

The Battle of Definitions

The search for an objective definition of the "global method" highlights two issues; the first, not surprisingly, involving Decroly, the other related to an American teaching method.

In discussing pedagogy, Decroly pleaded for "globalization," particularly in the case of reading. His goal was to put an end to fragmented learning, dissociated from any natural context, in favor of teaching large chunks within a functional context. Decroly's writings reflect the affirmation of a pedagogical principle accompanied by concrete examples more than an explicit pedagogical approach. The very term "global method" is not attributed to Decroly, but to a French school principal, Madame Rouquié (Hébrard, 1996).

The American method of teaching reading that trains children to visually recognize isolated words is known as "look and say." In a wider sense, one thinks of "whole language," but the concept is almost totally unknown to French teacher trainers and researchers. This approach has never been cited in the French context (except in Quebec).

Since the technical definition of the global method was not well developed by Decroly, and since its origin remains ambiguous, it is not surprising that its meaning for the general public is fuzzy. People speak of the "global method," but with little agreement on the precise meaning of the term.

As for dyslexia, it seems easier to define the term by what it is not than by what it is. In current usage, "global method" seems to mean any pedagogical practice reaching beyond "b–a–ba," that does not implement blending or combining small units, and is not strictly limited to decoding. From that standpoint, anything beyond the level of blending letters can be qualified "global"; words themselves are already "global." This first definition refers, then, to linguistic units. In a wider view, "global" may be perceived as not being traditional teaching; as such, "global" means "modern," or everything different from the method by which any given person learned to read.

The Battle of Numbers

Due to the lack of specifications for the global method, we wonder if it is a widespread phenomenon whose mysterious nature makes us feel uneasy, or a rare phenomenon that is only a minimal threat. The question posed here is the percentage of teachers and of classes using this method. Although it is true that, in Belgium, official instructions in 1937 encouraged teaching practices inspired by Decroly, quasi-officializing his pedagogy of globalization until 1957, nothing of the sort happened in France. The global method has never existed in French schools, at least in the early grades. Decroly's globalization might have had an effect in nursery schools, but a global approach to teaching reading, according to historians who have studied the question (Hébrard, 1996), never became a tangible reality in first grade, neither in the Belgian nor the American sense.

What percentage of classes today are inspired by an ideo-visual approach? In our national study on pedagogical practices in first grade, carried out under the aegis of the Ministry of National Education, 1,250 teachers responded; only 20 percent reported following a meaning-based approach (Fijalkow & Fijalkow, 1994; Fijalkow, 2003). Our study revealed that, contrary to widespread beliefs, what characterized the classroom practices of teachers using this approach was extreme prudence. Whereas traditional teachers act in very clear-cut ways, the innovative teachers showed far less radical behavior in implementing their approach. We hypothesize that the interest kindled by our first published results stemmed from the surprise of seeing that a maximum of 20 percent of teachers focused on meaning. This surprise paralleled the relief by both ordinary citizens and school inspectors, uneasy about meaning-centered teaching and inclined to overestimate the magnitude of the practice. Our study, replicated 20 years (without ministerial support and therefore on a smaller scale), showed a sharp drop in the percentage of innovative teachers, a clear result of de Robien's policies.

Every reading researcher who tries to compare the effects of innovative pedagogy to the dominant, traditional approach has difficulty in finding a classroom, even in large French cities, where ideo-visual pedagogy is the rule. In the long run, the global method seems to play the role of *Arlésienne,* a fictional character whom everyone talks about but never sees. Like illiteracy and dyslexia, the global method comes across as everyday reality, whereas its existence is an ideological myth and not an objective reality.

The State of Affairs

Opponents of the global method in its initial form often blamed it for children's difficulties in learning to read and spell, accusing it of being an elitist method, only valid for children who were highly developed intellectually. A few decades later, adversaries of the ideo-visual approach presented by the *AFL* similarly expressed their doubts as to its pedagogical effectiveness, but limited their criticism to learning to read.

This accusation, however, is a rhetorical exercise: it is not founded on precise facts based on any scientific study. The claim nonetheless benefits from a certain level of credibility allowing it to transfer the burden of proof onto the accused. The debate is oriented in such a way that makes it unnecessary to ground the accusation on proof. Similarly, existing practices for teaching reading are also not required to prove their effectiveness or their efficiency. Such asymmetry clearly shows that a climate of suspicion reigns where novelty is an issue, but not where established practices already benefit from previously won credibility.

In French-speaking countries, several assessments have been performed in schools, yielding contradictory conclusions. In French-speaking Switzerland, results analyzed by Cardinet and Weiss (1976) strongly plead the case for a wide-ranging approach to reading, whereas the French researcher Goigoux (2000) and unpublished work on meaning-oriented teaching methods by a Belgian team from the University Libre de Bruxelles conclude in a counter-productive sense. The bottom line—a classic one in terms of evaluating reading methodologies—is that neither enthusiastic affirmations, on the one hand, nor accusations, on the other, stand up to the test of facts, underscoring the inherent difficulty of such evaluations.

This is why research throughout the world has turned from studying the question in the field to an experimental approach, examining it variable by variable rather than as a whole. Among such studies, the most widely known pertain to phonemic awareness. Whether a result deliberately sought out or not by researchers, this focus has meant renewed legitimacy for a code-based approach, stressing the importance of phonemic awareness in learning to read. But this research, nonetheless, runs up against a double difficulty.

On the one hand, in the case of phonemic awareness, it is difficult to distinguish cause from effect. Phonemic awareness most likely facilitates learning how to read, at least in a context of traditional pedagogy. But since this consciousness also develops in a traditional teaching context, the causality link is too complex to draw simple conclusions. Causality may indeed be circular rather than linear, contrary to what researchers first thought.

It is also noteworthy that Bryant, one of the seminal researchers in the development of studies on phonemic awareness, in moving beyond his initial framework, led an experiment comparing a code-based and a meaning-based approach (Bryant, 1992; Rego & Bryant, 1993). Both gave positive results. Bryant thus underlined the sophism consisting of questioning meaning-based instruction from research conducted solely on code-based teaching, and advocated the development of studies based on meaning-oriented instruction. A door has been opened, but more research remains to be done.

Discussion

The global or ideo-visual method, or meaning-based teaching, seems, like dyslexia, to be more than anything else a paper tiger, a ghostly creature created primarily by the media to instill fear into the hearts of the well-meaning frightened by the pedagogical audacity of supposedly irresponsible teachers.

In the research currently available, the debate remains more ideological than scientific, opposing those who focus on meaning and those who do not. In France today, the turnaround produced by de Robien's initiative has translated into widespread support for code. Those who exclusively defend meaning, or even those who advocate moving beyond debate towards a more balanced view, are presently silent.

This situation can be explained in four ways. First, the researchers involved—cognitive psychologists and linguists—know about as much as the average educated citizen about teaching reading in school; their knowledge is not of a professional nature. Hence, they are inclined to take one part (cognitive psychology, language) for the whole (teaching and learning enabling children to accede to literacy). From this also follows the fact that didactic variables are not taken into account, so these researchers consider that results obtained express "learning reading" when, in fact, they express "learning reading" in specific didactic conditions. Furthermore, the strong drive to be in harmony with an overwhelmingly anglophone scientific community encourages an intellectual subordination to hard-line currents of thought.

Finally, it is well known that the political left wing cannot be confounded with the pedagogical left wing. Having progressive ideas in general does not stop people from thinking, in all good faith, that the traditional methods by which they themselves learned to read have proven their worth and need not be replaced.

To summarize: What is known as "*la méthode globale*" proves to be mainly a mythical method, an approach very rarely used in teaching practices. The reality is that there is no "global method," but at the most, a decreasing number of teachers who work from a meaning-based perspective.

Conclusion

Whose knowledge does and should count with regard to reading pedagogy? To answer the question in France, three specific groups stand out. First are people whose knowledge seems to really count. This group includes parents of school-age children, the most influential stakeholders in reading policies. Their role was particularly evident during the so-called war on "dyslexia" and on the "methods of teaching reading." In Japan, a research team led by sociologist Mimizuka Hiroaki speaks of "parentocracy" (Hiroaki, 2007). This concept most accurately describes the current state of teaching reading in France. Parents, as well as the Minister of National Education (a parent himself), strongly believe that there is no other way to learn to read than the way they were taught.

The knowledge most valued is that which has traditionally been transmitted from generation to generation. For parents:

- At school: Teachers should teach today the same way that parents were taught when they were children themselves.
- At home: Parents ought to help their children to learn in the same way that they were taught when children. It seems that the only people who believe that it is possible to learn otherwise are the reading professionals.

Another category whose knowledge really counts are members chosen by the Minister of Education to work in his cabinet. Most of them are inspectors of education (*IEN*), with knowledge grounded in their professional experience. They are knowledgeable, not necessarily as regards reading but of the French educational system; consequently, they know what should be maintained or what should be restored. Other cabinet members close to the minister (political advisors, communication specialists) are also important since reading first became a political problem in the last several decades.

The third group of influential individuals includes people from the world of health sciences: Physicians who today may prefer to be called "neuroscientists." Since the time of Molière, in the 17th century, this kind of knowledge can be quite influential in France. A specific example is the replacement of specialized reading teachers by speech therapists. The latter are called upon mainly for students who do not learn to read easily, since these medical professionals are considered competent by the Ministry of National Education in teaching emerging literacy.

A fourth group is statisticians and economists. The ministry is very confident about their evaluations on literacy and on the data from polls. Their knowledge is taken seriously because it is based on mathematics. These people are hired to evaluate reading and, occasionally, to discover what people think about reading problems.

People whose knowledge apparently counts are those whose knowledge seems to count, but whose knowledge may be limited. Linguists and cognitive psychologists are called upon for further expertise, but they are called in only after decisions are made, not before. These researchers are used to give a scientific cast to political decisions. They help to legitimize already-made decisions, not to inform decision-makers on strategic questions.

People whose knowledge does not really count, but should. First, in spite of over 100 years of data collection and studies, research from the human and social sciences such as sociology, social psychology, pedagogy, and didactics is not valued at all. Second, teachers' knowledge does not count either. We are not referring here to the traditionally minded teachers mentioned above, but to those teachers who teach differently and, fortunately and happily, succeed in doing so. Clearly there is an irony that leaves an important question unanswered: How do people with knowledge that should count make themselves heard?

Notes

1. L'Institut national de la statistique et des etudes économiques.
2. In France, this can refer to either ministerial technocrats or national inspectors for state education.

References

Bryant, P. (1992). Rapports entre les premières expériences de l'enfant et l'apprentissage de la lecture, In *Les entretiens*. Nathan. Paris : Nathan.

Cardinet, J., & Weiss, J. (1976). *L'enseignement de la lecture et ses résultats*. Frankfurt: H. Lang, P. Lang.

CRESAS. (1972). *La dyslexie en question*. Paris : A. Colin.

Critchley, M. (1970). *The dyslexic child*. London: Heinemann.

Espérandieu, V., Leon, A., & Benichou, J.P. (1984). *Des illettrés en France*, Rapport au Premier Ministre, Paris: La Documentation française.

Fauroux, R. (1996a). Pour l'école, Rapport de la commission présidée. Paris: Calmann-Lévy.

Fauroux, R. (1996b). Le combat de l'école, *Le Débat*, 5, 4–23.

Fijalkow, E. (2003). *L'enseignement de la lecture-écriture au Cours préparatoire, entre tradition et innovation*. Paris : L'Harmattan.

Fijalkow, E., & Fijalkow, J. (1994). Pratiques d'enseignement de l'écrit au cycle 2. *Revue Française de Pédagogie*, 107, 63–79.

Fijalkow, J. (1984/1996). *Mauvais lecteurs, pourquoi?* Paris: PUF.

GFEN. (1974). *L'échec scolaire, doué ou non-doué*. Paris: Editions sociales.

Goigoux, R. (2000). Apprendre à lire à l'école: Les limites d'une approche idéovisuelle. *Psychologie Française*, 45–59.

Goodman, K.S. (1976). Reading: A psycholinguistic guessing game, In H. Singer, & R.B. Ruddell (Eds.). *Theoretical models and processes of reading*, Newark, DE: International Reading Association.

Guilbaud-Witaszek, D. (2011). Les enfants ayant reçu un diagnostic de dyslexie sont-ils dyslexic? "Actes du colloque: psychopathologie et handicap chez les enfants et les adolescents", 3-5 Novembre 2011, Lyon, France.

Hébrard J. (1996). L'enseignement de la lecture en France: La conjoncture de l'après-guerre, Didactique de la lecture. Regards croisés. Actes de la rencontre lecture organisée le 6 avril 1994 à l'IUFM de Toulouse en hommage à Éveline Charmeux, Toulouse; Presses universitaires du Mirail et CRDP Midi-Pyrénées, 21–54.

Hiroaki, M. (2007). Shôgakkô gakuryoku kakusa ni idomu—Dare ga gakuryoku wo kakutoku suru no ka [Combattre les écarts de performance à l'école primaire—Qui acquiert les compétences scolaires?]. *Kyôiku shakaigaku kenkyû* [Recherche en sociologie de l'éducation], 80, 23–40.

INSEE. (2004). Available on-line: www.anlci.fr/fileadmin/Medias/PDF/EDITIONS/ Les_chiffres_de_l_illettrisme.pdf

International Dyslexia Association. (2012). Brain activity associated with dyslexia predates difficulty learning to read, *The Examiner*, February.

Junier, H. (2011). Dyscalculie, dysorthographie, dyspraxie ... Attention aux surdiagnostics!. *Sciences Humaines*, 232.

Le Monde de l'éducation. (2006a). *Assez de polémiques, des réponses sérieuses*

Le Monde de l'éducation. (2006b). *Lecture: Le point de vue de scientifiques*, (Mars). Accessed at ftp://trf.education.gouv.fr/pub/edutel/actu/2006/apprendre_a_lire_lettre.pdf

OECD. (1997). *Literacy skills for the knowledge society*. Paris: OECD.

Rego L.L., & Bryant, P. (1993). The connection between phonological, syntactic and semantic skills and children's reading and spelling. *European Journal of Psychology and Education*, 8, 235–246.

Russell, G., Norwich, B., & Gwernan-Jones, R. (forthcoming). When diagnosis is uncertain: Variation in conclusions after psychological assessment of a six-year-old child, *Early Child Development and Care*.

Taylor, H., Satz, P., & Friel, J. (1979). Developmental dyslexia in relation to other childhood disorders: Significance and utility. *Reading Research Quarterly*, 15, 84–101.

Veber, F., & Ringard J-C. (2001). Plan d'action pour les enfants atteints d'un trouble spécifique du langage: Propositions remises au Ministre de l'éducation nationale, au ministre délégué à la santé, au secrétariat d'Etat aux personnes âgées. Paris: Ministère de l'éducation nationale.

5

FLYING BLIND

Government Policy on the Teaching of Reading in England and Research on Effective Literacy Education

Henrietta Dombey

Editor's Note: In the United States, the Constitution leaves education to the states. During the civil rights era the courts began to insist that access to education was unequal, leading to federal support for measures to equalize educational opportunity. The Elementary and Secondary Education Act (ESEA) was passed in 1965 to deal with this issue. When ESEA was re-framed in 2002 as No Child Left Behind, federal support became contingent under Reading First on mandates for direct instruction in phonics, leading to a level of central control not thought possible before. In England, as in most other countries, control of education is in the central government as a matter of course. Curriculum, teaching methods, and instructional materials are all determined by a central education ministry. So in England the battle has been between informed professionals in the field and policy makers in London. In the United States, the absurdity was framing this as a contest between phonics and everything else loosely called whole language. In England, the question was not whether the focus should be on phonics, but rather which kind of phonics, synthetic, or analytic? That's a bit like deciding whether a paddle or a strap should be used in inflicting corporal punishment on children. Never mind that there should be no corporal punishment and never mind what the best research shows about phonics in reading instruction.

KSG

Testing Five-Year-Olds on Synthetic Phonics

As I write, in England, children have just gotten out of school for the Easter holidays. When they return, the five- and six-year-olds currently shouting in the park behind my house will, like their age-mates in England, have to undergo what the government terms its "Year 1 Phonics Screening Check." They will be confronted by a set of 40 words; half are one and two syllable "real" words with regular spelling, and half are pseudo words, constructed on similar spelling principles. These they have to pronounce in two sets, easier and harder, with the pseudo words presented first in each set. The Pass Mark has been set at 80 per cent correct. In a recent trial, only 32 per cent of the children out of 300 schools passed (DfE, 2011). Those who fail when the test is for real won't be retained (a practice thankfully not in favour in the UK) but they will be required to sit the test repeatedly until they pass. All this despite the fact that over 80 per cent of Year 2 children (six- and seven-year-olds) currently achieve the required level in a test of reading comprehension (see Chapter 2 for results of a similar test in African nations).

Unsurprisingly, the introduction of this test, buttressing the government's insistence on synthetic phonics as the one legitimate route into reading, has had a marked effect on classrooms in England. A number of head teachers (principals) have urged their colleagues teaching the youngest children to stop spending time on books and concentrate instead on reading. Money that would have gone to refresh school bookshelves is now being earmarked for synthetic phonics reading schemes and related materials. And any focus on rhyme or analogy is out, despite the fact that English orthography yields more easily to such an approach than it does to "sounding out" unknown words grapheme by grapheme. Nothing is to distract children from a disciplined use of grapheme–phoneme correspondences.

In this short chapter, I set out key research findings on characteristics of the most successful teaching of reading, many from studies of effective schools and effective teachers. I then examine the relevant section of the Coalition government's "White Paper" on education (DfE, 2010a) and the research it cites in support of the national policy on the teaching of reading. After discussing how we appear to have arrived at such a policy, I conclude by considering what might be the aims of teaching children to read.

Key Evidence on the Most Successful Reading Teaching

Before examining the UK government's approach to the teaching of reading in England (the other parts of the UK administer education themselves) I'd like to set out some important propositions that are supported by a range of research studies.

Learning to Read Means Learning to Make Sense of Text

We have known this for many decades. None of the research cited here is new, but none of it has been controverted by more recent work. Reading is much more than pronouncing written words. Children who become avid and accomplished readers focus on making sense (Clark, 1976; Durkin, 1966). They certainly need to identify words, but they develop a habit of mind that expects the words they decode to make sense (Clay, 1972). This allows them to monitor their own performance and to make corrections when they misread. This carries an important implication: assessment of children's reading needs to involve making sense of text. It is not enough to test their recognition of isolated words, much less their use of synthetic phonics. To find out whether children are learning to read, we must examine the extent to which they are putting aspects of reading together in the service of constructing meaning from text. To do anything less than that is to send children (and parents and teachers) a message that making sense is not an essential part of reading.

Really successful schools and teachers have much to teach us about the teaching of literacy. Studies of schools and classrooms where children are taught to read most effectively, where they actually like reading and do plenty of it, show consistently that high-achieving classes are characterised by three key features: A balanced approach, with attention to text features matched by attention to comprehension; attention to individual children as literacy learners; and high levels of engagement in reading. Most of the studies have been carried out in the US, but studies of English teachers have supported their findings.

Balanced Literacy Teaching is More Successful Than Phonics Alone

In extensive surveys in the US, Taylor and Pearson (2002) and colleagues (2000) have shown that balanced literacy teaching is more successful than phonics alone. In balanced classes, "the consistent message [is] that understanding and effective communication—not just word recognition—are what literacy is about" (Taylor & Pearson, 2002, p. 365). In England, this is borne out by the study carried out by Medwell, et al. (1998) for England's Teacher Training Agency, which showed that the most effective literacy teachers taught the technical aspects of reading and writing in the context of making meaning through text, continually emphasising the purpose of the whole complex process. Children need to be constantly encouraged and supported to focus on making sense of written text, and to see its uses in ordering, enlarging, enjoying and making sense of their lives. This means ensuring that classrooms are filled with interesting written texts – on screen as well as on paper – and that children are given rich experiences of putting these texts to use. Effective teachers treat children as individuals.

The children in British classrooms are more varied in terms of their backgrounds and experience of language and literacy than ever before. So it is more important than ever to recognise that children do not all learn at the same rate or in the same way. In the most effective classrooms, children recognise what they can do and build on it, moving forward into new territory; they are also helped to see what they can't do and tackle this in a productive spirit (Pressley, et al., 2001). Teachers construct and interpret their programmes of work to allow quicker learners to move ahead and slower learners to address their problems. They also recognise not just where their children are, but who they are – their experiences, interests, perceptions and conceptions. They recognise and value the language and literacy that children bring to school, even where these differ markedly from the teachers' own experiences (Comber & Kamler, 2004; Luke, 1993). Effective teachers make use of this knowledge, recruiting children's skills, experiences and interests through high-quality interaction and close monitoring of individuals (Medwell, et al., 1998). In this way, through responding to their interests and experiences they maximise children's learning potential. Teachers in the most effective schools constantly adapt to the children in the classroom, rather than faithfully following a plan. They demonstrate that a "one size fits all" approach does not address the wider challenges of increasing diversity in children's lives beyond school.

Effective Teachers Work to Engage Children in Their Learning

Engagement is increasingly seen by researchers as central to progress in reading. Children who do not feel interested or involved, who respond in a perfunctory way to their lessons, get less from them than children who participate eagerly and actively (Anderson, et al., 1988; Cunningham & Stanovich, 1998; Guthrie, et al., 1996). Effective schools are marked by eager students, who read more, both in and out of school, and become better readers as they do so, better at recognising the words and better at making sense of them. The contribution of engagement is significant: after parental background, it has the biggest effect on progress in reading. In addition to such studies of effective schools and classrooms, we have also learned much from effective readers, both adults and those learning to read.

How Readers Make Use of Their Phonic Knowledge When They Read for Sense

It has been known for well over 100 years that fluent readers do not process texts one word at a time, much less one letter at a time (Cattell, 1886). Fluent reading is not a matter of efficient bottom-up processing, but rather a complex multi-level, interactive process, involving the construction, amendment, refinement and confirmation of expectations set up by the preceding text and the context in which the reading takes place. The grapho-phonic information provided by the letters on the page is essential, both in prompting expectations and in testing them (Goodman, 1995).

Of course, young readers operate rather differently: They are, by definition, less experienced and hence less fluent. But young readers of English do not process every new word one letter at a time. They move between different sizes of unit (Brown & Deavers, 1999; Goswami, 2010). Sometimes they work words out letter by letter, sometimes they look at familiar groups of letters, such as "all", sometimes they look at whole word patterns, such as "little" or "bottle".

Naturalistic studies of children reading also have much to tell us. "Kidwatching" (Goodman & Goodman, 1994) taught us much about the processes of meaning construction that young children engage in. In particular, the procedures of "miscue analysis", which the Goodmans pioneered and developed, have provided a window on the reading process. Careful documentation and analysis of what children and adults actually do when they read has shown us that neither young readers nor proficient readers proceed in a linear, inductive way from letter perception, through word and phrase perception, to meaning. The knowledge of other texts, language patterns and the world shape how readers proceed and the meaning they construct from text.

Other studies, focusing on the grapho-phonic aspect of word recognition, have cast doubt on the "common sense" inductive view of reading. Children taught by various approaches nonetheless appear to attend to the letters on the page in a similarly eclectic way: Even those taught synthetic phonics sometimes use units of analysis larger than the individual grapheme–phoneme correspondence. But different approaches to early reading nevertheless appear to leave an enduring "cognitive footprint". When confronted with unusual or invented "words" fitting more complex English spelling patterns, adults taught to read through synthetic phonics tend to use a limited grapheme–phoneme rule set (Thompson, et al., 2009). Adults taught with a mainly textual approach are more likely to connect stimulus words such as "thild" to words they already know, such as "mild" or "child".

So we now know much about how children learn to read and how they can best be taught. With this in mind, I turn to England's policy on the teaching of reading in the early stages of formal schooling.

England's White Paper on Education

Apparently the weight of this evidence, gathered from effective schools and classrooms, and from studies of successful young readers, does not convince those who lay down policies framing literacy teaching in England. In the White Paper published in October 2010, there is no mention of balance, none of treating children as individuals, and the word "engagement" does not appear. Instead, a common sense notion dominates: that reading is essentially a bottom-up, inductive process and that to teach reading effectively you have to start with the basic units of graphemes and phonemes. The White Paper claims:

> 4.16 The evidence is clear that the teaching of systematic synthetic phonics is the most effective way of teaching young children to read, particularly for those at risk of having problems with reading.[56] Unless children have learned to read, the rest of the curriculum is a secret garden to which they will never enjoy access.

(DfE, 2010a, p. 43)

The research they cite in support of this proposition is presented in footnote 56, where four references are listed, which I quote as they appear:

> Ehri, L.C., Nunes, S.R., Stahl, S.A. and Willows, D.M. (2001), *Systematic phonics instruction helps students learn to read: Evidence from the National Reading Panel's meta-analysis*, Review of Educational Research, 71(3): 393–447.
> Camilli et al (2003). [sic]
> Torgerson, C. and Brooks, G. (2005), *A systematic review of the use of phonics in the teaching of reading and spelling*; DfES. National Institute for Child's Health and Human Development (2010).
> Torgerson, C., Hall, J. and Brooks, G. (2006), *A Systematic Review of the Research Literature on the Use of Phonics in the Teaching of Reading and Spelling*, DfES, University of York and University of Sheffield

The inclusion of these references adds less to the argument than the casual reader might suppose. These meta-studies appear to be chosen to give the impression that the bold statement "the teaching of systematic synthetic phonics is the most effective way of teaching young children to read" is supported by substantial research. But this support collapses when the references are examined closely. Taking them in turn, Ehri, et al. (2001) assess the evidence for the inclusion of systematic phonics teaching (analytic as well as synthetic) *as an element of* reading instruction programmes. They do not see synthetic phonics as superior to analytic phonics, neither do they see either as "a way of teaching children to read".

Like Ehri, et al., Torgerson, et al. (2006) do not interpret the evidence available as demonstrating a clear superiority of synthetic phonics over analytic phonics. Indeed they state clearly: "No statistically significant difference in effectiveness was found between synthetic phonics instruction and analytic phonics instruction" (p. 8).

Torgerson and Brooks (2005) does not exist.

The publication by Camilli, et al. (2003) is actually called "Teaching children to read: The fragile link between science and federal education policy". It argues strongly *against* phonics of any kind being seen as the dominant element in the teaching of reading: "Phonics, as one aspect of the complex reading process, should not be over-emphasized" (p. 2).

The civil servants who put the White Paper together were either disingenuous, or simply careless. They have taken the common sense idea of the Secretary of State, Michael Gove, and the Schools Minister, Nick Gibb, that the only effective route into reading is via sounding out the letters, and attempted to shore it up with evidence that actually points in a different direction.

Another set of studies, rather surprisingly not cited in the White Paper, has been much used in the defence of a synthetic phonics approach to early reading and actually does purport to do so. Present and recent governments in England have relied heavily on the research of Johnston and Watson in Clackmannan-shire, a small Scottish county, with a modest socio-economic profile (Johnston & Watson, 2004; 2005). In fact, both Labour and Conservative politicians have seized on this work, agreeing with its authors that it demonstrates incontrovertibly the superiority of a synthetic phonics approach. However, a careful examination of their publications and of relevant national test data and inspectors' reports shows something much less clear-cut. Perhaps this is why there is no mention of the Clackmannanshire research in the White Paper.

The Clackmannanshire research is much less substantial than its proponents would have us believe. In two studies, Johnston and Watson claim to demonstrate the superiority of synthetic phonics over analytic phonics in the early stages of learning to read. One is a two-year experimental study, the other a seven-year longitudinal study covering all the children in one age cohort in the small Scot-tish county of Clackmannanshire.

In terms of "reading" individual words, this research does indeed show dramatic gains for classes taught "synthetic phonics", but much smaller gains for compre-hension. As well as being hailed as an unqualified success by leading politicians, both Labour and Conservative, Johnston and Watson's synthetic phonics studies have been taken as gospel by the author of the Rose Report, commissioned by the Labour government to steer the teaching of early reading (DfE, 2010b; Rose, 2006).

The research is deeply flawed. In their study with the first two years of school-ing, an experimental study comparing classes taught by analytic and synthetic phonics, Johnson and Watson failed to:

- ensure a fairly matched "analytic group", taught with enthusiasm and struc-ture equal to that of the teachers of the experimental group;
- measure success in reading comprehension, rather than individual word recognition;
- demonstrate an absence of bias, since both investigators had published mate-rial for use in a synthetic phonics programme.

Their cohort study, which involved all the schools in the Clackmannanshire Local Authority adopting a synthetic phonics approach to early reading, shows sim-ilar weaknesses. Neither Johnston and Watson, nor those who cite their work so warmly make any mention of a number of initiatives also introduced in the Clackmannanshire schools at that time. These include:

- leadership training for head teachers;
- general discussion and staff development on effective literacy teaching (with a much wider range of concern than the teaching of phonics);
- home–school link teachers appointed to work with parents on literacy issues;

- further staff development on teaching comprehension and the development of reasoning;
- the introduction of a course of thinking skills;
- the injection of extra funds to buy more books.

In short, the authors' claims concerning the effectiveness of synthetic phonics cannot be said to be clearly demonstrated by these studies.

External assessment of the affected cohort confirms these doubts. Despite Johnson and Watson's intensive phonics teaching and all the other initiatives in which the schools took part, in the National Tests of reading taken in their last year of primary school, the cohort study children did not score significantly better than their predecessors (HMIE, 2003).

Perhaps the most damning indictment of the researchers' claim to have shown the power of synthetic phonics comes from Her Majesty's Inspectorate for Education (Scotland). A report on the Local Authority's schools pronounced the performance of Clackmananshire in reading and writing, after all these interventions, to be "below the average for comparator authorities" (HMIE, 2006, p. 4); that is, they were found to be below the mean of other Scottish Local Authorities with school populations from similar socio-economic backgrounds.

Synthetic phonics, which now dominates the reading policy for England, simply can't be said to have worked for the teachers and children of Clackmannanshire: the verdict of the inspectorate has not made the policy-makers waver from their course. The national policy remains as propounded in paragraph 4.16, quoted above. Every state-supported primary school in England now has to submit to a deeply flawed view of this vital area of the curriculum. And their Year 1 children have to endure a test that distracts them, their teachers and their families from the processes of learning, teaching and supporting reading as it is taught in the most effective schools.

So why have we got this policy?

When the National Literacy Strategy was introduced (DfEE, 1998), for all its faults of over-prescription, it did at least recognise that reading is a meaning-focused activity and that children learn to identify words in connected text by more than phonics alone. Since then, Britain's strong phonics lobby has striven ceaselessly to capture the ears of decision-makers. Successive waves of alarm about the standard of reading in our schools and our slide down international league tables have made our masters receptive to this alluringly simple solution. England's declining rank order and relatively low scores on the PISA and PIRLS tests are taken as arguments for increasing the emphasis on phonics in the early years of school (OECD, 2010; Twist, et al., 2007). Little notice is taken of the sad facts that our children's attitudes to reading declined markedly after the introduction of the more directive approach of the National Literacy Strategy (Sainsbury, 2003), and that children who like reading less do less of it and do not improve as much as children with a more positive attitude (OECD, 2010).

England's policy on the teaching of reading springs from a political desire to cut through the Gordian knot, to straighten out the teaching of reading at the start, in the way that seems obviously right to those who know little about the subject. Letters of the alphabet represent speech sounds, so surely children should learn these at the start and sound out all new words they come across?

But why was expertise ignored? Sadly, this is nothing new. The English have for centuries been noted for taking a pragmatic, untheorised, perhaps even uninformed approach to complex governmental problems, particularly where education is concerned. We call it being open-minded. Our civil service is constructed on the principle that expertise in subject matter is not desirable for most branches of government: apart from the elite at the Treasury and the Foreign Office, our civil servants are rotated between the Home Office, Education, Social Services and Health. Yet an important part of their job is to draft policy and guidance documents. This means constructing justifications for the preferred options of their uninformed political masters. Occasionally biddable "experts" are drafted in to provide justification for a course of action already decided on.

Why Do We Want Children to Learn to Read?

In this context, perhaps we should consider why we want children to learn to read at all. Do we want to teach them in order to make society run more smoothly, to speed up the processing of insurance claims? Do we want them to be able to interpret more complex documents, such as White Papers? Do we want them to read works of fact and fiction that help them to think about other places, other times and other points of view? Do we want them to use the printed word to see the familiar in new ways? Do we want them to critically evaluate what they read, asking searching questions about such matters as who the text speaks for and who it excludes?

Freebody and Luke's (1990) four resources model of literacy learning is a useful reminder of the different kinds of reading we might want to promote in our classrooms. As the authors state:

> The model posits four necessary but not sufficient 'roles' for the reader in a postmodern, text-based culture:
>
> * Code breaker (coding competence)
> * Meaning maker (semantic competence)
> * Text user (pragmatic competence)
> * Text critic (critical competence).
>
> (Luke and Freebody, 1999, p. 1)

In focusing teachers, children and parents on the first role (and an inadequate version of that), England's policy on the teaching of reading reduces the process of reading in the early stages to a pointless mechanical task that is rather poorly framed. The policy assumes that taking on the roles of meaning makers and text users will be unproblematic once the role of code breaker is established. Yet the research cited earlier in this chapter shows that the most effective schools balance their attention to word identification by simultaneously introducing children to these roles. And through these roles, effective schools and teachers engage children in the reading process, not through sugaring the pill of phonics learning with extrinsic rewards, but through showing them what reading can do for them, how it can enlarge and enhance their lives.

Our political masters care about the test scores of our ten-year-olds and 15-year-olds on PIRLS and PISA, those crucial international tests of semantic and pragmatic competence. However, they seem to believe that, to improve these scores, all that is needed is to ensure that the five- and six-year-olds learn fidelity to the letters on the page (at least to those in words with regular spelling). The development of England's children as text critics seems entirely outside governmental concerns. Thus we have to endure a policy that is likely to be deeply counter-productive. However, when the full impact of this policy becomes evident, when our slide down the international league tables continues, it will be teachers rather than the policy that will be held responsible. The challenge for the future is to change this state of affairs, by persistently calling attention to research and practice in England, and to the experiences of our colleagues elsewhere in the world.

References

Anderson, R.C., Wilson, P.T., & Fielding, L.G. (1988). Growth in reading and how children spend their time outside of school. *Reading Research Quarterly*, 23, 3, 285–330.

Brown, G.D.A., & Deavers, R.P. (1999). Units of analysis in non-word reading: Evidence from children and adults. *Journal of Experimental Child Psychology*, 73, 208–242.

Camilli, G., Vargas, S., & Yurecko, M. (2003). Teaching children to read: The fragile link between science and federal education policy. *Education Policy Analysis Archives*, 11, 15. Accessed on 31 March 2012 at: http://epaa.asu.edu/ojs/article/view/243

Cattell, J. (1886). The time it takes to see and name objects. *Mind*, 11, 63–65.

Clark, M. (1976). *Young fluent readers: What can they teach us?* London: Heinemann.

Clay, M. (1972). *Reading: The patterning of complex behaviour.* Auckland, NZ: Heinemann.

Comber, B., & Kamler, B. (2004). Getting out of deficit: Pedagogies of reconnection. *Teaching Education*, 15, 3, 293–310.

Cunningham, A.E., & Stanovich, K.E. (1998). What reading does for the mind. *American Educator*, 22, 1&2, 8–15.

Department for Education and Employment (DfEE) (1998). *The National Literacy Strategy: Framework for teaching.* London: Department for Education and Employment

Department for Education (DfE). (2010a). *The importance of teaching: Schools white paper 2010.* London: DfE. Accessed on 31 March 2012 at: www.education.gov.uk/b0068570/the-importance-of-teaching/

Department for Education (DfE). (2010b). *Reading at an early age the key to success.* Press Notice 22 November 2010. Accessed on 31 March 2012 at: www.education.gov.uk/inthenews/inthenews/a0068420/reading-at-an-early-age-the-key-to-success

Department for Education (DfE). (2011). *A third of children reach expected level in pilot of phonics check.* Press Notice 9 December 2011. Accessed on 31 March 2012 at: www.education.gov.uk/inthenews/inthenews/a00200672/a-third-of-children-reach-expected-level-in-pilot-of-phonics-check

Durkin, D. (1966). *Children who read early: Two longitudinal studies.* New York: Teachers College Press.

Ehri, L.C., Nunes, S.R., Stahl, S.A., & Willows, D.M. (2001). Systematic phonics instruction helps students learn to read: Evidence from the National Reading Panel's meta-analysis, *Review of Educational Research,* 71, 3, 393–447.

Freebody, P., & Luke, A. (1990). Literacies programs: Debates and demands in cultural context, *Prospect: Australian Journal of TESOL,* 5, 7, 7–16.

Goodman, K. (1995). *Phonics phacts.* Richmond Hill, Ontario: Scholastic Canada, Ltd (Canada), and Heinemann (USA) Portsmouth, NH.

Goodman, K., & Goodman, Y. (1994). To err is human: Learning about language processes by analyzing miscues. In R.M. Ruddell, & H. Singer (Eds.). *Theoretical models and processes of reading.* Newark, DE: International Reading Association.

Goswami, U. (2010). A psycholinguistic grain size view of reading acquisition across languages. In N. Brunswick, S. McDougall, & P. Mornay-Davies (Eds.). *The role of orthographies in reading and spelling.* Hove: Psychology Press.

Guthrie, J.T., Van Meter, P., Dacey-McCann, A., Wigfield, A., Bennett, L., Poundstone, C.C., Rice, M.E., Fairbisch, F.M., Hunt, B., & Mitchell, A.M. (1996). Growth in literacy engagement: Changes in motivations and strategies during concept-oriented reading instruction, *Reading Research Quarterly,* 31, 3, 306–332.

Her Majesty's Inspectors for Education (HMIE). (2003). *Inspection of the education functions of Clackmannanshire Council, September 2003.* Edinburgh: SEED. Accessed on 31 March 2012 at: www.hmie.gov.uk/documents/inspection/ClackmannanshireINEA2-9-03-a.html

Her Majesty's Inspectorate for Education (HMIE). (2006). *Pilot inspection of the Education Functions of Clackmannanshire Council in October 2005* Edinburgh: SEED. Accessed on 31 March 2012 at: www.hmie.gov.uk/documents/inspection/ClackmannanINEA2Pilot.html

Johnston, R., & Watson, J. (2004). Accelerating the development of reading, spelling and phonemic awareness skills in initial readers, *Reading and Writing: An Interdisciplinary Journal,* 17, 327–357.

Johnston, R., & Watson, J. (2005). The effects of synthetic phonics on reading and spelling attainment. A seven year longitudinal study. Edinburgh. Accessed on 31 March 2012 at: www.scotland.gov.uk/library5/education/sptrs-00.asp

Luke, A. (1993). The social construction of literacy in the primary school. In L. Unsworth (Ed.). *Literacy Learning and Teaching.* Melbourne: Macmillan Education Australia, 1–54.

Luke, A., & Freebody, P. (1999). *Further notes of the four resources model.* Accessed on 31 March 2012 at: www.readingonline.org/research/lukefreebody.html

Medwell, J., Wray, D., Poulson, L., & Fox, R. (1998). *Effective teachers of literacy*. Exeter: Teacher Training Agency.

OECD. (2010). *PISA 2009 results: What students know and can do—student performance in reading, mathematics and science*. Accessed on 31 March 2012 at: http://dx.doi.org/10.1787/9789264091450-en

Pressley, M., Wharton-McDonald, R., Allington, R., Block, C.C., Morrow, L., Tracey, D., Baker, K., Brooks, G., Cronin, J., Nelson, E., & Woo, D. (2001). A study of effective first grade literacy instruction, *Scientific Studies of Reading*, 5, 1, 35–58.

Rose, J. (2006). *Independent review of the teaching of early reading: Final report*. London: DfES.

Sainsbury, M. (2003). *Children's attitudes to reading*. Slough: National Foundation for Educational Research.

Taylor, B.M., & Pearson, P.D. (Eds.). (2002). *Teaching reading: Effective schools, accomplished teachers*. Mahwah, NJ: Lawrence Erlbaum Associates.

Taylor, B.M., Pearson, P.D., Clark, K., & Walpole, S. (2000). Effective schools and accomplished teachers: Lessons about primary grade reading instruction in low income schools, *Elementary School Journal*, 101, 121–165.

Thompson, G.B., Connelly, V., Fletcher-Finn, C.M., & Hodson, S.J. (2009). The nature of skilled adult reading varies with instruction in childhood, *Memory and Cognition*, 37, 223–234.

Torgerson, C., Hall, J., & Brooks, G. (2006). *A systematic review of the research literature on the use of phonics in the teaching of reading and spelling*. London: DfES.

Twist, L., Schagen, I., & Hodgson, C. (2007). *P I R L S Progress in international reading literacy study: Readers and reading. National Report for England, 2006*. Slough: National Foundation for Educational Research for the Department of Children, Schools and Families.

6

WHOSE KNOWLEDGE COUNTS, FOR WHOM, IN WHAT CIRCUMSTANCES?

The Ethical Constraints on Who Decides

Sue Ellis

Editor's Note: Once in a heated argument with a researcher with whom I strongly disagreed, my rival said "well at least we have to agree on the facts." But what the facts are is often the very essence of the disagreement. In this chapter, Ellis considers how the demand for "evidence-based" decisions in education often involves a narrow view of what the "evidence is" and who decides that. She shows how a highly publicized local study of which of two phonics approaches was more effective was misused to justify major changes in the national reading policy She also raises questions about the ethical issues created by narrowing what is considered evidence and what is excluded. Scotland and England, two separate educational authorities, show how the same evidence may be viewed quite differently.

KSG

Literacy is high on the agenda of politicians, policy makers, and the media, and it is an important issue for parents, educationalists, and researchers. The drive to increase literacy standards has focused on curriculum content, on ensuring teacher accountability through published test results and on making "evidence-based" decisions about education. Recent debates about evidence-based education began to gather force in the early 1990s.

In the UK, Hargreaves (1996) criticized educational research that lacked cumulative studies, did not make fundamental contributions to knowledge and was "irrelevant to practice . . . and which clutters up academic journals that virtually no one reads" (p. 7). Davies (1999) followed with calls for educational activity to be broadly evaluated by means of "carefully designed and executed controlled trials, quasi-experiments, surveys, before-and-after studies, high-quality observational studies, ethnographic studies which look at outcomes as well as processes, or conversation and discourse analytic studies that link micro structures and actions to macro level issues" (p. 109).

For Davies, evidence-based education was a set of principles or practices that would both influence how practitioners think about context and that alter the basis on which they deploy their judgment and build their expertise. Evidence-based approaches did not negate the need for professional decisions or experience, but supplemented them by providing a sound basis for action. He pointed out that evidence-based health care had not resulted in clinicians who referred to research to inform their daily practices, but it had helped them become clearer about the clinical problems for which solutions were required.

In the US, the argument took a different direction; one that focused on experimental paradigms and on evaluating replicable programs and practices (Slavin, 2002). In 1998, Congress made funding available to "proven, comprehensive reform models," an approach that was cemented further in the Government's *Strategic Plan for Education 2002–2007*, which criticized the lack of rigor in much educational research:

> unlike medicine, agriculture and industrial production, the field of education operates largely on the basis of ideology and professional consensus. As such, it is subject to fads and is incapable of the cumulative progress that follows from the application of the scientific method.
>
> (US Department of Education, 2002, p. 51)

Although US researchers initially proposed a complex and not necessarily hierarchical model, the federal No Child Left Behind Act mandate for "scientifically proven" instructional methods meant that research designs were ranked, with Randomized Controlled Trials (RCTs), at the top, followed by controlled cohort studies, case studies, individual case studies and, at the bottom, professional observation (Eisenhart & Towne, 2003). This model was rapidly exported around the world (Wiseman, 2010).

Now in both the UK and the US, research aims to have a direct impact on practice. The mission of the Institute of Education Sciences, the research arm of the US Department of Education, is:

> to provide rigorous and relevant evidence on which to ground education practice and policy and share this information broadly. By identifying what works, what doesn't, and why, we aim to improve educational outcomes for all students, particularly those at risk of failure.
>
> (Institute of Education Sciences, 2012)

In the UK, the Department for Education publishes research bulletins and powerpoint summaries of research which seek to: "make it easier for headteachers and teachers to have free access to high-quality research" (Department for Education, 2012).

For more than a decade, the definition of what counts as "gold standard" evidence in literacy education has fitted most easily with positivist paradigms of experimental investigations of literacy learning. This has led to a stronger emphasis on cognitive psychology paradigms and on program trials and evaluations in education research. Debates have focused on internal methodological issues such as the level of randomization (because children cannot be randomly allocated to schools and classes, or randomly allocated to follow different programs within a class). There has been less debate about how the shift has re-positioned policy making and research, or the new ethical guidance for researchers that this may require.

Literacy can be couched within several paradigms and the idea that the most powerful evidence for literacy teaching decisions is from RCTs and other quasi-experimental explorations of program content and design features has had a surprisingly easy ride in policy and media circles. It is surprising because large-scale survey evidence indicates that the major factors that affect how quickly and well children learn to read are not programs of teaching content but are external to schools and schooling, i.e. socio-economic status and gender. Moreover, evidence on factors within the school indicates that both teacher and school effectiveness trump program content for impact on learning (Hall, 2013).

The teacher's ability to integrate and balance such aspects as learning the codes of written language with meaningful activities that make literacy useful and purposeful is particularly important. In a review of the evidence, Hall (2013) reports that highly effective teachers are those who consciously integrate skills-based teaching with authentic tasks and are expert at scaffolding, monitoring understanding and at seizing the "teachable moment." They are excellent managers, well-planned, responsive and tenacious, weaving a curriculum that achieves both "instructional density" (Wharton-McDonald, et al., 1998), and meaningful activity.

The socio-cultural research would suggest solutions that focused on issues of social identity, pragmatic understanding, and cultural capital in literacy curriculum design. The teacher/school effectiveness research would suggest teacher- or school-focused solutions that illustrated how to create "noticing" teachers who weave programs and skills-based teaching into other, meaningful and authentic experiences to ensure coherent, engaging and responsive teaching and learning. However, the solutions that policy makers have "bought" are focused on program and content issues, and phonics programs have received a particularly high profile.

Today's mandates for "rigorous research" limit it to controlled experiments. RCTs manipulate tightly framed variables to address narrowly defined academic questions. They are less adequate for understanding the wide-ranging and complex interrelationships that need to be addressed during practical implementation. For example, evidence of impact on a general population is interesting for educators, but less useful than knowing about the effects on their own school community, which require cohort studies and case-study series (Sackett, et al., 2000). Policy makers and education managers require knowledge about issues such as the maintenance of gains, cost-benefit analyses and fit with current systems and practices.

Models of medical research in the UK encompass at least two stages beyond the RCT, and several stages before it. Investigations are "tested" as they move from theoretical insight through first case studies, then cohort studies to the third phase of RCTs. A fourth phase, however, beyond the RCT, investigates what happens when the intervention moves into "real world" contexts and a further fifth "efficiency" phase considers how the intervention can be made more cost-effective or time-efficient (Medical Research Council, 2008). These steps provide a clear and complete framework to help policy makers, clinicians and researchers to understand and assess the nature and breadth of the evidence they have and the knowledge generated, so that they can better judge what may work, for whom and under what circumstances.

Another consequence of the focus on psychology investigations and program trials is that it has skewed the discourse about the literacy curriculum. The recent heated arguments about whether synthetic or analytic phonics programs are better for helping children learn to read are a good example of this narrowing. In the late 1990s and early 2000s, robust arguments about the role of phonics and the type of phonics instruction that is most effective occurred across the English-speaking world (Goodman, 1993; Lewis & Ellis, 2006; Soler & Openshaw, 2007; Van Kraayenoord, 2003). In England, these conversations continue and have intensified (Dombey, 2010; Wyse & Goswami, 2008). In the US, the National Reading Panel Report on teaching children to read surveyed a narrow range of research evidence limited to experimental and quasi-experimental studies and concluded that "specific systematic phonics programs are all significantly more effective than non-phonics programs" (NICHD, 2000, p. 93). The Reading First Program (2009) was then implemented nationwide to promote direct instruction in phonological awareness and phonics.

In an analysis of UK literacy policy, Moss and Huxford (2007) argue that, having lost out to more balanced and integrated views of reading in the previous policy round (where the National Literacy Strategy had focused the teaching of reading on an interactive model of reading processes and promoted miscue analysis), phonics proponents simply out-maneuvered others in the policy arena. The "independent" Government inquiry that was established by the UK Labour Government in 2005 was chaired by Jim Rose and had three members, all academics: Morag Stuart, a staunch believer in synthetic phonics, who argued strongly for psychology researchers to have more influence in educational decisions about the literacy curriculum (Education and Skills Committee, 2005a); Greg Brooks, a strong advocate of phonics and of evidence-based education programs; and Kathy Sylva, a psychologist and expert in early years development. Given the composition of the committee, it was no surprise that the final report (Rose, 2006) favored phonics. Neither was it surprising that the report favored synthetic phonics.

Long-standing arguments interrogate the details, evidence-base and implications of different psychological models of phonics acquisition. They are perfectly appropriate and desirable academic debates, which will slowly evolve and help to advance psychological theory. But the current evidence about which model is best supported by the data is equivocal. The US National Reading Panel found that specific instructional approaches based on synthetic or analytic models "do not appear to differ significantly from each other in their effectiveness, although more evidence is needed to verify the reliability of effect sizes for each program" (NICHD, 2000, p. 93). In the UK, a systematic review of "gold standard" RCT evidence on trials of synthetic and analytic phonics concluded, "There is currently no strong RCT evidence that any one form of systematic phonics is more effective than any other" (Torgerson, et al., 2006, p. 49).

There are many influences on political decisions about the literacy curriculum. Research is one influence; another is professional opinion, but other influences are the media, political priorities, political and commercial interests, and lobbying. The emphasis on phonics within the Rose Review chimes with political statements at the time, while creating an ethical minefield for academics. Education is not the only policy area to face such issues. For example, in 2009 the UK's chief drug adviser, Professor David Nutt, was sacked when he criticized the Government's rejection of academic advice on the classification of cannabis, nicotine, alcohol, and other drugs. Other academics resigned from the committee, stressing that whilst the Government had the right to reject their advice, academics had the right to comment on this rejection.

Ethical Dilemmas

The next part of this chapter considers issues that arise for academics when their research is taken up by policy makers, the media, and politicians. It also discusses the pressures on academic researchers for their research to be seen to have impact and be relevant, so that they get promotion and enhance the profile of their university. To do this, I use, as a case study, one relatively small phonics intervention that received worldwide coverage after being given a high profile in the Rose Review, the study of synthetic phonics in Clackmannanshire, Scotland.

The Clackmannanshire experiment was carried out by Watson and Johnston as one part of three linked studies addressing the academic debate between analytic and synthetic phonics. The first two studies consisted of an RCT and an observational study. The actual sequence of these two studies is reported differently in different papers, as an RCT followed by an observation study (Watson & Johnston, 1998) but also as an observation study followed by an RCT (Johnston

& Watson, 2004). What is clear is that there was a ten-week RCT on 92 children to investigate "whether synthetic phonics was more effective than analytic phonics merely because letter sounds were taught at an accelerated pace" (Johnston & Watson, 2004, p. 343), and an observational study of how phonics was taught in 12 schools (Watson & Johnston, 1998). These studies reported large reading gains when children were shown how to decode CVC words (words with a consonant–vowel–consonant construction, such as "dog").

The third study, which attracted worldwide attention, was a longitudinal cohort study of almost 300 children in 13 classes in eight schools, which followed the cohort from age five years to 12 years, when the pupils moved to secondary schools. It was designed to further evaluate psychology models of analytic and synthetic phonics. One hypothesis was that "If training in phonological awareness is essential for young children learning to read, the analytic phonics program with phonological awareness training should be more effective than the other two programs" (Johnston & Watson, 2004, p. 330).

The first 16-week intervention trialed three training programs based on: (a) synthetic phonics; (b) analytic phonics; or (c) analytic phonics plus phonological-awareness training. The programs were introduced as part of the normal literacy curriculum in the first term of primary school. Standardized tests showed that after 16 weeks, the synthetic phonics classes were seven months ahead of chronological age expectations for word reading and seven months ahead of the other two groups. In spelling, the synthetic phonics groups were eight months ahead of the analytic phonics and nine months ahead of the analytic phonics+phoneme-awareness groups (Watson & Johnston, 1998, pp. 7–8).

At this point, all groups were transferred onto the accelerated synthetic phonics program. Toward the end of their second year, the word reading and spelling averages in all 13 classes were well above the children's chronological age. There were no significant differences in word reading or comprehension between the groups although the original synthetic phonics group was significantly better at spelling. After seven years, the Clackmannanshire children were reported as three years and six months ahead of their chronological age in decoding words; one year and nine months ahead in spelling; and three-and-a-half months ahead of their chronological age in comprehension (Johnston & Watson, 2005). These results caught the attention of the media and policy makers around the world. The Westminster Select Committee Enquiry, in the Rose Review stated, "In view of the evidence from the Clackmannanshire study ... we recommend that the Government should undertake an immediate review of the National Literacy Strategy" (Education and Skills Committee, 2005b, p. 23).

The success of the synthetic phonics experiment in Clackmannanshire influenced curriculum policy development around the world. In Australia, for example, the Government's National Enquiry into the Teaching of Literacy acknowledged the merits of both balanced and integrated approaches, but said:

Notwithstanding these assertions, findings from the seven-year study undertaken by Johnston and Watson (2005) clearly indicate the superior efficacy of synthetic phonics instruction, and are worthy of mention here. . . . Johnston and Watson note that although children from disadvantaged backgrounds typically had poorer literacy skills at school entry, the children from less disadvantaged backgrounds who had initially been taught synthetic phonics were still performing at or above chronological age on word reading, spelling and reading comprehension (Australian Government Department for Education, Science and Training, 2005, p. 35).

In England, the opposition MP, Nick Gibb (now Minister of State for Schools), used parliamentary questions about Clackmannanshire to challenge the governing Labour party's education policy. In Scotland,[1] however, where a devolved curriculum prevents national politicians from aligning themselves with particular teaching approaches to make political capital, praise was less effusive. Her Majesty's Inspectorate of Education (HMIE) wrote: "Whilst this programme had made a strong impact on pupils' ability to sound out, spell and recognise words, further work was required to link these skills to other aspects of reading such as comprehension" (HMIE, 2006, p. 4).

A Scottish Executive funding requirement for the Early Intervention projects, under which the Clackmannanshire experiment took place, was that bids should not address narrow aspects of literacy learning. The phonics study was thus part of a broader development in which the intervention schools also revised core reading schemes and library books and introduced a thinking and comprehension skills program (Robertson, 1999; 2005). Home–school liaison teachers in four of the most disadvantaged intervention schools were funded to make home visits to support literacy development, establish story clubs, library visits, after-school homework clubs, parent groups, and to create libraries and borrowing services in the schools (Clackmannanshire Council, 2003).

The curriculum and staff development for the phonics programs in Clackmannanshire was clearly excellent. Sensitive to local context and intellectually engaging, it was systematic, coherent, and delivered with conviction. It provided specific content knowledge about phonics, practical advice about lesson structures and resources, emphasised purpose, motivation, the importance of noticing and building on success, and it encouraged teachers to create opportunities for children to apply their knowledge and to reflect on what they had learnt (Robertson, 2005).

Follow-through and support by head teachers and local authority advisors was focused and practical. Individual pupil progress was monitored with support in the form of catch-up groups and homework clubs for anyone falling behind. This was a well-integrated intervention, in line with research on successful staff development and curriculum reform.

Johnston (2006) has argued, correctly, that these other programs cannot explain the advanced phonic decoding skills displayed—on average three-and-a-half years ahead of the children's chronological age. However, the focus on narrow questions of interest to psychologists and the lack of attention on other features in the implementation illustrates a tension and ethical dilemma for the researchers: There is little practical advantage in being able to sound out complex individual words as an isolated skill. Successful literacy education (as opposed to a successful result in the tightly delineated domain of a psychology experiment) must create readers who are significantly better at reading for meaning. This was the point made by the Scottish HMIE.

National test results provide a different lens through which to examine the reading attainment of the cohort. At that time in Scotland, small groups and individuals took tests at different points throughout the year, tests designed to reflect the literacy activities and reading content of normal classroom work. The system was biased in favor of the child and of teacher judgment; robust evidence from classroom work could be used as evidence to overturn a poor test result. In an attempt to ensure that national assessments did not skew teaching, school test results were not published and schools were not ranked. However, local authorities were told how their results ranked against those of other similar local authorities. The national test results of individual schools were used for internal monitoring and evaluation of school performance by local authorities and were part of the evidence of achievement submitted by the schools for HMIE inspections.

In 2005, a national newspaper obtained and published the Primary 7 national test results for every school and local authority in Scotland using the *Freedom of Information Act* (Fracassini, et al., 2005). These included the results of the Clackmannanshire phonics intervention schools and of the experimental cohorts, who graduated from primary school in 2003/2004. Table 6.1 summarizes the results for the eight schools involved in the intervention study. It provides the school national test data for the years before and after the research cohort graduated and for the year that the research cohort graduated. Most children were expected to attain Level D by their last year of primary school.

The schools serve very different communities. The percentage of Free School Meal (FSM) entitlement provides a broad indication of the socio-economic status of the families in the school. At this time in Scotland, those in the bottom quarter of the socio-economic scale were more than twice as likely to be among the bottom 25 percent for reading attainment (Scottish Executive Education Department, SEED, 2002). The school roll indicates the total number of children attending the school, which gives a rough approximation of the size of a particular year-group. This is important because it is clear that in all but the two most advantaged schools, the intervention cohorts were rather small. It is clearly problematic to report results in terms of pupil percentages for small schools, because if just one or two children under- or over-perform, it can create a relatively large percentage "swing" year-on-year. The percentage results for bigger schools are more robust.

TABLE 6.1 Reading Attainment in P7 (% Pupils Level D or Above)

	Roll	% Free School Meal entitlement in 2003/04	Year: 2002/03	Year: 2003/04 (intervention cohort)	Year: 2004/05
A	488	14	69	70	82
B	409	22	80	84	79
C	229	56	47	78	n/a
D	155	76	47	73	66
E	146	41	57	44	72
F	114	45	44	20	21
G	63	33	70	91	75
H	277	17	87	77	77

National average for P7 pupils at Level D or above in 2003/04 = 74.5%
National average for Free School Meal entitlement in 2003/04 = 21%

The between-school variability in data indicates why the Scottish HMIE may have been less enthusiastic about the intervention than the psychology researchers. The small schools C, D and G, with very high FSM entitlements of 56 percent, 76 percent, and 33 percent respectively in 2003/2004, attained or exceeded national literacy averages, which is an excellent result. Other small schools, E and F, did not. Significantly, school A, the largest school and the one serving the most advantaged community, only just meets national attainment levels.

This shows that "evidence" of reading achievement can look different when seen through different lenses; a different type of test produces a different picture. The psychology research paradigm, focused on individual-level scores, did not examine the school-level patterns. The Scottish policy makers, by way of contrast, would have been well-aware of the variations. Further, the number of small schools with very high FSM meant that the statement that "most of the intervention schools were in areas of severe economic deprivation" was correct, but this did not mean that most *children* in the study came from those areas.

The psychology researchers are also unlikely to have been aware of the schools' national test results at the time. Even had they inquired, the official "no publication" rule meant that it is unlikely they would have been told. This positions the academics in a difficult place: their work was funded under an "education" grant and their results publicized to educators and education policy makers, but the driving questions and the narrow data collection reflected the research paradigms of psychology, not education. Whereas medical researchers working in this situation are supported by a robust and complete Medical Research Council framework that locates their work within a broader setting, there is no clear and commonly agreed framework for psychologists working within education spheres. Although there are frameworks for implementation models, the hierarchical model promoted by the rhetoric of evidence-based education muddies the water for researchers, policy makers and the media. This makes it difficult for academics to exercise even limited control over how the media and policy forums report their work. It also makes it almost impossible to have meaningful conversations in the popular press about the value of different kinds of research.

Having a framework to facilitate such conversations is a particularly pressing matter in the current academic climate. The four-yearly Research Excellence Framework (REF) audit for the Higher Education Funding Council (HEFC) in the UK requires researchers to show "impact." Further, it makes impact a matter of importance, not just for the researchers, but for the universities that employ them. It is weighted fairly heavily, at 25 percent of the outcomes of the REF, to ensure that institutions take it seriously and it is non-transferrable: "The HEI where the research was undertaken should be credited with the impact; and impacts should not 'travel' with researchers should they move to a different institution" (HEFC, 2010, p. 21). Each REF panel is required to develop:

> more detailed guidance on what constitutes impact in their disciplines. This should include guidance about the types of impacts and indicators anticipated from research in their disciplines . . . The guidance should be flexible enough to allow for a wide variety of impacts and indicators, including impacts that panels may not anticipate (HEFC, 2010, p. 3).

The British Psychological Society (BPS), in its advisory Code of Ethics and Conduct (BPS, 2009), provides guidance for members. It acknowledges that problems do not necessarily result from deliberately unethical behavior and suggests that: "reflective practice, peer support and transparency of professional activity would prevent problems occurring or developing into serious concerns" (BPS, 2009, p. 7).

The limitations of psychology research are not always clear, even to policy makers and psychologists at the highest level. When Professor Morag Stuart was called to give academic evidence to Westminster Select Committee of Enquiry into Reading, she was asked by the Chairman: "So we should listen to psychologists more than educational researchers?" She replied, "The research on reading goes on in psychology departments" (Education and Skills Committee, 2005a, Q38–9, p. 5).

The British Educational Research Association (BERA) guidelines cover researchers' responsibilities to participants, sponsors, the community of educational researchers, education professionals, policy makers and the general public. However, the last section (covering responsibility to education professionals, policy makers and the general public) is rather short, consisting of just two sentences:

> Researchers have a responsibility to seek to make public the results of their research for the benefit of educational professionals, policy makers and a wider public understanding of educational policy and practice, subject only to the provisos indicated in previous paragraphs;

Educational researchers must endeavour to communicate their findings, and the practical significance of their research, in a clear, straightforward fashion and in language judged appropriate to the intended audience
(BERA council 2011, pp. 9, 10).

The guidelines acknowledge that sometimes research may be used to ill effect:
"Researchers have the right to dissociate themselves publicly from accounts of
the research that they conducted, the subsequent presentation of which they consider misleading or unduly selective." A more proactive approach would provide
and publicize a framework that links research designs to claims about impact in
complex investigations. This approach might inform and frame conversations in
helpful ways and make misinterpretations less likely.

The American Education Research Association (AERA) provides the most
detailed ethical guidance about research use outside of academe (AERA, 2011a).
It foregrounds the importance of public trust, respect and honesty and identifies
five principles: a) professional competence; b) integrity; c) professional, scientific
and scholarly responsibility; d) respect for people's rights, dignity and diversity;
and e) social responsibility. The values under "social responsibility" articulate that
researchers should "apply and make public their knowledge in order to contribute
to the public good. When undertaking research, they strive to advance scientific
and scholarly knowledge and to serve the public good" (p. 146). The potential
for commercial and economic exploitation is also acknowledged, as is the need
to think about how research is framed for consumption by the public and policy
makers:

When education researchers provide professional advice, comment, or testi-
mony to the public, the media, government, or other institutions, they take
reasonable precautions to ensure that (1) the statements are based on appropriate research, literature, and practice; and (2) the statements are otherwise
consistent with the Code of Ethics. . . . In working with the press, radio,
television, online media or other communications media or in advertising
in the media, education researchers are cognizant of potential conflicts of
interest or appearances of such conflicts (e.g. providing compensation to
employees of the media), and they adhere to the highest standards of professional honesty (AERA, 2011a, p.149).

What is interesting about the AERA approach is that it recognizes the need for
exemplification and frameworks, explicitly encouraging the committee to "develop materials and innovative means of access and dissemination to enhance the
relevance of ethics in the everyday work of the education research profession"
(AERA, 2011b, p. 121).

Perhaps the AERA guidelines are more comprehensive because the definition of evidence-based education has been in operation longer and the problems of how research is used and misused are more salient. The existence of policy entrepreneurs (Kingdon, 2002) who drive their own agendas or those of special interest groups for altruistic purposes or raw commercial and economic advantage have been around longer in the US. Educational researchers and policy makers have witnessed a range of groups keen to shape the education research that is presented, how it is published and to whom. Hall (2007) points out that, in England, education increasingly presents big political and economic business opportunities, although still a long way behind the American experience. The number of people interested in reading research has expanded from "just reading researchers" to a whole range of players, not all of whom are altruistic. Hall highlights the ethical holes in the Committee System of Enquiry at Westminster where, unlike in the US, those giving evidence do not have to declare any financial interest they might have in a particular form of outcome. Robins (2010) also outlines how commercial publishers of school materials in both the US and the UK strategically court not only those who might have political influence over the literacy policy and curriculum content, but academic researchers whose work might benefit the publisher.

Literacy educators and researchers are finding themselves in an increasingly tangled political and legal landscape, where frameworks that help to locate what *evidence* really means in the context of complex interventions are extremely important. Education is funded by public money and must be able to show it has been spent wisely. Policy development and implementation frameworks that encompass notions of empirical assessment and "best-evidence" scrutiny could provide some protection against charges of incompetence, cronyism and corruption. However, for them to have "bite" requires a clear definition of what counts as "*best evidence*" in education interventions. Moreover, pupils can, and do, sue for inappropriate literacy teaching (BBC 2000a; 2000b). The internet makes it easy to access up-to-date research knowledge and it facilitates stakeholder networks that share this information. Now is the time for a very clear and well-publicized framework, one that shines a light on what counts as good *education* research in complex implementation and investigations.

Note

1. For non-UK readers, the education systems of Scotland and England are separate.

References

AERA. (2011a). Code of ethics. *Educational Researcher*, 40, 3, 145–156.
AERA. (2011b). Council adopts new AERA code of ethics: Ethics committee to emphasize ethics education. *Educational Researcher*, 40, 3, 120–121.

Australian Government Department for Education, Science and Training. (2005). Teaching reading: Report and recommendations national enquiry into the teaching of literacy. Australia: Barton.

BBC. (2000a). Ex-pupil can sue over dyslexia. July 27. Available at: http://news.bbc.co.uk/1/hi/uk/852919.stm (accessed on October 12, 2012).

BBC. (2000b). Parents campaign for dyslexia action. BBC World Service, Education. January 11. Available at: http://news.bbc.co.uk/1/hi/wales/598752.stm (accessed on October 12, 2012).

BERA Council. (2011). Ethical guidelines for educational research. Available at: www.bera.ac.uk/system/files/3/BERA-Ethical-Guidelines-2011.pdf

BPS. (2009). Code of ethics and conduct. Ethics and standards. August. Available at: www.bps.org.uk/what-we-do/ethics-standards/ethics-standards (accessed on May 24, 2012).

Clackmannanshire Council. (2003). *My mum likes school: Evaluation of the effectiveness of home school liaison work in increasing parental involvement in four core schools*. Clackmannanshire: Clacks Council Early Learning Initiatives.

Davies, P. (1999). What is evidence-based education? *British Journal of Educational Studies*, 47, 2, 108–121.

Department for Education. (2012). Training and development: Research informed practice. Available at: www.education.gov.uk/schools/careers/traininganddevelopment/research-informedpractice (accessed on April 25, 2013).

Dombey, H. (2010). *Teaching reading: What the evidence says*. Royston: UKLA.

Education and Skills Committee. (2005a). Eighth report: Witnesses Monday 15 November 2004: Dr. M. Stuart. United Kingdom Parliament. Available at: www.thesundaytimes.co.uk/sto/news/uk_news/article155878.ece (accessed on April 15, 2013).

Education and Skills Committee. (2005b). *Teaching children to read: Eighth Report of Session, 2004–5*. London, HMSO.

Eisenhart, M., & Towne, L. (2003). Contestation and change in national policy on "scientifically based" education research. *Educational Researcher*, 32, 7, 31–38.

Fracassini, C., Farquharson, K., & Marney, H. (2005). Focus: Secrecy that fails Scotland (or what the executive, unions, councils—and even some parents—don't want you to know). *Sunday Times (Scotland)*, November 13. Available at: http://www.timesonline.co.uk/article/0,,2090-1870190_1.00html (accessed on March 21, 2006).

Goodman, K. (1993). *Phonics phacts*. Portsmouth, NH: Heinemann.

Hall, K. (2007). Literacy policy and policy literacy: A tale of phonics in early reading in England. In R. Openshaw, & J. Soler (Eds.). *Reading across international boundaries: History, policy, and politics*. Charlotte, NC: Information Age Publishing, Inc, pp. 55–71.

Hall, K. (2013). Effective literacy teaching in the early years of school: A review of evidence. In J. Larson, & J. Marsh (Eds.). *The handbook of early childhood literacy*, 2nd edition. Thousand Oaks, CA: Sage.

Hargreaves, D. (1996). *Teaching as a research based profession: Possibilities and prospects*. London: Teacher Training Agency.

HEFC. (2010). *Research excellence framework impact pilot exercise: Findings of the expert panels*. A report to the UK higher education funding bodies by the chairs of the impact pilot panels. London: Research Excellence Framework.

HMIE. (2006). *Pilot inspection of the education functions of Clackmannanshire council in October 2005*. Edinburgh: Scottish Executive Education Department.

Institute of Education Sciences. (2012). About IES: Connecting research, policy and practice. Available at: http://ies.ed.gov/aboutus/ (accessed March 1, 2012).

Johnston, R. (2006). Personal communication with the author.

Johnston, R., & Watson, J. (2004). Accelerating the development of reading, spelling and phonemic awareness skills in initial readers. *Reading and Writing: An Interdisciplinary Journal*, 17, 327–357.

Johnston, R., & Watson, J. (2005). The effects of synthetic phonics teaching on reading and spelling attainment: A seven year longitudinal study. Edinburgh: Scottish Executive Education Department. Available at: www.scotland.gov.uk/Publicati ons/2005/02/20688/52449 (accessed April 15, 2013).

Kingdon, J. (2002). *Agendas, alternatives, and public policies*. 2nd edition. New York: Longman.

Lewis, M., & Ellis, S. (Eds.). (2006). *Phonics: Practice, research and policy*. London: Paul Chapman Publishing and UKLA.

Medical Research Council. (2008). Developing and evaluating complex interventions: New guidance. Available at: www.mrc.ac.uk/complexinterventionsguidance (accessed March 29, 2012).

Moss, G., & Huxford, L. (2007). Exploring literacy policy-making from the inside out. In L. Saunders (Ed.). *Exploring the relationship between educational research and education policy-making*. London: Routledge.

NICHD. (2000). Teaching children to read: An evidence-based assessment of the scientific research literature and its implications for reading instruction. Available at: www.nichd. nih.gov/publications/nrp/upload/report.pdf (accessed May 24, 2012).

Reading First Program. (2009). Available at: www2.ed.gov/programs/readingfirst/index. html (accessed May 24, 2012).

Robertson, L. (1999). Report to learning and leisure committee of 27, October, 1999: Clackmannanshire Early Learning Initiative: third progress report. Clackmannanshire: Local Authority.

Robertson, L. (2005). Why synthetic phonics was a natural winner. *The Scotsman*, April 27. Available at: http://thescotsman.scotsman.com/education.cfm (accessed on March 26, 2006).

Robins, E. (2010). *Beginning reading: Influences on policy in the United States and England, 1998–2010*. Unpublished PhD thesis. Available at: http://www.nrrf.org/ dissertation-robins9–10.pdf (accessed on May 24, 2012).

Rose, J. (2006). *Independent review of the teaching of early reading: Final report*. Nottingham: DfES.

Sackett, D., Straus, S., Richardson, S., Rosenberg, W., & Haynes, R. (2000). *Evidence-based medicine*. Edinburgh: Churchill Livingstone.

SEED. (2002). Programme for International Student Assessment: Scottish Report (Education and Young People Research Unit). Edinburgh: Scottish Executive Education Department. Available at: www.oecd.org/education/33686029.pdf (accessed October 12, 2012).

Slavin, R. (2002). Evidence-based education policies: Transforming educational practice and research. *Educational Researcher*, 31, 7, 15–21.

Soler, J., & Openshaw, R. (2007). "To be or not to be?": The politics of teaching phonics in England and New Zealand. *Journal of Early Childhood Literacy*, 7, 3, 333–352.

Torgerson, C., Brooks, G., & Hall, J. (2006). *A systematic review of the research literature on the use of phonics in the teaching of reading and spelling*. London: DfES Research Report 711.

US Department of Education. (2002). Strategic plan for 2002–2007. Available at: www2.ed.gov/about/reports/strat/plan2002-07/plan.pdf (accessed on August, 2011).

Van Kraayenoord, C. (2003). Phonological awareness, phonemic awareness and phonics. *Education Views*, 12, 7, 14–15.

Watson, J., & Johnston, R. (1998). Accelerating reading attainment: The effectiveness of synthetic phonics. *Interchange 57*. Edinburgh: Scottish Executive Education Department.

Wharton-McDonald, R., Pressley, M., & Hampston, J. (1998). Literacy instruction in nine first-grade classrooms: Teacher characteristics and student achievement. *Elementary School Journal*, 99, 2, 101–128.

Wiseman, A. W. (2010). The uses of evidence for educational policymaking: Global contexts and international trends. *Review of Research in Education*, 34, 1, 1–24.

Wyse, D., & Goswami, U. (2008). Synthetic phonics and the teaching of reading. *British Educational Research Journal*, 34, 6, 691–710.

7

ABOUT THE DUBIOUS ROLE OF PHONOLOGICAL AWARENESS IN THE DISCUSSION OF LITERACY POLICIES

Renate Valtin

Editor's Note: In a sane and fair world, educational policies should be based on the kind of knowledge Renate Valtin brings together on the issue of phonological awareness. But in Germany, as elsewhere, decisions are made politically with agendas that have little to do with rational consideration of the available knowledge. Why do political authorities prefer the advice of those who offer simplistic solutions to societal problems? And why are the same political solutions offered in so many different countries? It is not a coincidence. This article is a good example of the extensive research done in other languages that American researchers should be aware of.

KSG

Kindergarten and the Educational System in Germany

Germany is a federal republic consisting of 16 federal states which have sole power over educational policy within their geographical area (Hornberg, et al., 2007). In most state schools, children start around the age of six. Preprimary education, usually offered as kindergarten, is neither part of the compulsory school system nor linked to it, and attendance is voluntary—but parents have to pay in most states (while university studies are usually free). As the term "kindergarten" implies, the goals and methods of these institutions are social–pedagogical in nature, involving playing, social activities, preparation in physical abilities, speech, language, creativity, music, and daily routines. More than 95 percent of children attend kindergarten at the age of five. Instruction in reading and writing is not included in the curriculum.

The PISA 2000 findings led to "PISA shock" in Germany because of the high correlation of achievement with social class, with a high proportion of failing pupils coming from lower socio-cultural and migrant backgrounds. The discussion that occurred relating to these figures acknowledged the relevance of preschool education as the foundation for literacy. The Standing Conference of Ministers of Education and Cultural Affairs suggested the improvement of early language development and training in kindergarten, a policy aimed at improving both family literacy (Hornberg & Valtin, 2011) and the quality of early childhood education and care.

While language training is acknowledged, there is controversy between two early literacy approaches: (a) integrative language learning and a literacy-rich environment, and (b) functional training with the focus on fostering phonological awareness. The concept of phonological awareness is popular in Germany and stems from educational psychologists who often disregard linguistic and educational knowledge about emergent literacy. They claim that phonological awareness is an important "prerequisite" skill for literacy learning; that "deficits" lead to difficulties in reading and spelling and should be compensated through specific training prior to the start of formal schooling. Interestingly, some of these authors have developed tests and training material for phonological awareness.

In this chapter, I present a critical analysis of the concept of phonological awareness for learning to read, and the empirical data used as evidence of its importance. I question the usefulness of phonemic training in kindergarten. I mainly refer to German studies. Actually, if phonological awareness has no use as a precursor to reading and spelling in German, then how could it be important in an even more irregular orthography such as English?

The Concept of Phonological Awareness in Educational Psychology

Schneider, et al. (2000, p. 284) define phonological awareness as "the ability to explicitly reflect on the sound structure of spoken language," and distinguish two components: the broad sense of phonological awareness refers to the "analysis of broader sound structures such as words and syllables," the narrow sense "concerns the ability to isolate phonemes within words and syllables" (p. 284). Adherents concede that phonological awareness is a "conglomerate of different sub-skills with different levels of complexity" (Mayer, 2011, p. 50). Mayer (2011) reported correlations between two tests of phonological awareness: TEPHOBE and BISC (developed by Jansen, et al., 2002), along with the subtests. The two tests showed a moderate correlation of .42. Only ten of the 25 correlations between subtests reached significance. Two subtests that are supposed to measure the same skill (synthesis of onset and rhyme, phoneme synthesis) only correlated between .38 and .45. This analysis shows that different tests and even similar subtests measure different (sub)skills. Thus it does not seem justified to speak in general of phonological awareness. The specific subskills should be named.

Empirical Evidence

Phonological awareness is regarded as the strongest predictor of learning written language in alphabetic orthographies. How firm is the empirical ground for this assumption? Most of the research studies are "theory free" and establish evidence from correlations between measures of phonological awareness and global measures of reading (reading fluency and accuracy) and spelling (number of errors). The measures of reading and spelling are output oriented and do not take into account the existing knowledge we have of strategies for learning to read and spell in the early phases of written language acquisition (see the developmental model in Table 7.1) and of qualitative analysis of spelling errors (Valtin & Hofmann, 2009).

The correlational studies show a highly variable picture: from no significance (Röhr, 1978) to low or moderate correlations (Martschinke, 2001). The correlations are similar to those for letter knowledge (Brügelmann, 2005), intelligence (Deimel, et al., 2005), and naming speed (Mayer, 2011), and are too low to be used for individual prognosis (Rackwitz, 2008). In one study by Grube and Hasselhorn (2006) phonological awareness, showed significant correlations with reading in grades 1 and 2 but not in grades 3 and 4; with spelling in grades 1, 2 and 4 but not in grade 3; and, surprisingly, with mathematics in grades 1, 2, 3 and 4. The authors concluded "that aspects of phonological information processing are not only relevant for learning to read and spell but also play a considerable role in acquiring mathematical competence" (Grube & Hasselhorn, 2006, p. 99, translated by R.V.). No further explanations are given. This study is an example of a general problem in this research tradition. The relation to written language learning is asserted, but not explained; how might the different subskills of phonological awareness be embedded in a theory of learning to read and spell?

Correlations refer to common variance between two measures and are not proof of a causal relationship. The common variance might reflect common factors, e.g. general intelligence, vocabulary knowledge or preschool reading competence. In a predictive study, Lundberg, et al. (1980, p. 166) concluded: "The most powerful determinant of reading achievement in grade one is the ability in kindergarten to analyze phonemes and reverse their order." However, my reanalysis of the data of this study, using factor analysis of the battery of variables and comparing poor and good readers at the end of first grade, showed that those children successful in the phonemic tasks were already readers when entering school and that preschool reading ability correlated more highly with later reading achievement than the ability to reverse phonemes did (Valtin, 1984b). Phonological awareness seems to be a product of reading, not a precursor.

Correlations between measures of phonological awareness and later reading achievement to establish the prognostic validity of the Bielefeld Screening Inventory (BISC) were difficult to replicate (Brügelmann, 2003; 2005). The BISC correctly identified less than 20 percent of children with reading and spelling difficulties in first and second grades (Marx & Weber, 2006). Moreover, most of the "at-risk" children developed normal reading and spelling competences (Brügelmann, 2003; 2005). There were both false positives and false negatives, a poor result for a supposedly diagnostic instrument. Similar results were obtained in another analysis of the predictive value of phonological awareness which found that sound-blending abilities in kindergarten had no predictive value for learning to read and spell (Rackwitz, 2011; Röhr, 1978).

One word of caution with regard to predictive validity:

> The underlying rationale of these studies assumes that children's scholastic achievement is a direct function of the abilities that they exhibit when entering school and that instruction does not provide a systematic, but rather a random effect. The role assigned to the teacher and his/her teaching methods seems to be merely ephemeral, which implies a very pessimistic picture of education. Whoever believes education has beneficial effects and considers compensatory effects as desirable must be suspicious of predictive correlations between preschool abilities and scholastic achievement (Valtin, 1984b, p. 238).

Some psychologists have begun to rethink the effects of teaching reading: "The instructional approach to reading in the first grades might affect the predictive validity of an early screening" (Marx & Weber, 2006, p. 251).

Another line of small- and large-scale research studies concerns the transfer effect from phonological training in kindergarten to later reading and spelling achievement. Not all studies have shown effects from such phonological training (May & Okwumo, 1999; Rothe, 2008; Wolf, et al., 2010) or even from training of phonological awareness combined with letter training (Hartmann, 2002). Marx, et al. (2005) reported that the preventive effects of the training existed for decoding only and not for reading comprehension. In the large EVES project (Roos & Schöler, 2007), there were no effects at the end of first grade, and in later grades mainly small effects in spelling, but only for girls, not for boys. Rackwitz (2008) found only small effects on spelling and concluded: "Phonological awareness is overestimated in its relevance as precursor and predictor of literacy development" (p. 1). Other studies did not succeed in demonstrating that isolated phonological training had an advantage over more comprehensive methods where children had a book-rich environment and many opportunities to gather experiences with written language (Franzkowiak, 2008; Lenel, 2005; May & Okwumo, 1999; Rackwitz, 2008).

There are also studies investigating the effect of phonological training in first grade parallel to reading instruction. No advantage of the trained group in comparison with untrained children was observed by Einsiedler, et al. (2002), and Kirschhock (2004). In a study by Hatz and Sachse (2011), "children at risk" (with low scores on a phonological test) who received phonological training in first grade showed no advantage in phonological awareness nor in spelling, compared with an untrained group at the end of first grade.

In several experimental studies carried out by researchers in colleges of education, teacher educators demonstrated that children learn phonemic synthesis and analysis through traditional methods of teaching reading in Germany, because children in the first months of school are encouraged to grasp the alphabetic code (Brügelmann, 2005; Röhr, 1978). To sum up, the empirical evidence provided in German studies for the relevance of phonological awareness is contradictive and not very convincing.

Critique of the Concept of Phonological Awareness

Phonological awareness, as the term is used by educational psychologists in Germany, does not refer to a unitary function (Andresen 2005, p. 232) but to a conglomerate of heterogeneous linguistic units and operations (Schmid-Barkow 1999). *Words* as parts of sentences belong to a grammatical category, and segmenting sentences into words is a grammatical operation that has nothing to do with the phonological level, because "words as components of speech are neither salient nor clearly marked" (Ehri 1984, p. 120). *Syllables* are elementary, articulatory units of speech and thus easily perceptible. *Phonemes* belong to a linguistic model of language and are highly abstract units (distinctive speech sounds which differentiate words) that categorize speech sounds into perceptual categories (e.g. in Japanese, the sounds /l/ and /r/, which are separate phonemes in German, are allophones of the same phoneme).

From a psycholinguistic point of view, the components subsumed under phonological awareness are components of language awareness, linguistic awareness, or metalinguistics, terms that appeared with increasing frequency in reading theory literature and research in the 1970s and 1980s. Over 30 years ago, language awareness and its relationship to the acquisition of written language were investigated theoretically and empirically, both in Germany (Andresen, 1985) and elsewhere in the world. In 1979, John Downing and I published a collection bringing together disciplines of linguistics, psycholinguistics, experimental and child psychology, and education (Downing & Valtin, 1984). Various studies at that time showed that children develop the understanding of syllables, words, and phonemes independently of one another and in different phases in their development (Andresen, 1985; Clark, 1978; Hakes, 1980; Valtin, 1984a).

Early in the preschool years, children are able to segment speech into *syllables*. They use rhymes either spontaneously or after brief instruction. They sometimes confuse the phonological and the semantic level, as the example of my niece, aged four years, shows: "House and mouse are rhymes—and apples and pears too."

The development of the concept of a *word* and the ability of children to segment utterances into words has been intensely investigated in developmental psychology and psycholinguistics, using a variety of procedures (e.g. counting words in sentences, interviews about the meaning of a word, giving examples of long and short words). The studies by Januschek, et al. (1979); Kirschhock (2004); and Valtin, et al. (1986/1994) show that children of the same age have quite different and multiple concepts of a "word," which are gradually narrowed under the influence of school and the learning of reading and writing. For preschool children, words and language in general are embedded in the context of action, and they have difficulty in differentiating between words and their referents (Homer & Olson, 1999). They think that, for example, *cow* is a longer word than *butterfly* (Bosch, 1937; Kirchhock, 2004; Valtin, et al., 1986/1994), and that *Blätter* (leaves) are many words (Januschek, et al., 1979). Because of this embeddedness, children have difficulty segmenting utterances into words, as the following example by Valtin, et al. (1986/1994) demonstrates. When asked how many words are in the sentence "Father goes into the garage," the children's answers showed these patterns:

- Inability to segment.
- Identification of semantic salient units ("Father goes"—"into the garage").
- Distinction between subject and predicate ("Father"—"goes into the garage").
- Differentiation between content words (nouns, verbs), on the one hand, and function words (articles, prepositions, and conjunctions), on the other hand, although the latter were not always identified as words.

Similar developmental sequences have been observed when studying Russian (Karpova, 1966) and Spanish children (Ferreiro, 1978), and appear to be related to experiences with print (Ehri, 1984).

The task of segmenting words into sounds or phonemes is very difficult. Training studies with preschool children demonstrate that at best they are able to identify the first phoneme of a word if it is a syllable (a-pron) or when it is a continuant (/s/, /f/, /m/). Children have more difficulty with stop consonants (/t/, /p/) (Bryant, 1993; Helfgott, 1976; Zhurova, 1973). Since the ability to segment words into phonemes and to combine phonemes into a word is only relevant when learning an alphabetic script, it should be useful to look at this skill within a framework of written language acquisition.

Phonological Awareness and Written Language Acquisition

Learning to read and spell is an active process in which children build theories by forming, testing, and modifying hypotheses about the function and features of written language (Downing & Valtin, 1984), and by forming strategies to deal and communicate with print. The complexity of the learning demands is very high because of the abstractness of written language, both from the acoustic aspect of language and from the conversational partner. Our alphabetic system is a relatively late human achievement, based on remarkable insights into the lexical, syntactic, and phonological structure of language.

A fruitful theoretical model for the acquisition of reading and spelling was outlined by Downing (1984) in his theory of cognitive clarity: the learner must reconstruct the linguistic insights possessed by the inventors of the alphabetic script, and rediscover for themselves the rules by which it is coded. During this process, the learner has to gain cognitive clarity or insight into the function of print (the squiggles on the page are a visual representation of language and not merely a set of symbols whose content is arbitrary), and into the structure of our alphabetic system, and the recognition that linguistic units are represented in print.

The longitudinal pilot study by Valtin (1989) and the intervention study by Kirschhock (2004) demonstrate that children entering school have vague concepts about both the function of reading and writing and the concepts of print (what is a letter, a word, a sentence?). Both studies administered Downing's LARR battery (Language Awareness in Reading Readiness). Average readers and spellers showed evidence of cognitive clarity during the first year in school while slower readers had difficulties at the end of first grade. Kirschhock (2004) showed that the development of these concepts varied with the teachers' reading instruction methods.

Learners have to acquire certain cognitive and linguistic abilities and insights that may be differentiated into four elements: (1) the ability to objectify language and to reflect on formal properties of language; (2) the concept of a word and the ability to segment sentences into words; (3) the analysis and synthesis of phonemes; and (4) the learning of orthographic principles and phoneme–grapheme correspondence rules.

First is *the ability to objectify language and to reflect on formal properties of language*. This is a real "prerequisite" for learning to read and write in an alphabetic code. Only when children are able to shift from content to form and to concentrate on the acoustic features of a word are they responsive to sounds rather than meaning. When a teacher asked "Listen, what does *car* begin with?" The child replied: "with a bumper."

The ability to concentrate on formal properties of language may be measured by syllable and rhyming tasks as well as comparison of long and short words and requires a certain level of cognitive decentration in Piaget's sense (Lundberg, 1982; Van Leent, 1983; Watson, 1984). Phonological awareness in a broad sense covers this ability. It is not justifiable, however, to also subsume the analysis of words under this category.

Second is *the concept of a word and the ability to segment sentences into words*. When learning print, the child has to grasp the concepts of the word as a linguistic unit and of word boundaries, i.e., that a written sentence contains all parts of speech, and that gaps are left between the words. These insights develop only gradually and reflect experience with print. In their invented spellings, preschool children and first graders leave no gaps between words and segment sentences into semantic units, often leaving out function words (see Figure 7.1).

Interviews with children about "What is written in a written sentence?" (Ferreiro, 1978;Valtin, 1989) show that children believe that only content words, such as nouns or verbs, are visually represented in print, but not articles and other function words.This is reflected in their dictations and their invented spellings Figure 7.1). In the sentence "OmaopALESA" (Grandma and grandpa are reading), for example, the function word "und" is missing and there are no word boundaries. It is during the process of learning to read and spell that children gradually acquire the knowledge of words and word boundaries (Ehri, 1984; Kirschhock, 2004; Valtin, 1989).

The third point is about *analysis and synthesis.* The learner has to gain an awareness of phonemes, i.e., that words can be divided into sound segments, and that one or more letters can be associated with these segments. In fact, this is an artificial operation, only needed when learning an alphabetic code. Beginning learners have great difficulty in analyzing spoken words because of the nature of the acoustic signal. In pronunciation, the speech sounds are not discrete units but overlap and are co-articulated, so that the phonetic properties of sounds are altered by adjacent sounds (Ehri, 1984, p. 120). Phonemes are abstract units, and so phonemic segmentation and synthesis are not simple associative memory tasks but highly demanding conceptual tasks (Andresen, 1985; Helfgott, 1976;Valtin, 1984a). Even when children have learned to match sounds with letters, they need many months of schooling to cope with phonemic segmentation of difficult words, especially those with consonant clusters. That the difficulty of phonemic segmentation depends on the position of the phoneme in a word has been demonstrated by Zhurova (1973) and Marsh and Mineo (1977).

Observation of children's spellings of unknown words demonstrates these difficulties and points to characteristic developmental stages:

a) *Recognition and representation of prominent speech sounds.* Consider ★L for *Elefant.*
b) *Rudimentary or skeleton writing.*With growing awareness of the sound structure of words, children begin to represent some phonetic elements, as in ★GBSA for *Geburtstag* (birthday).
c) *Phonetic-articulatory strategy.* Beginning learners, when analyzing sound structure, pronounce the word slowly trying to "catch" all sounds of their pronunciation, for instance, ★AIEN or ★AEIN for *"ein"*(a). When discovering the alphabetic principle children seem to develop the rule:"Spell as you speak," and start with an analysis of their articulatory cues, often affected by local accents. Slow articulation as well as local accents may result in artificially different sounds as well: ★ESCH for *"ich"* (I), ★BEN instead of *"bin"* (am). Children may omit sounds within clusters or may produce extra segments not symbolized in print as ★THROIMPTE for *"träumte"* (dreamed). Similar phenomena have been observed by Ehri (1984) with spellings as ★FEREND for "friend" and ★BALAOSIS for "blouses."

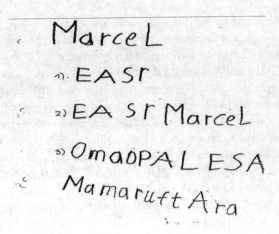

FIGURE 7.1 Writing Without Word Spaces

d) *Phonemic strategy with first use of orthographic patterns.* At this phase, children begin
   to segment phonemically. Experience with conventional spellings helps children to learn which phones to ignore (Ehri, 1984). According to German linguistics (Eichler & Bünting, 1976), German adult speakers produce about 120
   to 150 perceptually different speech sounds in their speech, but only 38 to 40
   phonemes have the function of indicating differences in meaning. Mainly under
   the influence of print, children develop the phonemic classification system and
   detect inconsistencies between the sounds and orthographic patterns of words.
   In their spellings, they begin to use orthographic regularities. The challenge in
   German orthography is that correct phonemic segmentation alone does not
   guarantee correct spelling. In a study by Löffler (personal communication),
   children who were able to correctly segment the word "Elefant" phonemically
   produced 106 variants of this word by assigning incorrect graphemes to the
   phonemes, e.g., ★Älefant, ★Ellefant, ★Elefannt, ★Ehlefant, ★Elevant, ★Ellefant.
   These examples demonstrate that the main difficulty in spelling is not phonemic analysis but the complexity of phoneme–grapheme correspondences.

The fourth *component of learning to read and write is learning phoneme–grapheme-
correspondence rules and principles of orthography.* Competence models of orthography
include two dimensions: phonographic abilities (phoneme analysis and assigning
of graphemes) and grammatical operations, including word and sentence level
(Löffler & Meyer-Schepers, 2005). In German orthography, about 40 phonemes
(including 16 vowels and three diphthongs) are represented by 86 graphemes,
each consisting of one, two or three letters (Thomé, et al., 2011, p. 54). So the
phoneme–grapheme-correspondence rules are complex. In addition, the principles of German orthography reflect phonemic, orthographic, morphemic, and
grammatical information.

Each stage of the child's development of reading and spelling competence may be characterized by a dominant strategy that reflects important insights into the nature of print. Observations of children (Dehn, 1987; Scheerer-Neumann, 2001), case studies (Scheerer-Neumann, et al., 1986), and pilot longitudinal studies (Valtin, 1997; Valtin, et al., 1986/1994) demonstrate the existence of a developmental sequence (Table 7.1), which results from interaction between the child's emerging insights, the structure of orthography, and the teaching method. Only at levels 3 and 4 is phonemic awareness relevant.

Comparing sequential patterns of spelling and reading, we find striking similarities. However, it is doubtful whether there is a strict parallel. As case studies show (Scheerer-Neumann, et al., 1986), some children learn the phonetic strategy when spelling but cannot read what they have written. Other children learn to sound out words when reading before being able to segment words into phonemes. In German, reading (or at least decoding) is easier than spelling. Since the grapheme–phoneme-correspondence rules are rather consistent, a "sounding-out" strategy leads to an articulatory code that is more or less similar to the real word. Thus decoding does not present as many problems as spelling, where the phoneme–grapheme-correspondences are less predictable and children have to shift from their phonetic-articulatory strategy to phonemic

TABLE 7.1 Developmental Model of Reading and Spelling

Level	Skills and insights	Reading	Spelling
1	Imitative behavior	Pretend reading	Scribbling
2	Knowledge of single letters in a figurative sense, but no insight into the relationship between letters and sounds	Naive-holistic reading children guess at words, orienting themselves at the context and figurative cues	Logographic strategy: Drawing arbitrary sequences of letters or letter-like forms (pseudo-words)
3	Beginning insight into the function of letters, knowledge of some letters/sounds	Beginning alphabetic strategy (phonetic cue reading)	Rudimentary or skeletal writings
4	Insight into the alphabetic principle, ability to segment words into speech sounds and phonemes	Sounding-out strategy (reading letter by letter), sometimes without understanding	Phonetic-articulatory strategy (I spell as I speak)
5	Knowledge and use of orthographic patterns	Alphabetic reading with use of chunks	Phonemic strategy with first use of orthographic patterns
6	Automatized processes	Automatized word recognition	Correct spelling

classifications, and also learn orthographic rules that cannot be solved by phonological knowledge.

Phonological Training as Preparation for Learning to Read and Write?

While some psychologists plead for preschool training combining phonological skills and letter knowledge in order to prevent reading difficulties, educators deny the usefulness and meaningfulness of such an approach and urge more comprehensive training in kindergarten. I have argued (Valtin, 2003), along with other experts in first grade reading instruction (Bosch, 1937) that isolated training of letters and sounds outside the context of reading and writing does not lead children to grasp the *function* of letters and sounds (let alone phonemes). At best children learn letters in a figurative way (discriminating visual features).

A close look at how Schneider, et al. (2000) proceeded in their letter-sound training in kindergarten illustrates the problems that arise from isolated learning of letter-sound combinations. Twelve letters were chosen because of their frequency in written texts (A,E,M,I,O,R,U,S,L,B,T,N). Each letter was introduced in combination with a sound story, e.g. when >A< (in German the /a/ is pronounced as in father) was presented, children had to remember that when visiting a dentist they say "/aaa/" (signalling pain—not to be mixed up with /aaa/ /aaa/—signalling that the child has to got to the toilet).

Children had to buzz like a bee (zzz) for the letter >S<. This so-called "interjection" method is a variety of the synthetic approaches to teaching reading that are no longer used in German schools; methods criticized by Bosch over 70 years ago (1937). He observed that children who had learned to associate letters with natural sounds when reading a word like >im< muttered: "Iiiii /eee/ cries the cock, mmm mumbles the bear." Children of low intelligence in particular were unable to "forget" the associations they had learned earlier. Bosch's main argument against synthetic approaches is that children are taught meaningless units (letters) and thus have difficulty in grasping the *function* of letters in words. For many years the so-called "analytic-synthetic method" which starts with meaningful words, each word analyzed into its graphemic and phonemic elements so that children grasp the function of letters and the alphabetic code, has been prescribed in most of the German states (Valtin, 2003). The learned words are embedded in a communicative situation. Children are also encouraged to invent spellings and to experience the communicative function of writing.

Newer studies show that these instructional methods also lead to phonemic awareness (Kirschhock, 2004; Marx & Weber, 2006). This seems to be a rather trivial insight because the alphabetic principle consists in the representation of phonemes by graphemes. Even if children start with "deficits" in phonological tasks, teachers can compensate for these (Brügelmann, 2005; Kirschhock, 2004; Rackwitz, 2008; Röhr, 1978).

If the synthetic approach (teaching isolated letters in combination with natural sounds) was abandoned in first grade for good reasons more than 30 years ago, why should this questionable approach be used in kindergarten? In the Schneider, et al. (2000) intervention study, some kindergarten teachers eventually refused to participate in the letter-sound training.

These examples of the negative effects of phonological training tasks, together with the limited evidence of transfer effects, support the view that phonemic segmentation and analysis should be learned in the context of whole words and embedded in a reading task and not in kindergarten. In both of the international literacy studies, IGLU (PIRLS) 2001 and 2006, the correlations between reading competence in grade 4 and preschool knowledge of reading and writing letters and words were non-significant (Bos, et al., 2007).

The Relevance of Preschool Education for the Foundation of Literacy

As PIRLS demonstrates, children who have spent at least two years in kindergarten have an advantage in reading and mathematics in grade 4 over children with less or no participation in kindergarten (Bos, et al., 2007). PIRLS also shows that children from low socio-cultural and/or migration backgrounds are the biggest group among poor readers. Preschool education thus has taken on particular importance.

Children need a comprehensive program to develop their oral language before entering school. Instead of teaching meaningless elements of written language, such as letter-sound associations in didactically questionable formats, time in kindergarten should be used for a comprehensive approach, with the aim of broadening children's vocabulary and grammatical knowledge as well as their communicative abilities. Kindergarten teachers should provide situations where children can experience different functions of language, in social play and role play (Andresen, 2005), in conflict situations, and problem solving.

The ability to shift attention from content to form may be fostered in language games, using rhymes, tongue-twisters, and poems. In addition, kindergarten teachers should provide a literacy environment in which children engage in communicative functions of reading and writing. Reading books aloud, telling stories, presenting picture books, using writing in communicative contexts are all well-known methods.

Conclusions

The vague concept of phonological awareness and the differentiation into broad and narrow senses needs to be embedded into a psycholinguistic theory of development of language awareness and literacy acquisition, as already achieved in the last century in Germany (Andresen, 1985) and in international research (Downing & Valtin, 1984). Educational psychologists still have the strongest impact on preschool programs in Germany, even though they disregard linguistic and educational knowledge about emergent literacy in school. In kindergarten, time should be devoted to oral language development and to experiences with the *functions* of written language by providing a rich literacy environment.

Acknowledgment

Some parts of this chapter are published in Valtin (2012).

References

Andresen, H. (1985). *Schriftspracherwerb und die Entstehung von Sprachbewußtheit.* Opladen: Westdeutscher Verlag.

Andresen, H. (2005). *Vom Sprechen zum Schreiben.* Stuttgart: Klett.

Bos, W., Hornberg, S., Arnold, K.-H., Faust, G., Fried, L., Lankes, E.-M., Schwippert, K., & Valtin, R. (Eds.). (2007). *IGLU 2006. Lesekompetenzen von Grundschulkindern in Deutschland im internationalen Vergleich.* Münster: Waxmann.

Bosch, B. (1937). *Grundlagen des Erstleseunterrichts.* Korrigierte Reprintausgabe. Frankfurt: Arbeitskreis Grundschule (1984).

Bryant, P. (1993). Phonological aspects of learning to read. In R. Beard (Ed.). *Teaching literacy balancing perspectives.* London: Hodder & Stoughton.

Brügelmann, H. (2003). Vorschulische Prädiktoren des Misserfolgs beim Schriftspracherwerb in der Schule. Abschlussbericht des Projekts LOGIK-R an das MWF/Düsseldorf. Available at: www.agprim.uni-siegen.de/logik-r/logik%5B1%5D.03.bericht_an_mswf.11–232.pdf (accessed April 13, 2011).

Brügelmann, H. (2005). Das Prognoserisiko von Risikoprognosen—eine Chance für "Risikokinder"? In B. Hofmann & A. Sasse (Eds.). *Übergänge. Kinder und Schrift zwischen Kindergarten und Schule* (pp. 146–172). Berlin: Deutsche Gesellschaft für Lesen und Schreiben.

Clark, E.V. (1978). Awareness of language: Some evidence from what children say and do. In A. Sinclair, R.J. Jarvella, & W.J.M. Levelt (Eds.). *The child's conception of language* (pp. 17–44). New York: Springer.

Dehn, M. (1987). Wie Kinder Schriftsprache erlernen. In I. Naegele & R. Valtin (Eds.). *Rechtschreibunterricht in den Klassen 1–6* (pp. 28–37). Frankfurt: Arbeitskreis Grundschule (3rd ed. 1994).

Deimel, W., Ziegler, A., & Schulte-Körne, G. (2005). *Modell Schriftsprach-Moderatoren (MSM). Zwischenbericht der wissenschaftlichen Begleitung nach zwei Jahren—Kurzfassung.* Available at: www.kjp.med.uni-muenchen.de/download/MSM-Zwischenbericht.pdf (accessed March 22, 2009).

Downing, J. (1984). Task awareness in the development of reading skill. In J. Downing & R. Valtin (Eds.). *Language awareness and learning to read* (pp. 27–56). New York: Springer.

Downing, J., & Valtin, R. (Eds.). (1984). *Language awareness and learning to read.* New York: Springer.

Ehri, L.C. (1984). How orthography alters spoken language competencies in children learning to read and spell. In J. Downing, & R. Valtin (Eds.). *Language awareness and learning to read* (pp. 119–148). New York: Springer.

Eichler, W., & Bünting, K.-D. (1976). *Deutsche Grammatik.* Kronberg, Ts: Scriptor.

Einsiedler, W., Frank, A., Kirschhock, E.M., Martschinke, S., & Treinies, G. (2002). Der Einfluss verschiedener Unterrichtsformen auf die phonologische Bewusstheit sowie auf Lese-Rechtschreibleistungen im 1. Schuljahr. *Psychologie in Erziehung und Unterricht*, 49, 194–209.

Ferreiro, E. (1978). What is written in a written sentence: A developmental answer. *Journal of Education*, 160, 25–39.

Franzkowiak, T. (2008). *Vom BLISS-Symbol zur alphabetischen Schrift. Entwicklung und Erprobung eines vorschulischen Förderansatzes zur Prävention von Lernschwierigkeiten beim Schriftspracherwerb*. Dissertation im FB 2. Universität: Siegen. Available at: http://dokumentix.ub.uni-siegen.de/opus/volltexte/2008/351/index.html (accessed February 3, 2010).

Grube, D., & Hasselhorn, M. (2006). Längsschnittliche Analysen zur Lese-, Rechtschreib- und Mathematikleistung im Grundschulalter: Zur Rolle von Vorwissen, Intelligenz, phonologischem Arbeitsgedächtnis und phonologischer Bewusstheit. In I. Hosenfeld, & F.-W. Schrader (Eds.). *Schulische Leistung: Grundlagen, Bedingungen und Perspektiven* (pp. 87–105). Münster: Waxmann.

Hakes, D.T. (1980). *The development of metalinguistic abilities in children*. New York: Springer.

Hartmann, E. (2002). *Möglichkeiten und Grenzen einer präventiven Intervention zur phonologischen Bewusstheit von lautsprachgestörten Kindergartenkindern*. Fribourg: Sprachimpuls.

Hatz, H., & Sachse, S. (2011). Prävention von Lese-Rechtschreibstörungen. Auswirkungen eines Trainings phonologischer Bewusstheit und eines Rechtschreibtrainings im ersten Schuljahr auf den Schriftspracherwerb. *Zeitschrift für Entwicklungspsychologie und Pädagogische Psychologie*, 42, 4, 226–240.

Helfgott, J. (1976). Phonemic segmentation and blending skills of kindergarten children: Implications for beginning reading acquisition. *Contemporary Educational Psychology*, 1, 157–169.

Homer, B.D., & Olson, D.R. (1999). The role of literacy in children's concept of word. *Written Language and Literacy*, 2, 113–140.

Hornberg, S., Bos, W., Lankes, E.-M., & Valtin, R. (2007). Germany. In A.M. Kennedy, I.V.S. Mullis, M.O. Martin, & K.L. Trong (Eds.). *PIRLS 2006 encyclopaedia: A guide to reading education in the forty PIRLS 2006 countries*. Chestnut Hill, MA: TIMSS & PIRLS International Study Centre, Boston College.

Hornberg, S., & Valtin, R. (2011) (Eds.). *Mehrsprachigkeit: Chance oder Hürde beim Schriftspracherwerb?* Berlin: Deutsche Gesellschaft für Lesen und Schreiben.

Jansen, H., Mannhaupt, G., Marx, H., & Skowronek, H. (2002). *Bielefelder Screening zur Früherkennung von Lese-Rechtschreibschwierigkeiten*. Göttingen: Hogrefe.

Januschek, F., Paprotté, W., & Rohde, W. (1979). The growth of metalinguistic knowledge in children. In M. Van de Vlede, & W. Vandeweghe (Eds.). *Sprachstruktur, Individuum und Gesellschaft. Akten des 13. Linguistischen Kolloquiums, Gent 1978*, 243–254. Tübingen: Niemeyer.

Karpova, S.N. (1966). The preschooler's realization of the lexical structure of speech. In F. Smith, & G.A. Miller (Eds.). *The genesis of language: A psycholinguistic approach*. Cambridge, MA: MIT Press.

Kirschhock, E.-M. (2004). *Entwicklung schriftsprachlicher Kompetenzen im Anfangsunterricht*. Bad Heilbrunn: Klinkhardt.

Lenel, A. (2005). *Schrifterwerb vor der Schule. Eine entwicklungspsychologische Längsschnittstudie*. Weinheim: Beltz PVU.

Löffler, I., & Meyer-Schepers, U. (2005). Orthographische Kompetenzen: Ergebnisse Qualitativer Fehleranalysen, insbesondere bei schwachen Rechtschreibern. In W. Bos, E.-M. Lankes, M. Prenzel, K. Schwippert, R. Valtin, & G. Walther (Eds.). *IGLU. Vertiefende Analysen zu Leseverständnis, Rahmenbedingungen und Zusatzstudien* (pp. 81–108). Münster: Waxmann.

Lundberg, I. (1982). *Longitudinal studies of reading and its difficulties in Sweden.* Unpublished manuscript. University of Umea, Sweden.

Lundberg, I., Wall, S., & Oloffson, A. (1980). Reading and spelling skills in the first school years predicted from phonemic awareness skills in kindergarten. *Scandinavian Journal of Psychology*, 21, 159–173.

Marsh, G., & Mineo, R.J. (1977). Training preschool children to recognize phonemes in words. *Journal of Educational Psychology*, 69, 748–753.

Martschinke, S. (2001). *Diagnose und Förderung im Schriftspracherwerb.* Bd. 1: Rundgang durch Hörhausen. Erhebungsverfahren zur phonologischen Bewusstheit. Donauwörth: Auer.

Marx, P., & Weber, J. (2006). Vorschulische Vorhersage von Lese- und Rechtschreibschwierigkeiten. Neue Befunde zur prognostischen Validität des Bielefelder Screenings (BISC). *Zeitschrift für Pädagogische Psychologie*, 20, 251–259.

Marx, P., Weber, J., & Schneider, W. (2005). Langfristige Auswirkungen einer Förderung der phonologischen Bewusstheit bei Kindern mit Defiziten in der Sprachentwicklung. *De Sprachheilarbeit*, 50, 6, 280–285.

May, P., & Okwumo, S. (1999). Effekte vorschulischer Trainings zur Schriftanbahnung auf das Rechtschreiblernen im ersten Schuljahr. Available at: www1.unihamburg.de/psycholo/-frames/projekte/PLUS/May_Okwumo_99_Eff_VS_Train.pdf (accessed April 13, 2011).

Mayer, A. (2011). *Test zur Erfassung der phonologischen Bewusstheit und der Benennungsgeschwindigkeit (TEPHOBE), Manual.* München: Max Reinhardt.

Rackwitz, R.-P. (2008). Ist die phonologische Bewusstheit wirklich Voraussetzung für einen erfolgreichen Schriftspracherwerb? *Erziehungswissenschaft und Bildungsforschung kontrovers.* Available at: http://nbn-resolving.de/urn:nbn:de:bsz:752-opus-12 (accessed April 13, 2011).

Rackwitz, R.-P. (2011). Phonological awareness: "necessary" prerequisite for the successful acquisition of literacy? Paper presented at the European Reading Conference, Mons. Available at: www.dgls.de/tagungen/119–17-europaeische-lesekonferenz-in-monsbelgien.html (accessed March 29, 2012).

Röhr, H. (1978) *Voraussetzungen zum Erlernen des Lesens und Rechtschreibens.* Dissertation. University of Münster.

Roos, J., & Schöler, H. (2007). *Zur Wirkung des Trainings der phonologischen Bewusstheit im Vorschulalter auf den Schriftspracherwerb: Abschlussbericht des Projektes EVES.* Available at: www.ph-heidelberg.de/wp/Schoeler/Datein/Abschlussbericht-Stadt-%20Heidelberg_January%20,2007.pdf (accessed July 13, 2011).

Rothe, E. (2008). Effekte vorschulischen und schulischen Trainings der phonologischen Bewusstheit auf den Schriftspracherwerb. *Wortspiegel, Fachzeitschrift von LOS*, 1/2, 3–5.

Scheerer-Neumann, G. (2001). Förderdiagnostik beim Lesenlernen. In I.M. Naegele, & R. Valtin (Eds.). *LRS—Legasthenie in den Klassen 1–10. Handbuch der Lese-Rechtschreib-Schwierigkeiten, Band 2* (pp. 70–86). Weinheim: Beltz.

Scheerer-Neumann, G., Kretschmann, R., & Brügelmann, H. (1986). Andrea, Ben und Jana: Selbstgewählte Wege zum Lesen und Schreiben. In H. Brügelmann (Ed.). *ABC und Schriftsprache: Rätsel für Kinder, Lehrer und Forscher* (pp. 55–96). Konstanz: Faude.

Schmid-Barkow, I. (1999). „Phonologische Bewusstheit" als Teil der metasprachlichen Entwicklung im Kontext von Spracherwerbsprozessen und Spracherwerbsstörungen *Die Sprachheilarbeit*, 6, 307–317.

Schneider, W., Roth, E., & Ennemoser, M. (2000). Training phonological skills and letter knowledge in children at risk for dyslexia: A comparison of three kindergarten intervention programs. *Journal of Educational Psychology*, 92, 2, 284–295.

Thomé, G., Siekmann, K., & Thomé, D. (2011). Phonem-Graphem-Verhältnisse in der deutschen Orthographie. In G. Schulte-Körne (Eds.). *Legasthenie und Dyskalkulie: Stärken erkennen—Stärken fördern* (pp. 51–64). Bochum: Winkler.

Valtin, R. (1984a). The development of metalinguistic abilities in children learning to read and write. In J. Downing, & R. Valtin (Eds.). *Language awareness and learning to read* (pp. 207–226). New York: Springer.

Valtin, R. (1984b). Awareness of features and functions of language. In J. Downing, & R. Valtin (Eds.). *Language awareness and learning to read* (pp. 227–260). New York: Springer.

Valtin, R. (1989). Prediction of writing and reading achievement—some findings from a pilot study. In M. Brambring, F. Losel, & H. Skowronek (Eds.). *Children at risk: Assessment, longitudinal research, and intervention* (pp. 245–267). Berlin, New York: Walter de Gruyter.

Valtin, R. (1997). Strategies of spelling and reading of young children learning German orthography. In C.K. Leong, & M. Joshi (Eds.). *Cross-language studies of learning to read and spell* (pp. 175–194). Series D: Behavioural and Social Sciences—Vol. 87, Kluwer Academic Publishers, Dordrecht/Boston/London.

Valtin, R. (2003). Methoden des basalen Lese- und Schreibunterrichts. In U. Bredel, H. Günther, P. Klotz, J. Ossner, & G. Siebert-Ott (Eds.). *Didaktik der deutschen Sprache. Ein Handbuch.* d.2 (pp. 760–771). Paderborn: Schöningh.

Valtin, R. (2012). Increasing awareness of phonological awareness—helpful or misleading? In S. Suggate, & E. Reese (Eds.) *Contemporary debates in child development and education* (pp. 227–237). London, New York: Routledge.

Valtin, R., Bemmerer, A., & Nehring, G. (1986/1994). Kinder lernen schreiben und über Sprache nachzudenken—Eine empirische Untersuchung zur Entwicklung schriftsprachlicher Fähigkeiten. In R. Valtin, & I. Naegele (Eds.). *"Schreiben ist wichtig!" Grundlagen und Beispiele für kommunikatives Schreiben(lernen)* (pp. 23–53). Frankfurt: Arbeitskreis Grundschule (4th ed. 1994).

Valtin, R., & Hofmann, B. (2009). *Kompetenzmodelle der Orthographie. Empirische Befunde und förderdiagnostische Möglichkeiten.* Berlin: Deutsche Gesellschaft für Lesen und Schreiben.

Van Leent, H. (1983). Auditieve analyse en leren lezen. *Pedagogische Studien*, 60, 13–27.

Watson, A.J. (1984). Cognitive development and units of print in early reading. In J. Downing, & E. Valtin (Eds.). *Language awareness and learning to read* (pp. 93–118). New York: Springer.

Wolf, K.M., Stanat, P., & Wendt, W. (2010). Evaluation der kompensatorischen Sprachförderung. Zweiter Zwischenbericht. Berlin, November 2010. Available at: www.isq-bb.de/uploads/media/ekos-bericht-2-endfassung.pdf (accessed April 10, 2013).

Zhurova, L.Y. (1973). The development of analysis of words into their sounds by preschool children. In C.A. Ferguson, & D.I. Slobin (Eds.). *Studies of child language development*. New York: Holt, Rinehart & Winston.

PART 2

Aspects of Literacy:
The Knowledge Base

8

THE ROLE OF STORY AND LITERATURE IN A WORLD OF TESTS AND STANDARDS

Kathy G. Short

Editor's Note: Short explores the major role of story and how it represents the lives, experiences, and ambitions not only of students but of teachers in developing curriculum and in addressing the broader political context of public policy and mandates. Through classroom examples, she demonstrates how story provides opportunities for children to make sense of their experiences and information. Story also provides opportunities for learners to make connections with their histories, communities, and cultures if the curriculum includes the time and space for creating and sharing stories within a literate classroom community. At the same time she critiques how mandates that focus on instructional experiences such as a specified number of informational texts, the reading of short excerpts, and the emphasis on close reading can trivialize the experience of literature in the classroom.

KSG

We live storied lives. Stories fill every part of our daily existence. We talk about events and people, read books and news reports, gossip with a friend, send text messages, listen to music, watch YouTube videos, and catch up on favorite television shows. Stories are woven so tightly into the fabric of our everyday lives that it is easy to overlook their significance in framing how we think about ourselves and the world.

Stories are much more than a book or movie. They are the way our minds make sense of our world. We work at understanding events and people by constructing stories to interpret what is occurring around us. In turn, these stories create our views of the world and the lenses through which we construct meaning about ourselves and others. We tell stories to make connections and form relationships. Stories bind us together in community.

Stories are also used to influence us, to provide views of the world that manipulate our emotions and perceptions, as often occurs in political ads and debates during elections. The public story about education and teachers has been unrelentingly negative—public schools are in desperate straits and failing economically and academically; teachers are incompetent and willing to be mediocre; adults are entering the workforce unable to perform basic literacy tasks. The public story is that new tests and standards are needed to force teachers to raise the level of their teaching because high school graduates are not college or career-ready. The answers can be found in mandating more focus on informational text, close reading, text complexity, and performance measures.

As teachers, we often feel battered by public stories that crash upon us like tidal waves, pounding and pummeling, washing the ground from beneath our feet. We try to stand our ground and tell our stories about what matters but our voices are lost in the storm. Sometimes we respond by trying to *cope* with the standards and tests so that students can be successful within those mandates without sacrificing what we know about learning. For example, Santman (2002) immersed her middle school students in studying tests as a genre and in an inquiry on test-taking strategies as a way to prepare for high-stakes tests instead of limiting her curriculum to low-level skills. Sometimes, we respond by engaging in *innovation* in order to grow our teaching and create more effective learning contexts, believing that if students become inquirers and critical thinkers they will be able to critically engage with the tests. We also respond by *resisting* and publicly working for change by challenging the policies that locate success within tests and standards and ignore existing educational research and scholarly work.

Since stories play an integral role in how we think about ourselves and the world as well as in how others perceive us, educators need to understand the role of story. We need to understand why stories are important and why they matter to our students as learners and human beings and to our work as educators, both in developing curriculum with students and in addressing the broader political context of public policy and mandates.

Why Stories Matter

If we step back from the pressure of tests and standards and consider why story matters and the ways in which story *is* thinking and world-making, we have time to reconsider and recapture the role of story and literature in classrooms (Short, 2012). Focusing on why stories are significant provides insights into how the public story about schools and teachers frames policies, and provides an opportunity to consider how we can participate in telling a different story.

Story is How We Make Sense of Our Experiences

Story is the way we make sense of the world. Harold Rosen (1986) argues that stories move us from the chaotic "stuff" of daily life toward understanding. An endless flow of experiences surrounds us on a daily basis, and we invent beginnings and endings to organize those experiences by creating a meaningful sequence of facts and interpretations. Stories impose order and coherence on the stream of experiences and allow us to work out significance. Stories thus provide a means of structuring and reflecting on our experiences (Bruner, 1988). We tell our stories to others to invite them to consider our meanings and to construct their own, as well as to better understand those experiences ourselves. Stories are what distinguish us from other living beings. Stories make us human. The nature of a life is that it is a story.

Story is thus a mode of knowing—one of the primary ways in which we think and construct meaning. Story captures the richness and nuances of human life, accommodating the ambiguity and complexity of situations in the multiplicity of meanings inherent to any story (Carter, 1993). Although traditionally thought is seen as an instrument of reason, there are forms of thought that are narrative in nature rather than logical. Barbara Hardy (1968) believes that story is a primary act of mind:

> For we dream, remember, anticipate, hope, despair, believe, doubt, plan, revise, criticize, construct, gossip, learn, hate, and love by narrative. In order to really live, we make up stories about ourselves and others, about the personal as well as the social past and future.
>
> (p. 5)

Our views of the world are a web of interconnected stories; a distillation of all the stories we have shared. We connect to these interconnected past stories in order to understand new experiences (Rosen, 1986). This web of stories becomes our interpretive lens for new experiences so that story is our means of constructing the world, of world-making.

Sometimes the stories we tell are delusional. In our need to make sense of experiences, we may construct stories that lead us deeper into mental illness, conspiracy theories, and construction of a world that doesn't exist but is "true" in our minds (Gottschall, 2012). If we cannot find meaningful patterns in the world, we make them up, a reflection of the essential role that story plays in cognition.

Story is How We Make Sense of Information

Rosen (1986) argues that the distinction between expository text and narrative text, and between theories and stories, is an artificial one, noting that theories are just big stories. Scientists, for example, create theory by using current information to tell a story that provides an explanation of a natural phenomenon such as black holes. They change their stories over time as new information and perspectives become available. A story is thus a theory of something; what we tell and how we tell it reveals what we believe (Carter, 1993).

Information does not tend to be retained unless it is connected to a story (Gottschall, 2012). When we attend a lecture or conference presentation, we tune in when the speaker tells a story and the ideas and information connected to those stories are what we tend to remember. Most information bounces off, with little impression and no recollection. Stories engage our curiosity and emotions and make that information understandable and memorable.

Story is How We Connect to Each Other and to Our Histories

Stories of the past are particularly significant in framing our thinking about the world. Milton Meltzer (1981), the author of many nonfiction history books on social issues, argues that history *is* memory, consisting of stories about our past that provide us with a sense of humanity. Without these stories of the past, we are nothing, adrift and unable to compare and contrast our current experiences with the past in order to make sense of those experiences. We are locked in the current moment, deprived of memory, and so blinded from understanding the present. Meltzer argues that governments in totalitarian countries outlaw the collective memory by burning books and imprisoning writers. In the U.S., we neglect it, and so fail to see ourselves as part a larger continuum of life that stretches far behind us and far ahead as well. We need stories of the past to locate ourselves and to envision a reason to take action for social change to create a better world. Without the stories of the past, we are unable to see the possibility of change.

Story is Where We Explore Our Fears and Our Futures

Many people dismiss story as escapism and believe that we tell and read stories for pleasure to escape the stress of daily life. Gottschall (2012) points out that the problem with this belief is that the stories primarily focus on trouble. Oral folklore and written novels are full of conflict and struggle that go way beyond what we encounter in daily life. Stories are not about our lives as actually lived, which would be quite boring and not useful to readers; instead, stories focus on conflict and crises that lead to some kind of resolution.

The same focus on crisis characterizes our dreams. We often think of dreams as positive, as wish fulfillment, but Gottschall (2012) cites research studies that indicate our night dreams can be horrorscapes, full of discord, violence, and flight or fight responses to situations that reflect our greatest fears. Horrible things happen in our dreams to those we love or catch us in embarrassing situations (standing naked in front of the classroom). He argues that the purpose of the stories we play out in our dreams is to cope with the anxieties of our waking lives.

The stories we read and live out in our dreams allow our brains to play out events and emotions without risk and test possible responses to those events. Just as pilots train on flight simulators to develop strategies for safely flying and landing planes, we use story as our flight simulator for social interactions. Young children engage in story through play in much the same way that they rehearse for adult life (Engel, 1995). Story gives us the benefit of practice for the big dilemmas of life and that practice, in turn, improves our ability to engage in more effective problem-solving in daily life. Gottschall (2012) points to research showing that our neurons fire as much during the experience of a story as in a real life experience, challenging the assumption that story is a vicarious experience—story *is* experience.

Story is Where We Develop Values and Community

Not only are stories full of conflict and crisis, but they are also moralistic, with strong messages that reinforce the values and norms of our society and connect us as a community. Stories allow us to construct a vision of the world as a place which goodness is usually rewarded and endorsed and badness is condemned and punished (Bettelheim, 1976). We come to believe in justice and a just world because of story, even though justice does not always prevail in real life. Story is the center that holds us together despite our individual differences and agendas. Gottschall (2012) argues that story is the glue that binds us within groups and makes it possible for us to form communities around common core values.

Story is a Way to Change the World

One of the most powerful examples of how story can change the world is *Uncle Tom's Cabin* (Stowe, 1852), a compelling and heart-rending novel that changed the way in which Americans viewed slavery. The facts about slavery did not influence public perception or awaken a strong voice for change, but the story of a human being caught in the inhumanity of slavery incited a nation to take action. Story can also have a negative effect in changing the world. Hitler's view of himself as saving the world grew, at least partially, from his immersion in the musical stories of Wagner's operas (Kohler, 2000). Story constantly nibbles and kneads us as one of the primary sculpting forces of individuals and societies.

Another way in which story changes the world is by influencing our global perspectives and understandings. Story provides a way for us to move between local and global cultures and to explore the ways in which people live in cultures that differ from our own. Through story, we can challenge stereotypes and go beyond a tourist perspective of just gaining information about another country. When readers immerse themselves in story worlds, they gain insights into how people feel, live, and think in other parts of the world (Short, 2009). They can come to see themselves as connected to people around the world through common humanity and, at the same time, come to value the differences that make each culture unique. We need more than facts to understand the storied lives of people in diverse global cultures.

Story is a Strength for All Learners

The ways in which we create and tell stories are culturally-based. Our human need to story our experiences may be universal, but there is no one way to tell stories (Bruchac, 2003). Our stories are always intertextualized and interwoven with the stories that exist within our own cultures, both in content and in the style and structure of the telling. All children come to school with stories, although the types of story that they are familiar with and the ways in which they tell stories may be quite different from school norms. Shirley Brice Heath (1983), for example, found that children coming from an African American community had learned to tell fanciful stories in order to get adult attention and to aggressively push their way into conversations in order to get their turn. These children were viewed as rude and as telling "tall tales" at school, a misunderstanding of the cultural context of their homes and stories.

The challenge for teachers is not to judge children by what they are lacking, but instead to build on their strengths through the stories they bring to school from their families and communities. Children from families where they have not been read aloud to on a regular basis are often labeled as "disadvantaged" or "at risk," instead of drawing upon the wellspring of their stories. Their stories may be based in daily life and television rather than in oral tradition or books, but they are still stories. If the culture of the community is to enter the culture of the school, that community's stories must be viewed as a valued form of meaning-making.

Story and Literature within Classrooms

The broader context for story as meaning-making provides a way to reexamine the significance of story and literature within classrooms. Descriptions of children's literature in elementary classrooms typically focus on how to *use* children's books to teach something else (Short, 2010). Literature is viewed as a material used to teach reading, math, science, or social studies, a means of teaching comprehension or writing strategies, celebrating cultural diversity, or raising issues of social justice and equity. Even scholars who argue for the significance of reading aloud and providing time to read for enjoyment in an independent reading time do so from the perspective that these engagements will help students become more proficient readers, rather than because reading literature adds significance to a child's life.

What is often overlooked is that literature and stories are a way of knowing the world. Literature illuminates what it means to be human and makes accessible the most fundamental experiences of life–love, hope, loneliness, despair, fear, and belonging. Literature is the imaginative shaping of experience and thought into the forms and structures of language. Louise Rosenblatt (1938) argues that children read literature to experience life; they live inside the world of the story to engage in inquiry that transforms their thinking about their lives and world. These stories can take many forms and the increasing variety of digital and interactive formats invite a greater range of readers and so are cause for celebration, not concern, as they invite the active participation of readers in the worlds of story.

Reading literature to learn content more effectively or to experience life is not an either/or proposition. Literature can encourage student interest in certain topics and help them understand information and issues. Literature can provide a vehicle for learning about written language and engaging in curricular inquiries, and, at the same time, these experiences can occur within the context of literature as a way of knowing and critiquing the world.

Literature and Story as Transformation

Charlotte Huck (1982) often reminded us that literature provides experiences that go beyond entertainment or instruction by offering the potential to transform children's lives, connecting their hearts and minds to integrate reason and emotion. Children find themselves reflected in stories and make connections that transform their understandings of themselves and the world. Literature offers a tool for children in re-envisioning their lives in Leslie Kahn's sixth grade classroom (Short & Harste with Burke, 1996). Gangs and racism were such a common part of their neighborhood that students accepted them without question. Kahn decided that looking at history to take a more distanced perspective on racism might support students in bringing new perspectives on their lives, and so we developed an inquiry around the genocide and racism of the Holocaust. The students' initial questions were disquieting, focusing on the horrors of death, and so we immersed them in stories including novels about Holocaust experiences, visits by Holocaust survivors, and dramatic engagements of victims, bystanders, aggressors, and rescuers.

The students' final investigations reflected the transformations in their perspectives on racism to their lives. For example, several surveyed children in their school to find out how they chose their friends and whether those friendships crossed racial lines. One particularly powerful inquiry was a boy for whom gang membership was a valued and accepted practice in his family. His previous focus had been on which gang to join, not whether to join, because he had uncles in opposing gangs. The stories of the Holocaust survivors led him to question gangs as he investigated the similarities and differences between gangs and the Nazis and Hitler Youth.

Literature expands children's life spaces through inquiries that take them outside the boundaries of their lives to other places, times, and ways of living to see alternative ways to live their lives and to think about the world. Kathryn

Tompkins (2007) read aloud *When My Name Was Keoko* (Park, 2002) to her fourth grade students, a book about the Japanese occupation of Korea during World War II, and the loss of freedom for Sun-hee and her family as they are forced to take on Japanese names, language, culture, and history. The students connected powerfully with issues of freedom and their own struggles with the limits imposed on them by parents and teachers and engaged in inquiries about this time period and Korean culture. Sun-hee's story took them outside of their own cultural experiences and transformed the ways in which they thought about freedom and responding to limitations on freedom.

Literature stretches children's imaginations and encourages them to go beyond "what is" to "what might be." Hope and imagination make it possible for children to be resilient and to rise above their circumstances, to challenge inequity and to envision social change. Jennifer Griffith read aloud to her first graders *You Be Me, I'll Be You* (Mandelbaum, 1990), the story of a biracial child who is concerned that she does not look like either of her parents. Many of the children came from multi-racial Latino families and this discussion facilitated their awareness that members of their family who had darker skin were treated differently in the community. Because they loved these family members, they were deeply concerned and questioned the way in which our society judges people by the color of their skin.

Transformation occurs as children carry their experiences and inquiries with literature and story back into their worlds and lives. This potential for transformation is also available in reading informational books that are written from the perspective of one enthusiast sharing with another to "light fires" in children's minds, rather than from the perspective of textbooks written to instruct. Literature includes fiction and nonfiction; they are not in opposition to each other.

Louise Rosenblatt (1938) argues that "literature makes comprehensible the myriad ways in which human beings meet the infinite possibilities that life offers" (p. 6). They participate in another's vision, transforming that vision as well as their own sense of possibility, made possible because literature provides readers with a "living through" and not just "knowledge about" life.

Reading literature and listening to stories encourages readers to put themselves in the place of others, to use imagination to consider the consequences of their decisions and actions. Imagination and the balance of reason and emotion are further developed when readers move from personal response to dialogue where they wrestle with their differing interpretations of a story. These discussions are not just a better way to learn, but essential to democracy. Rosenblatt's vision of democracy is equitable social relationships in which people choose to live together by valuing individual voices within recognition of responsibility to the group. She believes that people need to have conviction and enthusiasm about their own cultural perspectives, while remaining open to alternative views and becoming aware of other's needs.

Dialogue about literature provides a significant context within which students learn to live with the tension of recognizing and respecting the perspectives of others without betraying their own beliefs. Through dialogue, students develop faith in their own judgments while continuing to inquire and remaining open to questioning their beliefs. Paulo Freire (1970) argues that dialogue has the fullest potential to support transformation and social change in the world.

Story and Literature Within a World of Standards and Tests

The Common Core State Standards (CCSS) have created new conversations around literacy and the types of reading experience and material that are valued in classrooms. Although some of these conversations result from misconceptions of the standards, the outcomes are administrative mandates and literacy programs that influence the ways in which story and literature are accessed in classrooms.

One major emphasis of the CCSS is a focus on informational text at all levels, with a call for a 50/50 split of literature and informational texts at Kindergarten and a gradual increase in informational texts as students move through the grade levels. Fiction is viewed as appropriate for classrooms, but not essential to success in college and careers. The problem with this dichotomy is that informational texts frequently make use of narrative to tell a story and engage readers. Straight information, a list of facts, is boring and not compelling for readers, except to use these texts to locate information needed for a task—as a reference tool, rather than a reading engagement. When these narrative structures are missing from an informational text, readers will often create their own narratives around the information, such as a young boy who reads the facts on a baseball card and imagines himself inside the life of that player. What this false dichotomy also ignores is that fiction often contains a great deal of information, so that readers of historical fiction, for example, gain many facts and insights. Children's literature is defined as both fiction and nonfiction so many of the texts that the standards label as informational text in opposition to literature are actually literary texts. A dichotomy between expository and narrative texts has been created that does not reflect the actual text structures of literature or the ways that readers engage with these texts.

Another major instructional trend is a reliance on instructional tasks that require students to read short text excerpts, followed by comprehension exercises that involve a close reading of the text to develop text-based answers. The problem with this emphasis is that students are not reading whole texts and stories. Reading one chapter from a novel or an excerpt from a longer text does not provide enough context or story to engage readers and draw them into the world of that story in order to develop complex interpretations. Readers cannot make the connections necessary to go beyond a surface level understanding and are being taught to read all texts as phone books or a set of directions to search for information, not to understand at a deep level. When reading adds nothing of significance to readers' lives, the danger is that they will develop the perspective that reading is not important except when needed for a task. If what they read never challenges them to think in new ways, then reading becomes a chore to get through, a task to complete, rather than something of value in their lives.

Rosenblatt (1938) argues that the stance we take as readers is influenced by what we are asked to do with a text. When readers know they will be asked literal level text-based questions or will be required to give a summary or retelling to make sure they have "comprehended" that text, they often read from an efferent stance to get information to take away. They read a story as if it were a reference source. Many of us read high school history textbooks in this way, not actually reading the chapter but skimming for answers to the questions on the study guide.

The problem is that an efferent stance involves staying outside the world of that story and readers can walk away with details but not construct a sense of the larger themes or ideas—they miss the story. When they read from an aesthetic stance, they immerse themselves in the story world and experience the story. They construct a complex understanding of that text, even though they may not have all of the details. The details are addressed as they become relevant in their dialogue about the story, rather than as the focus of the initial sharing. Rosenblatt's theories challenge traditional hierarchical taxonomies, such as the Bloom taxonomy, that assume that readers start at literal comprehension and then move to inferential and evaluative thinking. Most adults in book clubs have experienced coming to the group with a deep experience around a book and complex understandings of the issues, only to realize that they missed important details that other readers point out and that may support or challenge their interpretations.

A third instructional trend related to the CCSS is an emphasis on close reading and teaching reading and writing strategies. Teachers are being given the message that any text read to or by students should be used for instructional purposes, to teach something. If students respond to a text by talking about what it reminds them of from their lives, teachers are told to steer students back to the task and ask them to talk about what the story is about—to get the details and to support their statements by citing evidence in the text (Calkins, et al., 2012). Teachers are to ask text-dependent questions and value evidence, not connection.

Rosenblatt (1938) reminds us that first we need to respond as human beings, to share our experiences of that story, *before* we use the text to teach. Literature was not written to teach a strategy but to illuminate life. The first questions we should ask are, "What are you thinking?" "What connections did you make?" instead of "What was the text about?". These personal connections and responses are essential, but not sufficient, as readers then need to dialogue about their interpretations, critiquing those interpretations and examining whether they are supported by evidence from their lives and the text. Our first response to a text should not violate the nature of the text itself as an experience of life. The second response can then move into close reading of that text.

Teaching something from a text should come after personal response and dialogue, after readers have a chance to see that text as significant. That teaching should focus on one aspect of a text or one reading strategy. Beating a text to death with skill after skill is counterproductive—the reader walks away determined never to return to the text again and with little retention of the skills. By choosing one text structure or reading strategy, teachers provide a focus for students to explore and come to understand without destroying the text. It is much more useful for students to examine one or two significant metaphors in a particular work of Shakespeare, for example, than to identify every metaphor in that work.

Another instructional emphasis as a result of the focus on close reading has been to teach one text at a time, digging repeatedly into that text. The problem is that readers need to be able to build connections and complexity across texts in order to think conceptually and critically. If students are only reading one text at a time and each is separate from the next, they remain on the surface of each text. By making connections across texts, they build on the knowledge and insights gained from each text to construct complex interpretations and understandings.

Surrounding a novel with many short texts or gathering a set of related picture books to read aloud to young children over time supports this greater complexity of connection and understanding. A historical novel such as *When My Name Was Keoko* (Park, 2002), about the Japanese occupation of Korea, can be surrounded by informational texts such as maps of Korea and Asia, time lines of events, old newspaper clippings, examples of the two written languages, images of Korean cultural symbols, current newspaper articles on negotiations between Korea and Japan, and artifacts such as flags. Contemporary fiction, such as *Wonder* (Palacio, 2012), can be surrounded with books that connect to the theme of bullying as well as articles and internet postings. Rather than "read a paragraph closely," it is more consistent with the CCSS for students to surround a good book with other texts, with fiction, nonfiction, and informational texts.

As educators, we need to keep reminding ourselves that our goal for students is that they become literate—we aim too low by only focusing on literacy. Literacy involves being able to function and carry out the tasks of daily life at home and in our jobs. To be literate is to be able to think and use what we read to transform our minds and lives. Students do not become literate without extended opportunities to read and talk about their reading, to discuss what a book or text means and how it means. They also need to read works that are worth the effort. Students have no reason to value a process that is difficult and has little personal significance. We can drill them into literacy but can only invite them to become literate; they make the choice. The experiences that many students are having around reading in our schools are leading them to reject a literate identity.

Stories as Professional Identity and Possibility

Ludwick Fleck (1935) argued that we form thought collectives as we interact and talk with others to create a history and language with each other. All of us know that when we gather within our thought collectives, we talk story. As educators, we make sense of our classroom experiences by sharing stories in teacher lounges as well as in conference presentations, workshops, and publications. By immersing ourselves in stories of practice, we are able to envision the possibilities of those ideas in our own settings.

Story can also determine how we are viewed as teachers, teacher educators, and researchers. The public story about education in schools and universities has taken a consistent negative stance in recent years. We may choose to close our classroom doors and teach, but that allows others to tell the stories that define our lives, while we are closed out from that storytelling. Many of us complain about how public policies and mandates ignore research and the knowledge base we have built in education and instead go with what politicians view as "common sense." Their programs and solutions often make better stories—we understand the complexity of learning and teaching but they provide a simple story that makes a good sound bite. The simple story wins out and we fail to tell our story.

We need to teach the public to re-author their stories of school, a difficult task because negative habits of mind are deeply embedded in our consciousness and society. Jerome Bruner (1988) noticed that members of the same family spoke about the same events but in completely different ways. Some only had memories of problem-filled experiences and filtered out everything else, taking away hope and capability, while other family members related that same story as change and possibility. He argues that the ways we tell stories are so habitual that they become recipes for structuring experience itself—life *is* narrative. Our identities are thus a story subject to revision, and we may need to re-author our stories in order to re-author our lives.

This same re-authoring is needed for stories of school. Frameworks Institute is a nonprofit organization that identifies communication strategies to advance public understanding and action on social problems. This organization is looking at ways to re-author the "core story" that defines public conversations about educational reform in the U.S. (Bales, et al., 2012). They point out current stories of education and the problems inherent in cultural models framed around consumerism, the basics, naturalism, effort, and compartmentalization. The naturalism cultural model, for example, contains the idea that a good teacher is a "caring person," who intuitively engages students' inherent desire to learn. Since good teachers are naturally caring individuals, teacher education and professional development are not valued. The public conversation instead is around better recruitment of these "natural" teachers. The consumerism model focuses public attention on education as a limited commodity; any achievement that one group gains takes away from your child when the focus is on individual achievement rather than the benefits of education to society. Through focus groups, the Institute has found that framing reform around the value of progress provides a more compelling story for the public than other values, and so they are working at telling the education story around this value and developing easy-to-understand metaphors around progress.

We live in a world in which stories are used against us as educators while, at the same time, our own stories are no longer valued or welcomed. Qualitative research, which is based in stories constructed around data, is not considered rigorous, replicable or reliable for making decisions or establishing policies. Textbooks, basal readers, and facts are again replacing books and taking away the time for experiences around books from which children can construct significant stories and memories. School and public libraries are being closed or cut back in hours, certified librarians, and purchases of books. Even in innovative literacy instruction, we are so busy teaching comprehension strategies, units of study, and mentoring with texts that we are losing sight of reading as a way to immerse ourselves in the world of the story simply for the sake of what that story adds to our lives. We stand on top of the story and send down probes to mine the richness for other purposes.

Although there is a great deal of merit in these approaches to literacy and the ways in which real books are used to think about reading and writing, an emphasis on teaching with every book that is read aloud by the teacher or read by a child violates story as life-making. Stories are supposed to provide us with shattering, hopeful encounters that allow us to experience deep emotions and make us richer, more compassionate human beings. They cannot accomplish that purpose when they are always used to teach something else, no matter how important that something else is.

Stories as Democracy of the Intellect

Katherine Paterson (2000) argues that books and stories provide the basis for the democracy of the intellect, a term she borrowed from Jacob Bronowski (1974). When people can read freely and widely and engage in dialogue with others about that reading, they begin to question, something not necessarily valued by politicians and those in control. Public policies and laws that close libraries, limit the availability of books, impose narrow definitions of literacy and research, and dictate what happens in classrooms are a response to the threat posed by the democracy of the intellect.

We do not "require" stories; they can be little more than a frill, unless we believe passionately in the democracy of the intellect and in providing the time that children need to gain the experiences necessary to make wise decisions and develop freedom of imagination. A true democracy of the intellect breaks open the narrowness of the spirit and challenges the selfish interests of the privileged few. This democracy of the intellect supports us in critiquing society to question what is and who benefits as well as to consider what might be in order to take action and work toward a more just and equitable world (Freire, 1970).

Stories summon us to wisdom, strength, and delight and make the richness of imagination available to all of us in order to envision a better world and to take action that makes a difference. Stories have the power to direct and change our lives and world—*if* we provide the time and space for creating and sharing those stories within a literate community.

References

Bales, S., Kendall-Taylor, N., Lindland, E., O'Neil, M., & Simon, A. (2012). *Talking about skills and learning.* Frameworks Institute Message Memo. Retrieved October 24, 2012, from www.frameworksinstitute.org/assets/files/talking_about_skills_and_ learning_core_story_mm.pdf

Bettleheim, B. (1976). *The uses of enchantment.* New York: Knopf.

Bronowski, J. (1974). *The ascent of man.* Boston, MA: Little Brown.

Bruchac, J. (2003). *Our stories remember.* Golden, CO: Fulcrum.

Bruner, J. (1988). Research currents: Life as narrative. *Language Arts,* 65, 6, 574–583.

Calkins, L., Ehrenworth, M., & Lehman, C. (2012). *Pathways to the common core.* Portsmouth, NH: Heinemann.

Carter, K. (1993). The place of story in the study of teaching and teacher education. *Educational Researcher,* 22, 1, 5–12.

Engel, S. (1995). *The stories that children tell.* New York: Freeman.

Fleck, L. (1935). *Genesis and development of a scientific fact.* Chicago, IL: University of Chicago.

Freire, P. (1970). *Pedagogy of the oppressed.* New York: Herder & Herder.

Gottschall, J. (2012). *The storytelling animal: How stories make us human.* Boston, MA: Houghton Mifflin.

Hardy, B. (1968). Towards a poetics of fiction: An approach through narrative. *Novel: A Forum on Fiction,* 2, 1, 5–14.

Heath, S.B. (1983). *Ways with words.* Cambridge, MA: Cambridge University Press.

Huck, C. (1982). "I give you the end of a golden string." *Theory into Practice,* 21, 4, 315–321.

Kohler, J. (2000). *Wagner's Hitler: The prophet and his disciple.* London: Polity.

Mandelbaum, P. (1990). *You be me, I'll be you.* La Jolla, CA: Kane/Miller.

Meltzer, M. (1981). Beyond the span of a single life. In B. Hearne (Ed.). *Celebrating children's books* (pp. 87–96). New York: Lothrop.

Palacio, R.J. (2012). *Wonder.* New York: Knopf.

Park, L.S. (2002). *When my name was Keoko.* New York: Clarion.

Paterson, K. (2000). Asking the question. *The New Advocate,* 13, 1, 1–15.

Rosen, H. (1986). *Stories and meanings.* London: NATE.

Rosenblatt, L. (1938). *Literature as exploration.* Chicago: Modern Language Association.

Santman, D. (2002). Teaching to the test?: Test preparation in the reading workshop. *Language Arts,* 79, 3, 203–211.

Short, K. (2009). Critically reading the word and the world: Building intercultural understanding through literature. *Bookbird: A Journal of International Children's Literature,* 47, 2, 1–10.

Short, K. (2010). Reading literature in elementary classrooms. In S. Wolf, K. Coats, P. Enciso, & C. Jenkins (Eds.). *Handbook of research on children's and young adult literature* (pp. 48–62). New York: Routledge.

Short, K. (2012). Story as world-making. *Language Arts*, 90, 1, 9–17.

Short, K., & Harste, J. with Burke, C. (1996). *Creating classrooms for authors and inquirers.* Portsmouth, NH: Heinemann.

Stowe, H.B. (1852/2007). *Uncle Tom's cabin.* New York: Norton.

Tompkins, K. (2007). Creating lifelong relationships: Children's connections to characters. *WOW Stories: Connections from the Classrooms,* 1 (1). Retrieved January 15, 2012, from http://wowlit.org/on-line-publications/stories/storiesi1/6/

9

THE STAIRCASE CURRICULUM

Whole-school Collaboration to Improve Literacy Achievement

Kathryn H. Au and Taffy E. Raphael

> *Editor's Note: What if teachers were to plan together using their own professional knowledge to construct a coherent curriculum, avoiding repetitions and adapting state and federal mandates to fit their own classrooms and school community? This chapter reports examples from a school that did just that.*
>
> KSG

"We decided to change our assessment," a third grade teacher announced at the start of her presentation to the entire school. She went on, "Because our whole school has been working on reading comprehension for a while now, the students are coming in knowing story elements. They do well with comprehending fiction. At third grade we think we need to spend more time helping them comprehend nonfiction."

After the third grade teachers had finished sharing their new assessment task, as well as their students' pretest results, a second grade teacher spoke up. "Our grade level needs to meet with your grade level," she said. "We want to spend more time working with our students on comprehension of nonfiction, to get them ready for their work with you."

This exchange is representative of those we observe after teachers have been engaged in building their school's own staircase curriculum for a year or two. Our approach to whole-school improvement in literacy is called the Standards Based Change (SBC) Process (Au, 2005; Raphael, 2010; Raphael, et al., 2009). In this process, we help teachers come together as a school-wide professional learning community for the purpose of building a staircase curriculum to improve students' literacy achievement.

When teachers make comments such as those above, we can tell that they have gained a solid understanding of the staircase curriculum. Our purpose here is to elaborate on this key concept. We have structured this chapter around issues that arise when we guide teachers to build their school's own staircase curriculum in reading or writing. These issues arise primarily because administrators and teachers in many schools have come to believe that the way to improve literacy achievement is to purchase a packaged program (Dillon, 2003). With the SBC Process, we propose instead that literacy achievement can best be improved by guiding teachers to create their own curriculum. As discussed below, the staircase curriculum may be built around a school's existing reading program. However, the curriculum will always be broader than this program. It will be customized to address the literacy learning needs of the students served by the school.

What is a Staircase Curriculum?

Our concept of a staircase curriculum builds on research on curriculum coherence (Newmann, et al., 2001; Smith, et al., 1998). We find that visualizing the curriculum as a staircase (Taba, 1962) helps teachers to understand why they will want to collaborate within and across grades to coordinate and align their goals for student learning, assessment, and instruction.

Across grade levels, teachers strive to adjust and align their particular steps to eliminate any gaps and inconsistencies. When a school has a staircase curriculum, teachers know the goals for student learning at other grade levels. Having this knowledge enables teachers at each grade level to build systematically on what students learned in the grades below, as well as to prepare students for what is to come in the grades above.

We developed the concept of the staircase curriculum because of our work in Hawai'i and Chicago schools enrolling a high percentage of students of diverse cultural and linguistic backgrounds. Many of these students were reading and writing far below the expectations for their grade. To become strong readers, these students needed consistent instruction, coordinated across all the grades in elementary school. Having a staircase curriculum allows schools to address this need for consistency.

Each grade is responsible for helping students accomplish the goals represented by its step in the staircase, which leads to the vision of the excellent reader who graduates from the school. The vision statement developed by teachers at Philip D. Armour School in Chicago calls for graduates to acquire the "necessary skills and strategies to communicate effectively in all realms of literacy for the purpose of being a critical thinker, problem solver, and advocate in a continuously changing world." Think of all the learning that can take place from a curriculum reaching toward such a vision. The kindergarten teachers help students accomplish the learning goals represented by the first step, the first grade teachers help students accomplish the learning goals represented by the second step. This process continues all the way up to the school's last grade and the highest step where, if all has gone according to plan, students are able to fulfill the vision of the excellent reader.

The Fragmented Curriculum

Perhaps the easiest way to appreciate the benefits of a staircase curriculum is by considering its opposite—a fragmented curriculum. Wonderful things may be happening at different grade levels, but the teachers have not coordinated their efforts. This lack of coordination means that there are gaps, overlaps, and inconsistencies in the curriculum. Although the resulting disjunctions may pose no problem for capable students, they can slow or even derail the progress of students who find literacy learning challenging.

Having worked with leadership teams at 130 schools spanning the elementary, middle, and high school levels, we know from documentation that not one of these schools had a staircase curriculum in reading or writing before they began work with the SBC Process. Instead, all had fragmented curricula with bright spots in various grade levels and departments, but little or no coordination across these structures.

The following example of the situation at a K-6 school in Hawai'i illustrates this point. The teachers had decided to focus on reading comprehension. Kathy asked the teachers to work within grade levels to identify their end-of-year goals for student learning in this strand. When their charts were posted, the teachers were surprised to see that all grades had the goal that students should know story elements. This discovery led the teachers to a discussion of how story elements were defined at each grade level, the literature each grade level was using to teach story elements, and whether it was really necessary for all grade levels to have this focus. Over time, the teachers agreed that story elements would be taught in kindergarten and first grade, with an exploration of more sophisticated elements of literature, such as author's message and character development, beginning at second grade. The teachers realized that they were placing too great an emphasis on fiction and literature and too little emphasis on nonfiction and content area texts. Eventually, nonfiction and content area text became the focus for teachers in grades 3 and above.

As this example suggests, once a school makes a commitment to building its staircase curriculum, teachers can communicate systematically across grades and departments about their goals for student learning, instructional strategies, assessments, and rubrics. This communication enables teachers to build on the teaching and learning that took place in earlier grades or courses. Teachers are also able to prepare students with the background needed for success in the grades and courses that follow.

Alignment and Rigor

To build a staircase curriculum and accelerate the advancement of struggling learners requires coherent, sustainable actions. To accomplish this goal, teachers in a school must meet two challenges. The first challenge is alignment. Teachers must agree upon strands, such as ownership, comprehension, and vocabulary, which can flow across all grade levels. They must reach consensus about the definitions of these strands. For example, what concepts, strategies, and skills should be included in our school's comprehension strand? Teachers will want to make sure that expectations at each grade level build on those of the grade level below and lead up to those of the grade level above, so that the curriculum flows consistently from one grade to the next.

The second challenge in creating a staircase curriculum is rigor. Teachers must not only achieve alignment through the agreed-upon strands. They must also make sure that their grade level's step in the staircase, as defined by their expectations for students' end-of-year performance, is appropriately steep and ambitious. For example, Kathy worked at a school where the teachers in grade K-3 had high and demanding expectations for their students. However, the steps in the staircase were much less steep in the upper grades, with the end-of-year expectations for grades 4–6 being only slightly different from one another. The curriculum at this school was aligned but lacked rigor. Not surprisingly, this school had weak writing test scores in the higher grades. Working together, Kathy and the school's curriculum coordinator helped the upper grade teachers elevate their expectations for students' end-of-year performance. These teachers revisited state writing benchmarks for their grade levels, and examined writing samples of other Hawai'i schools and on other states.

Relationship to External Standards

As discussed earlier, the steps of a school's staircase curriculum are based on the benchmarks drafted by teachers at each grade level. The drafting of these benchmarks is the most difficult part of the SBC Process for teachers at most schools. We define benchmarks as demanding but achievable end-of-grade expectations geared to the hypothetical average student. We discuss issues surrounding benchmark development at some length here because teachers' willingness to draft their own benchmarks is critical to construction of the curriculum.

In the SBC Process, we make certain that each school's curriculum is carefully aligned to national, state, and other relevant external standards, such as the Common Core State Standards (NGA/CCSSO, 2010), in terms of the content and strategies addressed and the level of student performance expected at each grade level. However, we begin by asking teachers to "think their own thoughts first." The SBC Process is based on the idea that teachers must construct their school's own staircase curriculum for sustainable curriculum improvement. Our research suggests that literacy achievement improves and is sustained when teachers take ownership of their school's literacy improvement efforts and become creators, not just receivers, of curriculum (Au, 2005; Raphael, 2010).

All states now have standards for the English language arts, and these standards will likely converge over time under the influence of the Common Core State Standards Initiative (CCSSI). Many teachers may well wonder why they should go through the process of "reinventing the wheel" when external standards and benchmarks, those from their state and the CCSSI, already exist. This concern is understandable given educational trends, such as an over-reliance on packaged programs, which have tended to de-professionalize and disempower teachers (Dillon, 2003).

In the SBC Process we ask teachers to treat external standards and benchmarks with respect, while recognizing that they are not sacrosanct. To strengthen teachers' knowledge base for constructing their own benchmarks, aligned with those of external sources, we make sure to bring teachers up to date on the latest definitions and results from international comparisons such as the Programme for International Student Assessment (PISA, 2010) and Progress in International Reading Literacy Study (TIMMS and PIRLS International Study Center, 2010), and national projects such as the CCSSI and NAEP (National Assessment of Educational Progress, 2010). Teachers in most schools are quite familiar with their state standards and benchmarks, but if they are not, these too are presented. We also provide overviews of current research on key topics about which teachers have expressed concern, the most common being phonics, comprehension strategies, and vocabulary.

In addition, we help teachers to understand that external standards and benchmarks, while cloaked with an air of authority, are always developed through a human process requiring a large measure of professional judgment. We make this point by describing our own experiences with developing standards, but it is more effective when teachers hear it from their fellow teachers. At a school in Hawai'i, Kathy asked two second-grade teachers to describe their experiences while working on the state's standards and benchmarks. "When we looked around the room," one teacher said, "we realized that we were the only second-grade teachers there and that we were supposed to be representing all the second-grade teachers in our state." While these teachers agreed with the benchmarks eventually selected, they pointed out that other benchmarks could have served just as well.

Other points that help teachers appreciate the benefits of constructing their own benchmarks include the following:

- External standards and benchmarks are written to apply across a wide range of settings, not to address the needs of students at any particular school. Yet the most appropriate curriculum for a given school will be one tailored to its students' own needs as literacy learners. In creating their school's own staircase curriculum, teachers must draw on their knowledge of the students, school, and community, as well as on the professional resources mentioned above.

- The people who have the best understanding of any set of external standards and benchmarks are those who constructed them. To gain a deep understanding of standards and benchmarks, teachers must engage in an active process of construction, rather than a passive process of reception. The background gained by drafting their own benchmarks enables teachers to evaluate external benchmarks critically and create their own for sustainable improvements to their literacy curriculum, assessment, and instruction.
- Our research suggests that schools where teachers show a willingness to construct their own staircase curriculum, including grade level benchmarks, progress quite quickly in improving students' literacy achievement. In contrast, schools where teachers are unwilling to undertake this task progress much more slowly.

At a few schools, where teachers had not received professional development beyond that necessary for the implementation of packaged programs, we encountered considerable resistance from teachers unwilling to draft their own grade level benchmarks. In these cases, we did allow teachers to select from the benchmarks available through external sources, but continued to support their professional knowledge and ability to analyze standard documents critically.

For example, Kathy worked at a school in Hawai'i where the third-grade teachers asserted that they did not have the expertise to develop their own grade level benchmarks and instead wanted to adopt those in state documents. A year and several workshops later, these teachers asked to meet with Kathy to discuss their progress. "Who wrote these benchmarks?" they asked. "We know our students are able to identify the author's message and provide a justification for their choice. But these benchmarks don't include anything about the author's message." They further criticized the existing benchmarks for being too narrow and asked if they could combine several benchmarks into one larger statement. These teachers ended up constructing their own reading benchmarks, including one about the author's message, but it took time for them to develop the insight and confidence to do so.

After teachers have the agreed-upon strands for their literacy curriculum and have drafted their grade level benchmarks for these strands, we ask them to compare their benchmarks to those in state documents for the purposes of alignment. During this alignment activity, we have teachers consider two questions:

- Content: Do the benchmarks you drafted address all of the content in the state standards and benchmarks?
- Rigor: Are the benchmarks you drafted at least at the same level of rigor as state benchmarks?

We have worked with the SBC Process at a wide range of schools, from those that have consistently made adequate yearly progress (AYP) according to state test results, to those with a history of low achievement and a challenge to reach AYP targets. We delivered the same message to all schools: State standards and benchmarks are the floor, not the ceiling. The reason for this statement is that, in schools that have had their own staircase curriculum in place for a number of years, teachers find themselves gradually raising their expectations for student performance over time.

This situation was illustrated at a K-6 school where teachers created their own staircase curriculum in writing. After four years, Kathy and the curriculum coordinator compared the "meets" exemplars for each of the grade levels to the exemplars provided in new state documents. This analysis showed that the school's exemplars looked like the state exemplars for the grade above (i.e., the school's kindergarten exemplars looked like the state's grade 1 exemplars, the school's grade 1 exemplars looked like the state's grade 2 exemplars, and so on). When the results of this analysis were shared with teachers, they immediately recognized what had happened. A fourth grade teacher explained, "Now when the students come up to me, they are much better prepared than in previous years." The other teachers nodded in agreement, because many of the students had experienced a staircase curriculum in writing in grades K-3. This consistency in instruction made the students much more capable writers by grade 4 than students in earlier cohorts. "Because they're coming up as stronger writers," the fourth grade teacher continued, "we know we can move them farther along in writing than we used to. We adjusted our benchmarks upwards last year, and we're planning on doing the same thing again this year."

In short, there is a strong relationship between a school's staircase curriculum and external (including state) benchmarks. At the outset, the school's curriculum, the state standards and benchmarks are often quite similar. Because we have involved teachers in alignment activities, they have checked to make certain that the school's staircase curriculum addresses all the content and strategies in the state standards, and that the outcomes in their curriculum are at the same level of rigor as the state standards and benchmarks. Over time, however, the school's curriculum and the state standards and benchmarks begin to diverge, with the school's staircase curriculum having expectations considerably higher than those of the state.

Packaged Programs and the Staircase Curriculum

We frequently encounter the situation where educators believe that they have solved the problem of students' low achievement because they have just adopted a new packaged program. These educators assume that a new reading program has automatically given their school a staircase or coherent curriculum, an assumption that does not find support in the research.

A study by Newmann, et al. (2001) showed that Chicago schools with packaged basal reading programs did not automatically ensure consistency in reading instruction across the grades. Inconsistencies resulted because teachers could interpret a program differently or choose to emphasize certain parts over others. Adopting a packaged program can save teachers a great deal of time and effort, and in fact nearly all the schools that have worked with the SBC Process have used packaged programs. However, teachers at schools successful in the SBC Process viewed these programs as resources used to support the implementation of their staircase curriculum. Administrators at successful schools understood that adopting a packaged program did not remove the need for teachers to engage in detailed discussions about the staircase curriculum within and across grade levels.

In the SBC Process, we make a distinction between a school's adopted packaged reading program and its reading curriculum. We define a curriculum as all of the planned learning experiences for students within a particular domain such as reading. A curriculum is always broader than any particular packaged program. For example, we urge teachers to attend to students' ownership of literacy as the overarching goal of their language arts curriculum (Au, 1997). While ownership and the affective dimension are highly important to students' growth as readers (Guthrie & Wigfield, 2000), all the packaged programs known to us give insufficient attention to aspects of motivation. To cite another example, packaged programs almost always pay considerable attention to lower-level skills, including word identification, but give much less attention to reading comprehension, including students' critical evaluation of texts. In short, packaged reading programs rarely cover the dimensions that research and teachers' own experience show to be important to students' literacy development.

Focused discussions, for the purpose of constructing and strengthening the staircase curriculum, are central to effective classroom instruction and a school's success in improving literacy achievement. Research by Smith, et al. (1998) found that in low-performing schools there was inconsistency in the content and strategies teachers taught within grade levels as well as between grade levels. At high-performing schools, this inconsistency was greatly reduced because teachers had the opportunity to engage in professional conversations with their colleagues to ensure consistency of instruction within and between grade levels.

When we begin work at a new school, we ask the leaders and teachers not to make an immediate decision about adopting a new program. The goal is for the school to maintain the status quo while teachers build an understanding of their school's reading curriculum that is broader than their school's reading program or, indeed, any packaged program.

Furthermore, we want to take advantage of the fact that those teachers who have been working with a packaged program for a year or more have a clear idea of that program's strengths and weaknesses. If the school were immediately to adopt a new program, at least a year would have to pass before the teachers gained this same degree of insight about the new program. Our strategy, then, is to guide teachers to identify and build on the strengths of their present instruction in reading, while taking the opportunity to correct any weaknesses.

Kathy worked at a Hawai'i school that had used a highly structured, scripted program for six years. When Kathy met with the teachers to discuss what they saw as the strengths and weaknesses of this program, they clearly had answers. One of the third-grade teachers replied, "Well, our students are very good at decoding, but they don't understand the meaning of what they are reading." Other teachers verified that students were indeed strong in the area of word identification but lacking in the area of comprehension. A fifth-grade teacher pointed to another problem, stating that students lacked the motivation to read. This lack of enthusiasm for reading was particularly evident at grade 3 and beyond.

As the discussion progressed, the teachers agreed that they were satisfied that they had a sufficiently strong staircase curriculum for word identification. They knew how to teach students phonics and other word identification skills. However, they noted significant weaknesses in the staircase curriculum for reading comprehension. At the primary grades, teachers recognized that they needed to pay more attention to comprehension. At the upper grades, teachers recognized that, while they did more work with comprehension, many of their lessons focused on the literal level and did not foster students' ability to interpret and evaluate texts or make text-to-self, text-to-text, and text-to-world connections. At this school, the work of Kathy and her colleagues focused on helping teachers create a staircase curriculum in the two strands they had identified: (1) reading comprehension and (2) habits and attitudes toward reading.

Conclusion

Professional development that enables teachers to construct their school's own staircase curriculum is an important counterbalance to what has become an over-reliance on packaged programs and the equating of program with curriculum. Perhaps the most insidious effect of this over-reliance is that administrators and teachers in some schools have come to believe that it is the program, rather than the teachers' expertise and agency, that has the greater impact on students' literacy achievement. In the SBC Process to whole school literacy improvement, we follow the opposite logic. We argue that it is teachers' expertise and agency that makes the greater difference to students' literacy achievement. When teachers own the curriculum, high levels of instruction can be sustained over time. Through the SBC Process, teachers participate in professional development that strengthens their knowledge of literacy, instruction, and assessment for the purposes of constructing their school's own staircase curriculum, then provide instruction and monitor student progress within the framework of this curriculum.

A staircase curriculum offers many benefits to a school's administrators, teachers, and students. Administrators are often concerned about whether teachers, who have seen many initiatives come and go, will commit themselves to a new school improvement effort or simply go through the motions. By being involved in the SBC Process and constructing their school's staircase curriculum, teachers have the opportunity to take ownership of literacy improvement efforts, a benefit to administrators who might otherwise face yet another fleeting initiative. Teachers benefit because they have the chance to create a curriculum tailored to the literacy learning needs of their students, rather than being required to follow a packaged program that may not address these needs. Teachers appreciate having the time to engage in detailed discussions of curriculum within their grade levels, as well as the time to meet with teachers at other grades for the purpose of coordinating their steps in the staircase. Teachers describe their work with the SBC Process as some of the most worthwhile of their careers. Students benefit because they receive literacy instruction that flows consistently from grade to grade, enabling them to achieve at higher levels and, in many cases, to reach the school's vision of the excellent reader and writer.

Acknowledgment

An earlier version of this chapter appeared in the *New England Reading Association Journal*. Permission to reprint this material is gratefully acknowledged.

References

Au, K. (1997). Ownership, literacy achievement, and students of diverse cultural backgrounds. In J.T. Guthrie & A. Wigfield (Eds.). *Reading engagement: Motivating readers through integrated instruction* (pp. 168–182). Newark, DE: International Reading Association.

Au, K. (2005). Negotiating the slippery slope: School change and literacy achievement. *Journal of Literacy Research, 37,* 3, 267–286.

Dillon, D.R. (2003). In leaving no child behind, have we forsaken individual learners, teachers, schools, and communities? In C.M. Fairbanks (Ed.). *52nd yearbook of the National Reading Conference* (pp. 1–31). Oak Creek, WI: National Reading Conference.

Guthrie, J.T., & Wigfield, A. (2000). Engagement and motivation in reading. In M.L. Kamil, P.B. Mosenthal, P.D. Pearson, & R. Barr (Eds.). *Handbook of reading research,* Vol. III. (pp. 403–422). Mahwah, NJ: Erlbaum.

National Assessment of Educational Progress. (2010). National Assessment of Educational Progress (NAEP). Retrieved December 28, 2010, from http://nces.ed.gov/nationsreportcard/

Newmann, F.M., Smith, B., Allensworth, E., & Bryk, A.S. (2001). Instructional program coherence: What it is and why it should guide school improvement policy. *Educational Evaluation and Policy Analysis, 23,* 4, 297–321.

NGA/CCSSO, Common Core State Standards Initiative. (2010). About the standards. Retrieved December 21, 2010, from www.corestandards.org/about-the-standards

Programme for International Student Assessment. (2010). What PISA is. Retrieved December 28, 2010, from www.pisa.oecd.org

Raphael, T. (2010). Defying gravity: Literacy reform in urban schools. In K. Leander, D. Rowe, D. Dickinson, R. Jimenez, M. Hundley, & V. Risko (Eds.). *Fifty-ninth yearbook of the National Reading Conference* (pp. 22–42). Oak Creek, WI: National Reading Conference.

Raphael, T., Au, K., & Goldman, S. (2009). Whole school instructional improvement through the Standards-Based Change Process: A developmental model. In J. Hoffman, & Y. Goodman (Eds.). *Changing literacies for changing times* (pp. 198–229). New York: Routledge.

Smith, J., Smith, B., & Bryk, A. (1998). Setting the pace: Opportunities to learn in Chicago's elementary schools. Chicago, IL: Consortium on Chicago School Research.

Taba, H. (1962). *Curriculum development: Theory and practice*. New York: Harcourt, Brace & World.

TIMMS and PIRLS International Study Center. (2010). About PIRLS 2011. Retrieved December 28, 2010, from http://timss.bc.edu/pirls2011/index.html

10

DIVERSITY IN CHILDREN'S LITERATURE

What Does It Matter in Today's Educational Climate?

Rudine Sims Bishop

Editor's Note: The multicultural education movement grew out of the mid-century Civil Rights Movement, and by the 1990s incorporated a focus on "multicultural children's literature." The focus of this chapter is on historical developments relating to including diverse literatures in the curriculum and on the challenge inherent in maintaining an emphasis on such literature in a climate in which literature itself appears to be pushed to the back burner of educational reform.

KSG

Recently I read some stories from classroom teachers that, as a children's literature professional, I found disturbing because they indicate that, in the current political and social climate, our educational leaders may well have lost sight of the importance of literature in the education of our children. One story in the *New York Times* (Winerip, 2011) featured my NCTE (National Council of Teachers of English) colleague, Linda Rief. Linda teaches in a New Hampshire school in which 85 percent of the students are rated "proficient" on the state standardized test, but where the school has been deemed "failing" because about a dozen of its 126 special education students did not score high enough. This has resulted in an all-out focus on test preparation at her school, to the detriment of the kind of real learning experiences that Linda has been providing for 25 years, such as her semester-long genre study project.

The second piece, actually a series of stories, is an appendix to Rothstein, et al.'s *Grading Education: Getting Accountability Right* (2008). Several teachers were interviewed about the impact of the implementation of current accountability programs on their classroom teaching. A third grade teacher in an urban California school reported that she was not able to read aloud very often because the commercial program the school adopted crowded out all other reading experiences. "The children are missing out on real literature," she noted (Brekke-Brownell, cited in Rothstein, et al., 2008, p. 186). A K-1 teacher in an urban school in New York state reported that her school is using a heavily scripted commercial program, and "in the first grade we all have to be on the same page on the same day." She further reports that, "the children who do poorly on the test have to go on 'direct instruction,' which has no literature. I don't believe the children know what reading is any more" (Curto, cited in Rothstein, et al., 2008, p. 192).

These stories, and there are many more, suggest that well-intentioned government policies are having a deleterious effect on the teaching of literature in the classrooms of the United States. I argue that literature is essential to educating children to become productive, intelligent, participatory citizens of a democratic society. It expands their horizons, provides insight into human behavior, holds up for them the values and ideals we hold dear, and lets them know what we think it means to be a decent human being in this society. When the body of literature they are offered is diverse and inclusive, it also offers multiple perspectives on how to solve problems, invites critical thinking, and helps children find their connections to all other human beings. My concern is that, in the process of trying to drive all children to meet "common core standards," and "close the achievement gap" between white and minority children, government policies squeeze out that which is extremely important but extremely difficult to assess with standardized, easy-to-score, multiple-choice tests.

The federal policy initiative that is said to have revolutionized the role of the federal government in education was Johnson's Elementary and Secondary Education Act of 1965. It is the "granddaddy" of the current policy initiative, No Child Left Behind. The ESEA (1965) was part of Johnson's War on Poverty, and an element in his attempt to create "The Great Society." In 1965, a bit more than a decade after the Supreme Court had outlawed "separate but equal" schools because they are inherently unequal, educational opportunities were still not equally available to all school children. The framers of the ESEA understood that the children of the poor were suffering from a lack of adequate resources both in their home communities and their educational institutions. The overall purpose of the ESEA was, therefore, to address the problem of inequality by improving educational opportunities for poor children.

Title I of the ESEA provided funds for schools with high concentrations of low-income families. Of particular interest to me with regard to the impact of the ESEA on children's literature, however, was Title II, which made available funds for library, textbooks, and other instructional materials. One result was that, at the elementary level, per pupil expenditures on library resources increased 85 percent from 1965–1966. ESEA expressly stated that the federal government could have no say in the specific materials that were purchased.

Coming as it did in 1965, Title II coincided with social movements that together spurred the diversification of children's literature. Civil Rights activists, and a bit later, advocates of multicultural education, demanded that the voices and images of non-white children and other under-represented groups be represented in the literature and other curriculum materials offered in the schools. With ESEA money as an incentive, publishers responded by producing and promoting multicultural children's literature. School curricula began to be opened to diverse perspectives that invited critical discussions about where we have come from as a nation, and who we are today.

The ESEA has been re-authorized and changed several times over the decades since 1965, but it is important to note that, in its original form, it was an effort to put federal money where the federal mouth was, so to speak. Having decided that poverty presented a major obstacle to scholastic achievement, and that education was the "hope factor" for poor children, the federal government tied monetary resources to the creation of equal educational opportunity for poor and urban children.

The 2001 version of ESEA, "No Child Left Behind" (NCLB), while still claiming to improve educational opportunities for underserved children, focuses on a different set of priorities. Its impossible-to-reach goal was to have all students become proficient as measured by tests by 2014. Its strategy for reaching that goal was based on the premise that the solution to the so-called crisis in education consists in: 1) incentivizing states to adopt a set of "common core standards," 2) testing children annually using standardized tests of basic reading and math, 3) labeling schools that fail to make "adequate yearly progress" as failing, 4) sanctioning such schools by replacing their teachers and administrators, and 5) encouraging parents to remove their children from "failing" schools and to place them in alternative settings, especially charter schools. Thus, if the 1965 ESEA offered schools a carrot, the 21st century version was much more of a stick.

The most recently proposed version of the ESEA is Education Secretary Duncan's "A Blueprint for Reform: The Reauthorization of the Elementary and Secondary Education Act" (ESEA, 2010). Its goal is to make all students "college and career ready" by 2020. It proposes to accomplish this outcome by making available competitive grants to states that meet certain criteria. Although the Blueprint proposes offering funds for states to broaden their curricula, and recognizes that factors outside the schools impact children's achievement, in the end it proposes to continue the high-stakes testing and punitive sanctions that are at the core of the problems with NCLB. In fact, it appears that, in keeping with the intent to foster broader educational experiences, the blueprint encourages and offers to fund the development of assessments beyond the basic skill focus on reading and math of the NCLB. But the bottom line remains more tests.

My concern was with the likely effect of federal educational policies on classroom experiences with literature, and in particular the opportunities for youngsters to engage with a diverse body of literature for children and youth. In that regard, I believe we are in challenging times. Here are some of my concerns:

The Blueprint Discussion of Literacy. The Blueprint continues some of the emphasis found in NCLB. It requires states to "develop comprehensive, evidence-based, preK-12 literacy plans." The focus here is clearly on reading instruction, on the techniques of reading, on those aspects of reading that can be measured. There is reference to "identifying effective instructional materials" and to giving priority to states that have adopted common standards, and to states that use technology. Although none of this language precludes a focus on literature, none of it prioritizes literature either. Hence my concern about the possible interpretation of the term "evidence based," since NCLB allowed only a restricted definition of "evidence."

The Common Core Standards. Another entry into national policy is the arrival of the Common Core State Standards Initiative (CCSS, 2010). Although these standards are ostensibly not federal but state standards, much of the funding of the proposed new initiative is tied to states adopting college and career-ready standards. Since the vast majority of states have adopted the common core standards, it appears that they are close to becoming national educational standards in reading and math. One concern, shared by many critics of NCLB, is that the adoption of these standards motivates schools and school districts to use them as the curriculum guide for the teaching of reading and literature. And since high-stakes assessments appear to be tied to meeting the standards, the school curriculum tends to become narrower, not broader. Curricula narrowed to reflect a set of measurable standards tends not to emphasize learning experiences that are difficult to measure and quantify, such as engagement with literature.

Another concern with the standards is that, in offering a list of texts "illustrating the complexity, quality and range of student reading," they provide the temptation to make that list the required reading list for some schools. In all fairness, it should be noted that educators are warned that this is absolutely not the intent of the list. But I wonder if schools that are strapped for resources, including funds for libraries and librarians, and in danger of losing their staff or even being closed, won't reason that it couldn't hurt, and it might help, to expose children to books that are clearly sanctioned by the powers that be. I took a quick look at the K-5 lists (literature and informational texts). I have no quarrel with the quality of the texts listed, but I did note that diversity was apparently not one of the main criteria for the selections.

Challenge Schools. The Blueprint proposes to identify as "Challenge Schools" the lowest 5 percent of schools, based on "student academic achievement, student growth, and graduation rates, that are not making progress to improve." In these schools, states and districts will be required to implement one of four "school turnaround" models, to provide better outcomes for students. These turn-around models range from changing the principal to closing the school. In all likelihood, many, if not most, of the Challenge Schools are going to be those that serve poor and urban children. Although the intent of the "turn-around" is to improve the educational experiences of these children and to close the so-called "achievement gap," the reliance on high-stakes tests to measure student achievement and student growth is a strong incentive for teachers and administrators to focus on helping students to pass the tests. We all have heard horror stories about what can happen when administrators focus on test results. Once again, the children of the poor, the children who most need enriched educational experiences, who most need affirmation of their own worth, will again be short-changed. I see it as another case of paving the road to hell with good intentions.

Given the political agendas that too frequently drive policy decisions, I would urge local, state, and federal policy makers to think long and hard about what it is we want education to do for our children, and how proposed policies will advance or hinder those goals. Before we sit down at the table of school reform, I suggest we move with caution and ask, as Joyce Carol Thomas (1993, unpaged) suggests in a one of her poems, "Who has set this table?"

References

CCSS (2010). Common core standards initiative. Retrieved July 27, 2012, from www.core standards.org/

ESEA (1965). Elementary and secondary education act of 1965, background material with related presidential recommendations. Retrieved July 27, 2012, from www.eric.ed.gov/PDFS/ED018492.pdf

ESEA (2001). The no child left behind act of 2001. Retrieved July 27, 2012, from www2.ed.gov/policy/elsec/leg/esea02/107-110.pdf

ESEA (2010, March). A blueprint for reform: The reauthorization of the elementary and secondary education act. U.S. Department of Education. Retrieved July 27, 2012, from www2.ed.gov/policy/elsec/leg/blueprint/blueprint.pdf

Rothstein, R., Jacobsen, R., & Wilder, T. (2008). *Grading education: Getting accountability right.* Washington, DC: Economic Policy Institute.

Thomas, J.C. (1993). *Brown honey in broomwheat tea.* New York: HarperCollins.

Winerip, M. (2011). "In a standardized era, a creative school is forced to be more so." *New York Times*, October 30. A–11.

11

EXAMINING THREE ASSUMPTIONS ABOUT TEXT COMPLEXITY

Standard 10 of the Common Core State Standards

Elfrieda H. Hiebert and Katie Van Sluys

Editor's Note: One of the bad old ideas that keeps coming back in reading is that it is possible to arrange texts on a scale of reading difficulty (readability) and then create a calibrated series of reading experiences appropriate for all learners. The latest incarnation of this is in the Common Core Standards (CCSS Initiative, 2010) being widely imposed on teachers and students. What is missed by those who pursue this idea is that reading is a transaction between a reader and a text. What the reader brings to the text is at least as important as the difficulty of the text in determining how readable it will be for any given reader. This chapter provides a detailed critique of this policy and the dangers of building a reading program on the simplistic notion of readability.

KSG

At its core, reading involves a text and texts vary greatly in complexity—their structures, vocabularies, styles, and topics. Standard 10 of the Common Core State Standards (CCSS Initiative, 2010) calls for students to grow capacity in reading texts of ever increasing complexity over the school years, culminating in high school graduates' ability to read the complex texts of college and careers. The CCSS is the first standards document to recognize this fundamental feature of literacy. The writers of the CCSS are to be applauded for their recognition of a central feature of reading instruction that has often been ignored.

As is always the case in a human endeavor, translating vision to practice means that tough choices need to be made. That was so in the CCSS writers' description of a staircase of text complexity where decisions were made about such thorny issues as ways to measure text complexity and which texts exemplify complexity at different points along the staircase.

In this response, we consider three assumptions about the view of text complexity as operationalized by the CCSS. We are concerned that these assumptions, if left unexamined, could increase the achievement gap, as they become part of state and national policies. At the outset, we emphasize that we support strongly the goal of increased reading of complex texts and accompanying reading practices. A complex view of text complexity, however, is needed to ensure that appropriate texts and instruction are provided so such students can increase their capacity to engage with complex texts. Before addressing the three assumptions and their potential consequences, we describe why text complexity was included as a distinct standard within the CCSS.

Overview: Why Text Complexity as a Standard?

Previous standards documents of states and national organizations described students' comprehension or their recognition of features such as figurative language with respect to grade-level texts but grade level was never identified. An unarticulated assumption underlay these documents that the texts with which seventh graders would be applying a compare–contrast strategy would be more challenging than those that were used to measure third graders use of a compare–contrast strategy on state assessments, and so forth. Without an index of text complexity, establishing grade-appropriate text was determined by publishers and test-makers.

The results of leaving text levels ill-defined are evident from three groups of analyses. First, comparisons of students' performances on assessments administered by their states and those of the National Assessment of Educational Progress (NAEP) showed that grade-level proficiency varied greatly from state to state (e.g., Bandeira de Mello, 2011). Second, American students failed to perform at appropriate levels on international comparisons of literacy proficiency (Mullis, et al., 2003). Finally, the ACT's (2006) study of the preparedness of high school students for College Board examinations and the relationship of these performances to their grades in college showed that students needed to achieve benchmark scores on tasks with *complex* texts, not complex tasks with simple or uncomplicated texts to pass college courses. Unfortunately, only 51 percent of high school students achieved this benchmark level.

The response of the CCSS writers was to make the ability to read increasingly more complex text a centerpiece of the standards with an entire standard devoted to increased capacity with complex texts over the grades. The CCSS includes an appendix (B) where exemplars of complex texts are provided for different grade bands, beginning with the grade 2–3 band but the core of the definition of text complexity is in Appendix A where a tripartite model is provided as the basis for establishing text complexity. This model includes qualitative dimensions (i.e., levels of meaning or purpose, structure, language conventionality and clarity, and knowledge demands), reader and task dimensions (i.e., elements of instruction that teachers address in assignments and lesson planning), and quantitative dimensions. Within Appendix A, the CCSS suggest that further guidance on qualitative dimensions would be forthcoming but, within the document that was distributed, only one quantitative system was well described and operationalized. The readability system that was the focus of Appendix A was the proprietary Lexile Framework (MetaMetrics, 2000) which uses, as is typical of readability formulas, a semantic component (frequency of vocabulary) and a syntactic component (number of words in a sentence). Specific levels were identified within the Lexile Framework for grade bands, starting with grade 2–3. The point of initiation for the grade 2–3 band (450 on the Lexile scale) implicitly also establishes an expectation for grade 1.

In the almost two years since the release of the CCSS, the promise of additional guidance on qualitative systems has not materialized. Further, the organization responsible for the writing of the standards—Student Achievement Partners (SAP)—has supervised a grant from the Gates Foundation to establish the comparative predictive validity of different readability formulas. The report from this project includes co-authors from SAP and suggests an even stronger rationale for the use of readability formulas (Nelson, et al., 2012). Actions to date suggest a need for further examination of the assumptions about text complexity within the CCSS, including: (a) Text levels need to be accelerated at every level of students' school careers, including the primary grades; (b) Students at all proficiency levels can be rapidly "stretched" to read substantially harder texts; and (c) Readability formulas provide sufficiently valid assessments of text complexity that can be used as a guide for selections in instruction and assessment. We examine each assumption, related research, and potential consequences for young readers in the United States.

Assumption 1: Text Levels Need to be Accelerated at Every Level of Students' School Career, Including the Primary Grades

> K-12 reading texts have actually trended downward in difficulty in the last half century . . . quantitative measures should identify the college- and career-ready reading level as one endpoint of the scale.
>
> (CCSS Initiative, 2010, p. 8)

The CCSS is recommending a reconfiguration of grade-level readability standards in order to prepare high school graduates for the texts of college and careers. Table 11.1 shows how the CCSS proposes to achieve this goal—by raising text levels in all grades, starting with second grade. There is another way to achieve this goal, which would be to create a strong foundation in the early grades and then raise the difficulty exponentially in the upper grades, so that the increase, if it were graphed, would look like an up-sweeping curve. We believe that the research supports this second approach. But first, we'll examine what the CCSS proposes and the claims and sources used to support their recommendations: (1) that texts in

TABLE 11.1 Original and Recalibrated Lexile Ranges for CCSS Grade Bands

Text complexity grade band	Original Lexile ranges	Recalibrated Lexile ranges
K–1	—	—
2–3	450–725	450–790
4–5	645–845	770–980
6–8	860–1010	955–1155
9–10	960–1115	1080–1305
11–CCR	1070–1220	1215–1355

Note. Summarized from CCSS, Appendix A, p. 8.

all grades, including primary-level, have trended downward in difficulty over the years so that all students are reading easier material than they used to, and (2) that by accelerating difficulty in primary-level texts, students will be better positioned to meet college and career readability expectations by high school graduation.

First, the CCSS recommendations assume that readability levels of texts at every grade level have trended downward over the past 50 years. Several papers refute the idea that primary-grade texts have been simplified: in kindergarten (Hiebert, 2011a), in first grade (Hiebert, 2010), or in third grade (Hiebert, 2012a), and those arguments are summarized here. First, with regard to kindergarten, it is impossible that expectations could have declined over the past 50 years, since kindergarten texts were not part of core reading programs until after Reading First mandates in the first decade of the 21st century.

With regard to first grade, the first study cited is Chall's (1967/1983) reports on first-grade texts that summarized the features of texts in core reading programs with copyrights from 1956 to 1962. Massive changes occurred in first-grade texts in the subsequent decades (Foorman, et al., 2004), including the elimination of controlled vocabulary in first-grade texts that resulted in substantial increases in the number of unique and rare words.

The second study cited by the CCSS with implications for the primary grades is an analysis conducted by Hayes, et al. (1996) of texts from grades 1–8 and across three time periods (1919–1945, 1946–1962, 1963–1991). Hayes, et al. showed numerous changes in texts over these three periods, including evidence of school-book simplification. But this pattern of simplification did not hold for the primary grades. In grade 3, vocabulary difficulty was *highest* for the final period in that study.

CCSS also cites Williamson's (2008) analysis of a cohort of North Carolina students in grades 3–8 to show texts had become easier between the years 1999 and 2004. The end-of-the-year level for third grade on this curve was 700L. Table 11.1 shows that the exit level of the grade 2–3 band of the CCSS is 790, 1.6 standard deviations above the 700L level at which proficient third graders in North Carolina were performing.

The most recent evidence that the CCSS brings to bear on this claim of decreasing text difficulty is the ACT (2006) study that has already been described. The ACT research does not speak to primary level readabilities; the study begins with eighth-grade students.

To review, the data point only to a text-complexity gap at the middle and high school levels. None of these studies provides any evidence that primary-grade text difficulty has declined or that increasing grade-level reading expectations for the second and third graders will boost their trajectories as successful readers in the secondary grades—which brings us to the next claim associated with the CCSS assumption that "the earlier children learn to read, the better they will do." Despite substantial investments in early reading through No Child Left Behind/ Reading First, gains have not been evident in higher grades (Gamse, et al., 2008; Jackson, et al., 2007). These findings are echoed by international data that track the effects of early reading instruction on later reading achievement (Suggate, 2009). Differences are not evident in the reading achievement of students at the end of elementary school in different countries as a result of different school entry ages. However, in countries with earlier starting ages, the achievement gap between those who were proficient and those who were not grew larger among 15-year-olds.

Potential Consequences

The stance of the CCSS to have students reading earlier and at higher levels will probably neither help, nor hurt, those who come to school ready to read, but it could make literacy a greater challenge for the very students who most depend on America's public schools for their literacy instruction. At the present time, two-thirds of an American fourth-grade cohort does not meet current reading goals on the NAEP—one-third of the cohort falls below the basic standard, another third below the proficiency standard (National Center for Education Statistics, 2009). According to this framework for determining reading proficiency, students in the middle of fourth grade who could recognize the majority of what is considered fourth-grade vocabulary (Daane, et al., 2005) were considered proficient readers. Students scoring in the below-basic and basic groups fail to read a portion of these words or read them too slowly to be proficient readers. Therefore, when increasingly difficult text is presented, students on the low end of either the proficient or basic groups drop down into basic and below basic, respectively, as *A First Look* (ACT, 2010) study verifies with eleventh graders.

CCSS recommendations could also increase the downward movement of formal reading instruction into kindergarten. As Pearson and Hiebert (2010) have illustrated, the proficiency distribution in kindergarten mirrors the pattern of fourth grade cohorts: one-third enters kindergarten having mastered literacy content, another third has incomplete knowledge of this content, and the final third is entirely dependent on kindergarten to deliver this content.

Knowing student experiences and current performance is essential when making informed curricula decisions such that learning can occur for all learners. If we fail to do this and instead craft ill-informed and/or arbitrary expectations, the result will likely be separating, sorting, and labeling students who "can/can't" meet such expectations instead of the kinds of teaching and learning opportunity students really need.

Another consequence could be that the age at which children begin school will play a greater part in determining early academic success, as children born in the winter or spring will have 6–9 months advantage over their summer- or fall-born peers. Holding children back for an extra year will be a luxury that only some parents who can afford the childcare can indulge—another way in which this trend hurts students who depend upon public services. Finally, apart from any generalized group tendencies, there are individual differences in cognitive development rates that are not indicative of intelligence or future achievement. Any children given some breathing room in their early years of school might be able to catch up to grade-level standards. The pressure of higher expectations in the early grades may mean no grace period for these students.

Students will quickly come to know who is succeeding and who isn't. Such branding, whether it comes from the system or the students own observations about who is successful in class, can have long-lasting and often intractable effects on students' confidence as readers, which can, in turn, diminish their interest and willingness to engage in reading activities (Guthrie, et al., 2007).

While deeper reading of primary-grade focused research cited in the CCSS shows that texts have not grown easier over the years, there is research that points to another way—ensuring that primary-level students are meeting current expectations. Research shows that students in third grade who achieve proficient literacy levels (under existing not new and increased standards) are less likely to drop out of high school (Hernandez, 2011). Our energies would be better focused on attaining this useful goal that reflect the standards that are already in place, rather than grasping after an unsupported, aspirational standard that is even further out of reach.

Assumption 2: Students at All Levels Can Be Rapidly Stretched to Read Substantially Harder Texts

> Students in the first year(s) of a given band are expected by the end of the year to read and comprehend proficiently within the band, with scaffolding as needed at the high end of the range. Students in the last year of a band are expected by the end of the year to read and comprehend independently and proficiently within the band (CCSS Initiative, 2010, p. 10).

This quote from the CCSS suggests students are to be stretched to read texts within an identified grade-level band—first with scaffolding, and then on their own with the expectation that they can do so proficiently. Taking a closer look at this suggestion and the texts recommended within Appendix B as exemplars raises questions and concerns including issues of how texts are defined, how text complexity/difficulty is measured, and how the outcomes of interactions between readers and texts are defined and measured.

When it comes to texts and text selection, reading instruction in many contexts has long been influenced and shaped by frameworks that focus on texts and ways of leveling texts and then pairing particular texts with particular readers. For example, Betts' framework (1946), which assumes links between oral reading accuracy, reading comprehension, and possible emotional response (e.g. frustration), continues to influence instructional decisions within classrooms, schools, and policies (Halladay, 2008). A recent instantiation of this line of thinking is reflected in the CCSS reference to text complexity and subsequent recommendations of grade-level anchor texts that further define particular perspectives toward texts, readers, learning, and instruction. One could challenge the footings on which this document attempts to stand in a number of ways, but we think it is more productive to think about *readers* who walk into our schools and the kinds of *reader* we need to participate in present and future society.

The CCSS work with the notion of generic x-grade readers. Readers are far from clones of other age peers. Readers of any age come to text with distinct histories and diverse experiences with the purposes of reading; types and nature of different reading task; cultural and background knowledge; experience with words, print, and language(s); and academic positioning (including their own and others definitions of successful reading). It is imperative that any conversation or decision aiming to match readers and texts in ways that support and lead readers' development consider reader, context, and interactions with texts as well as text-based factors to create ideal instructional scenarios that offer the potential for engaging and teaching readers.

Readers come to texts with particular ideas and expectations often grounded in their cultural lives (Murata, 2007). Links between readers' prior and/or background knowledge and comprehension in first and/or additional languages has long been on the mind of educators and is well studied by researchers (Gee, 2000). In a recent study of fifth graders' social awareness, Dray and Selman (2011) showed that readers' social knowledge and experience, while moderated by reading skill, influenced comprehension. For good readers, there was almost no effect. But for those classified as poor readers, there was a fairly strong positive effect suggesting that readers' experiences influenced their comprehension of the focal text. While the study does not claim to illustrate causality, inferences suggest that the relationship between the text content and the lived experiences of the reader matter, especially for less experienced readers.

Readers not only vary in the experiences they bring with them into class-rooms, they vary in terms of how they approach reading—which may be based on their definitions of success, repertoire and use of reading strategies, social position, or engagement. Halladay's (2008) research into the lives of early readers finds that often young people's visions of successful reading varies from expectations for success held by other stakeholders, namely family, educators, or policy makers. Findings from a study conducted by Blaxall and Willows (1984) highlight the ways readers vary in terms of known strategies as well as how/when to orchestrate known strategies. Their findings suggest that more skilled readers have greater flexibility when it comes to using reading strategies as evidenced by more syntactically or semantically acceptable miscues. Less experienced readers lean on graphophonemic cues that result in the dominance of graphically similar substitutions likely to disrupt meaning making. The findings of Bomer and Laman (2004), who focus their research primarily on young learners' writing lives, challenge linear and purely cognitive development trajectories. Their research emphasizes the complex social work in becoming literate which includes the ways in which learners are perceived and positioned by others and their goals for any given literacy event. Cambourne's (1995) and Guthrie, et al.'s (1996) works focus on the social conditions that foster engagement and findings that suggest that engaged readers are knowledgeable, strategic, motivated, and socially interactive. These findings point to the complexity of readers—their histories, expectations, skills, motivations, and surrounding learning conditions that influence what they do with texts, the needs and experiences they bring to a reading event, and the diverse range of what they need for the best learning to transpire.

Another part of the puzzle concerned with making informed decisions about matching readers with texts, which was alluded to in the discussion of the Dray and Selman (2011) study but merits direct consideration, has to do with definitions, knowledge, actions, and contexts of reading. In other words, some research examines particular dimensions of reading practices and may or may not take into consideration all or enough factors to use such research to support claims about what makes a text "right" or appropriately "complex" for particular readers.

Consider research into the role of vocabulary. In one study, findings suggest that the percentage of high frequency words in a given text was a predictor of performance for low and average ability readers in terms of decoding, reading accuracy, and fluency (Compton, et al., 2004). Unfortunately, comprehension was not examined and we therefore do not know what sense readers made of text, even when the percentage of high frequency words impacted performance in measured areas.

Or, consider what has been found about matching readers and reading material in independent reading contexts. Carver and Leibert's (1995) research suggests that mere reading of easy or instructional matched books individually is insufficient for increasing readers' skills. This may mean that such texts, placed in the hands of novice readers, are insufficient for increasing readers' skills. This could be taken to mean that learning to read requires more "complex" texts. But, questions can be raised with regard to ways in which independent reading may have impacted engagement and/or how level "determinations" were made or how reading skills were designed and measured. A sweeping decision about the role of "easy" or "instructional" texts, or the merits of independent reading, also seems unwise as other, related, research suggests that there may be some gain for older readers who engage in independent reading (Krashan & McQuillian, 2007), or less fluent marginalized readers with the least access to print in their homes (Kim, 2006).

Findings like these may push some to shift from "determining the right text" to inviting readers to choose. More studies reveal partial insights into the merits and concerns of such a shift. Donovan, et al.'s (2000) findings suggest that the most emergent readers, when presented with choice of text, more often make text selections that are difficult. However, this research which tracked first-grade student-selections in relation to determined reading level did not gather data with regard to the nature of reading experiences, hence we do not know what readers took away from and/or learned during/from their interaction with texts that were classified as difficult. But, this research does raise questions about the roles' interest and motivation as well as conceptual and genre knowledge play in drawing readers to texts and engaging readers with texts for extended periods of interaction/reading. When Kim and Guryan (2010) examined choice in their study of fourth-grade Latino students' summer reading, they found that self-selected reading alone or with minimal support in the form of family literacy workshop impacts growth in reading ability. Again, this research points to the complexity of matching texts, readers, and instruction.

Potential Consequences

Focusing exclusively on texts, identified level of complexity, and accompanying expectations for achievement ignores the nuances of being and becoming a reader. It is probable and possible that raising the bar to a particular height and then asking children to jump harder and higher could result in children who can say the words in a text or get through identified texts and these same children growing into people who can decode but choose not to actively read. Furthering the distance between where learners are and where they are expected to be will likely further marginalize or deny access to the literacy club for students whose experiences, interests, and cultures are not part of a leveled canon. As reading begets better readers, turning students off to reading affects our national aspirations as well. Already, United States' students rank among the lowest of any country in their interest in reading (Mullis, et al., 2003). We also predict that the CCSS staircase will result in less proficient students spending less time reading. The CCSS advise that students who are reading at the low end of their grade band be exposed to the texts at the high end of their grade band. Often, exposure to difficult texts takes the form of read-alouds or read-alongs (either facilitated by teachers or digital devices) so that students who cannot read difficult texts independently can experience them with scaffolding. Research shows that read-alouds can support students' listening comprehension, but to date, we do not know if such experiences help students develop independent reading proficiency. Depending on the distribution of instructional time, such expectations may disadvantage the most emergent readers.

An early emphasis on increasingly difficult texts, as outlined in CCSS, could also create and reify simple definitions of what it means to read to the point where students are miles away from critically engaging with a wide range of texts today's young readers are bound to encounter in their reading lives. Given this modest examination of research, it can be argued that a focus on the text alone in the hands of emergent or novice readers will not produce the gains envisioned/called for by CCSS. It follows that while we need to think more about what is meant by "complex" when it comes to text, it's likely we ought to think more about the meaning of "complex" when it comes to readers, acts of reading, and reading instruction.

Assumption 3: Readability Formulas Provide Sufficiently Valid Assessments of Text Complexity That They Can Be Used as a Guide for Selections in Instruction and Assessment

> quantitative measures should identify the college- and career-ready reading level as one endpoint of the scale. MetaMetrics, for example, has realigned its Lexile ranges to match the Standards' text complexity grade bands and has adjusted upward its trajectory of reading comprehension development through the grades to indicate that all students should be reading at the college and career readiness level by no later than the end of high school (CCSS Initiative, 2010, Appendix A, p. 8).

We can all agree that text complexity is critical and that there needs to be progression in text complexity across the school years (although we can disagree where the points of greatest change need to be and also the ways to support struggling and beginning readers in increasing their capacity). As with so many things in education, it is the measurement of text complexity that can influence greatly what happens. As the adage goes, the medium can be the message.

The tripartite system of the CCSS was described at the beginning of the chapter where qualitative and reader-task features are part of a system for establishing text complexity with quantitative measures. The assessments of readers and tasks are viewed to be within the purview of classroom teachers working with students, although particular features of readers and tasks can be presented within a rubric to support teachers in making these choices (see, e.g., Hiebert, 2011b).

With respect to support for qualitative measurement of texts, the CCSS writers (CCSS Initiative, 2010) indicated that examples of such systems would be forthcoming. At this point, fulfillment of the promise has been indirect through endorsement by CCSS writers of an effort developed by the Kansas state department of education (Pimentel, 2012). Within the Kansas rubric (Copeland, et al., 2012), four traits (levels of purpose, structure, language conventionality and clarity, and knowledge demands) are described with generic descriptions at each of four levels (low, middle-low, middle-high, and high) for the two text types (narrative and informational). The Kansas system is at a nascent stage of development with vague descriptions, no examples of features instantiated in real texts, or evidence on reliability of the scheme. The offering of this system, after almost two years since the launch of the CCSS and the involvement of key CCSS writers in the already described predictive validity study of readability formulas (Nelson, et al., 2012) suggest that readability formulas are likely to loom large within the evaluation of text complexity in assessments and also text selection.

Nearly all readability formulas, regardless of small differences, analyze two main features of texts: (a) syntax and (b) vocabulary. Measurement of syntax is fairly straightforward, typically based on number of words per sentence, although occasionally number of syllables is used. For vocabulary, some formulas (e.g., Spache, 1953) compare the words in a text to an index of words that have been keyed to different grade levels, while others (e.g., Fry, 1968) use the number of syllables in words as an indicator of difficulty.

Until recently, readability formulas had to be applied manually by counting words or syllables and consulting word indices. Because of this, what was being measured by the readability formula was abundantly clear to all who used them. The Lexile and several other digitized readability formulas take a different tack, which is to establish vocabulary complexity by taking the average frequency of all words in a sample of text (Smith, et al., 1989). The frequency of a word is established relative to its rank relative to all of the words in a digital database.

A readability formula is a good first resource in sorting large groups of texts. Hiebert and Pearson (2010) obtained Lexiles (L) of a large group of beginning reading texts that were sorted by text levels as assigned by publishers. The progression across seven levels showed a steady increase in complexity: 87L for the first level, 238L for the middle level, and 489L for the final level. Within a level, however, the variation was substantial. For the texts classified as the mid-point of beginning reading programs, Lexiles had a range of 760L (610L to -160L). This range is almost equivalent to growth expected through the end of grade third, according to the accelerated levels in Table 11.1.

Explanations for at least some of the discrepancies in readability levels are evident in a comparison of the Lexiles assigned to two texts within the exemplar texts in Appendix B of the CCSS (CCSS Initiative, 2010): *Boy, Were We Wrong About Dinosaurs* (*Boy*; Kudlinski, 2005) and *In the Time of the Butterflies* (*Butterflies*; Alvarez, 1994). The Lexiles of the two texts fall closely to one another (within 60 Lexile points, the standard deviation in the Lexile Framework): 960L for *Boy* and 1000L for *Butterflies*). The CCSS writers offered these texts as exemplars for quite different levels, however: *Boy* for the grade 2–3 band and *Butterflies* for the grade 9–10 band.

One feature of readability formulas that can explain such disparate outcomes is text genre. *Boy* is an informational text, while *Butterflies* is a narrative text. Narrative texts often contain dialogue and people typically speak in relatively short sentences. Further, a writer of narrative often uses fairly straightforward vocabulary, sprinkled with rare vocabulary that provides nuance to the text. *Butterflies* contains words such as *anachuita* (name of a tree) and *guanabana* (name of a juice) but most of the words in the text are quite common. The mean of the frequency of words in a sample of *Butterflies* is 3.59 on a scale of 1 (hardest) to 5 (easiest) according to the Lexile Analyzer. The mean for word frequency in *Boy*—3.49—indicates that the vocabulary is somewhat more difficult than that in *Butterflies*, even though *Boy* is intended for primary-level students. Rare words such as *iguanodon* (a type of dinosaur) are repeated often in this informational text, reflecting the need to use precise vocabulary to convey particular concepts (Cohen & Steinberg, 1983). Most, if not all, readability formulas do not compensate for this repetition of rare vocabulary within informational texts, even when repetition is known to support word learning (Finn, 1978). Readability formulas, then, can overestimate the difficulty of even a fairly straightforward informational text such as *Boy*, just as they underestimate the difficulty of a narrative with complex themes and content such as *Butterflies*.

Another feature of measuring vocabulary within digital readability formulas is also reflected in similar levels assigned to *Boy* and *Butterflies*. This feature is the use of relative rankings of words in large databases as the source for the vocabulary component within the formula. Using average word frequency is a tricky business because a few hundred words in English, about 2 percent, account for approximately 80 percent of the words that appear in texts (Zeno, et al., 1995). The remaining 98 percent of the corpus appear much less frequently. In the Zeno, et al. (1995) corpus, approximately 86 percent of the almost 150,000 unique words appeared less than once per million words of text.

Even when algorithms are used to normalize a distribution, the distribution is so skewed that many texts receive a similar index for vocabulary. For example, the mean of the vocabulary index within the Lexile equation for the exemplar CCSS texts is 3.5 and the standard deviation is 0.21. The measure of sentence length shows considerably more variation: X = 14.95, SD = 4.8. As a result of so many words with similar ratings, more pressure within the readability formulas is on sentence length (Deane, et al., 2006). Within the sample of CCSS exemplar texts, the correlation between the Lexile and mean sentence length is 0.92, while that for the vocabulary measure is -0.46 (a negative correlation is expected since hard texts have lower vocabulary indices).

This heavy reliance on sentence length to define text difficulty creates its own set of problems; among them is the lack of knowledge as to how syntactic patterns can be taught, especially to English learners. Further, what we do know about syntax runs counter to assumptions made by readability formulas. According to the research, shorter sentences do not always make text easier. Short sentences tend to have fewer context clues and fewer links between ideas, requiring the reader to make more inferences. Even more troubling is the fact that sentence length is very easy to manipulate quickly. The consequences of such manipulation have been documented, as is discussed in the following section.

Potential Consequences

The temptation to rely on quantitative indices can be all too easy. When a policy document provides specific ranges, the temptation can move to an imperative. Quickly, we could return to the instructional and assessment contexts prior to *Becoming a Nation of Readers* (Anderson, et al., 1985) when writers were often asked to write texts to satisfy readability formula by using highly frequent words or short sentences (Davison & Kantor, 1982). The provision of specific quantitative ranges within the CCSS (see Table 11.1) could mean that states and large-city districts mandate particular readability levels in new assessments and textbook programs. Students could be reading inappropriate texts. For example, sixth graders (rather than high schoolers) could be asked to read texts such as *In the Time of the Butterflies* (Alvarez, 1994) and fifth graders (rather than second graders) given texts such as *Boy, Were We Wrong About Dinosaurs* (Kudlinski, 2005).

A second potential, unintended consequence is that publishers could return to rewriting texts to comply with readability formulas, rather than using the readability formulas as a general guideline (Davison & Kantor, 1982). A quick review of websites on the internet shows that some publishers are claiming to offer sets of CCSS-appropriate texts that have the same content but are at all of the grade bands in Table 11.1. How would a publisher achieve such a feat, when the vocabulary of texts at different levels varies considerably across grades? Hiebert (2012b) has illustrated how a classic text—*The Wind in the Willows*—can be transformed from college and career readiness to first grade Lexile levels by simply manipulating syntax.

The third potential and unintended consequence of specific quantitative indices is perhaps the most egregious. An easy to obtain measurement of a text's complexity can give educators the sense that they have identified appropriate texts and matched particular students with the texts. To provide texts that support students on the staircase of text complexity, educators need to understand the features of text that contribute to students' challenges with comprehension, vocabulary, and word recognition. Quantitative data may be quickly obtained but they fail to support teachers in understanding the features of complexity that challenge students at particular points on the staircase of reading.

Summary

By including a stand-alone text complexity standard, the CCSS shines a light on an issue worthy of research, discussion, professional learning, and informed classroom decisions with regard to texts and accompanying teaching practices. The effort was put together quickly—as is almost always the case with large-scale projects. We are hopeful, in writing this chapter, that there is an opportunity to consider potential consequences before their effects change the opportunities for thousands of students, especially those who live in high-poverty communities, to achieve high levels of literacy. The collective wisdom of scholars within the field of literacy needs to be brought to bear to the issues raised in this chapter—as well as to other issues (e.g., definitions of close reading). National conversations are needed to ensure that teachers can make informed decisions that support as well as challenge readers so that they not only learn to navigate over time increasingly more complex texts but also become readers who engage with sophisticated texts as active citizens.

References

ACT. (2006). *Reading between the lines: What the ACT reveals about college readiness in reading.* Iowa City, IA: Author.

ACT. (2010). *A first look at the Common Core and college and career readiness.* Iowa City, IA: Author.

Alvarez, J. (1994). *In the time of the butterflies.* Chapel Hill, NC: Algonquin.

Anderson, R.C., Hiebert, E.H., Scott, J.A., & Wilkinson, I.A.G. (1985). *Becoming a nation of readers: The report of the Commission on Reading.* Champaign, IL: The Center for the Study of Reading, National Institute of Education, National Academy of Education.

Bandeira de Mello, V. (2011). *Mapping state proficiency standards onto the NAEP scales: Variation and change in State Standards for reading and mathematics, 2005–2009* (NCES 2011–458). Washington, DC: National Center for Education Statistics, Institute of Education Sciences, U.S. Department of Education, Government Printing Office.

Betts, E. (1946). *Foundations of reading instruction, with emphasis on differentiated guidance.* New York: American Book Company.

Blaxall, J., & Willows, D. (1984). Reading ability and text difficulty as influences on second graders' oral reading errors. *Journal of Educational Psychology, 76,* 1, 330–340.

Bomer, R., & Laman, T. (2004). Positioning in a primary writing workshop: Joint action in the discursive production of writing subjects. *Research in the Teaching of English, 38,* 4, 420–466.

Cambourne, B. (1995). Toward an educationally relevant theory of literacy learning: Twenty years of inquiry. *The Reading Teacher, 49,* 182–192.

Carver, R., & Leibert, R. (1995). The effect of reading library books at different levels of difficulty upon gain in reading ability. *Reading Research Quarterly, 30,* 1, 26–48.

Chall, J. (1967/1983). *Learning to read: The great debate*, 3rd ed. Fort Worth, TX: Harcourt Brace.

Cohen, S., & Steinberg, J. (1983). Effects of three types of vocabulary on readability of intermediate grade science textbooks: An application of Finn's transfer feature theory. *Reading Research Quarterly, 19*, 1, 86–101.

Common Core State Standards (CCSS) Initiative. (2010). *Common Core State Standards for English Language Arts & Literacy in History/Social Studies, Science, and Technical Subjects.* Washington, DC: CCSSO & National Governors Association.

Compton, D., Appleton, A., & Hosp, M. (2004). Exploring the relationship between considering the reader-text match in first graders' self-selections during recreational reading. *Reading Psychology, 21*, 309–333.

Copeland, M., Lakin, J., & Shaw, K. (2012). *Text complexity and the Kansas Common Core Standards for English Language Arts and Literacy in History/Social Studies, Science, and Technical Subjects.* Retrieved from www.ccsso.org/Resources/Digital_Resources/ The_Common_Core_State_Standards_Supporting_Districts_and_Teachers_ with_Text_Complexity.html

Daane, M., Campbell, J., Grigg, W., Goodman, M., & Oranje, A. (2005). *Fourth-grade students reading aloud: NAEP 2002 special study of oral reading* (NCES 2006–469). Washington, DC: Institute of Education Sciences, U.S. Department of Education.

Davison, A., & Kantor, R. (1982). On the failure of readability formulas to define readable texts: A case study from adaptations. *Reading Research Quarterly, 17*, 2, 187–209.

Deane, P., Sheehan, K., Sabatini, J., Futagi, Y., & Kostin, I. (2006). Differences in text structure and its implications for assessment of struggling readers, *Scientific Studies of Reading, 10*, 3, 257–275.

Donovan, C., Smolkin, L., & Lomax, R. (2000). Beyond the independent-level text: Considering the reader-text match in first-graders' self-selections during recreational reading. *Reading Psychology: An International Quarterly, 21*, 4, 309–333.

Dray, A., & Selman, R. (2011). Culture and comprehension: A mixed methods study of children's responses to a fictional story about interracial conflict. *Reading and Writing Quarterly, 27*, 48–74.

Finn, P. (1978). Word frequency, information theory, and cloze performance: A transfer theory of processing in reading. *Reading Research Quarterly, 13*, 4, 508–537.

Foorman, B., Francis, D., Davidson, K., Harm, M., & Griffin, J. (2004). Variability in text features in six grade 1 basal reading programs. *Scientific Studies of Reading, 8*, 2, 167–197.

Fry, E. (1968). A readability formula that saves time. *Journal of Reading, 11*, 513–516, 575–578.

Gamse, B., Jacob, R., Horst, M., Boulay, B., & Unlu, F. (2008). *Reading First Impact Study Final Report.* Washington, DC: National Center for Education Evaluation and Regional Assistance, Institute of Education Sciences, U.S. Department of Education.

Gee, J. (2000). Discourse and sociocultural studies in reading. In M.L. Kamil, P.B. Mosenthal, D. Pearson, & R. Barr (Eds.). *Handbook of reading research v. 3* (pp. 195–207). Mahway, NJ: Lawrence Erlbaum.

Guthrie, J., Hoa, A., Wigfield, A., Tonks, S., Humenick, N., & Littles, E. (2007). Reading motivation and reading comprehension growth in the later elementary years. *Contemporary Educational Psychology, 32*, 282–313.

Guthrie, J., McGough, K., Bennett, L., & Rice, M. (1996). Concept-oriented reading instruction: An integrated curriculum to develop motivations and strategies for reading. In L. Baker, P. Afflerbach, & D. Reinking (Eds.). *Developing engaged readers in school and home communities* (pp. 165–190). Mahwah, NJ: Lawrence Erlbaum.

Halladay, J. (2008). *Difficult texts and the students who choose them: The role of text difficulty in second graders' text choices and independent reading experiences.* (Doctoral dissertation). Retrieved from ProQuest. (1685138491).

Hayes, D., Wolfer, L., & Wolfe, M. (1996). Schoolbook simplification and its relation to the decline in SAT-Verbal Scores. *American Educational Research Journal, 33,* 2, 489–508.

Hernandez, D. (2011). *Double jeopardy: How third-grade reading skills and poverty influence high school graduation.* Baltimore, MD: The Annie E. Casey Foundation.

Hiebert, E.H. (2010). *Have the texts of beginning reading been dumbed down over the past 50 years?* Retrieved from http://textproject.org/frankly-freddy/

Hiebert, E.H. (2011a). *Is reading in kindergarten the means for ensuring college and career readiness?* Retrieved from http://textproject.org/frankly-freddy/is-reading-in-kindergarten-the-means-for-ensuring-college-and-career-readiness/

Hiebert, E.H. (2011b). *Benchmark texts: Stepping up complexity.* Santa Cruz, CA: TextProject. Retrieved from http://textproject.org/teachers/benchmark-texts-stepping-up-complexity/

Hiebert, E.H. (2012a). The common core's staircase of text complexity: Getting the size of the first step right. *Reading Today, 29,* 3, p26–27.

Hiebert, E.H. (2012b). *Transforming texts from college-career to first grade: Effects of syntactic changes on quantitative measures of text complexity.* Retrieved from http://textproject.org/frankly-freddy/

Hiebert, E.H., & Pearson, P.D. (2010). *An examination of current text difficulty indices with early reading texts* (Reading Research Report 10.01). Santa Cruz, CA: TextProject, Inc. Retrieved April 1, 2011, from www.textproject.org/research/an-examination-of-current-text-difficulty-indices-with-early-reading-texts/

Jackson, R., McCoy, A., Pistorino, C., Wilkinson, A., Burghardt, J., Clark, M., Ross, C., Schochet, P., & Swank, P. (2007). *National evaluation of early Reading First: Final report.* Washington, DC: U.S. Department of Education, Institute of Education Sciences.

Kim, J. (2006). The effects of a voluntary summer reading intervention on reading achievement: Results from a randomized field trial. *Educational Evaluation and Policy Analysis, 28,* 4, 335–355.

Kim, J., & Guryan, J. (2010). Efficacy of a voluntary summer book reading intervention for low income Latino children from language minority families. *Journal of Educational Psychology, 102,* 1, 20–31.

Krashan, S., & McQuillian, J. (2007). The case for late intervention. *Educational Leadership, 65,* 2, 68–73.

Kudlinski, K. (2005). *Boy, were we wrong about dinosaurs.* New York, Dutton.

MetaMetrics. (2000). *The Lexile framework for reading.* Durham, NC: Author. Retrieved from www.lexile.com/about-lexile/lexile-overview/

Mullis, I., Martin, M., Gonzalez, E., & Kennedy, A. (2003). *PIRLS 2001 international report: IEA's study of reading literacy achievement in primary school in 35 countries.* Chestnut Hill, MA: International Study Center, Boston College.

Murata, K. (2007). Unanswered questions: cultural assumptions in text interpretation. *International Journal of Applied Linguistics, 17,* 1, 38–59.

National Center for Education Statistics. (2009). *The Nation's Report Card: Reading 2009* (NCES 2010–458). Washington, DC: Institute of Education Sciences, U.S. Department of Education.

Nelson, J., Perfetti, C., Liben, D., & Liben, M. (2012). *Measures of text difficulty: Testing their predictive value for grade levels and student performance.* New York: Student Achievement Partners.

Pearson, P.D., & Hiebert, E.H. (2010). National reports in literacy: Building a scientific base for practice and policy. *Educational Researcher, 39*, 4, 286–294.

Pimentel, S. (2012). *The Common Core State Standards: Supporting districts and teachers with text complexity.* Webinar presented through the Council of Chief State School Officers. Retrieved from www.ccsso.org/Resources/Digital_Resources/The_Common_Core_State_Standards_Supporting_Districts_and_Teachers_with_Text_Complexity.html

Smith, D., Stenner, A., Horabin, I., & Smith, M. (1989). *The Lexile scale in theory and practice* (Final report). Washington, DC: MetaMetrics. (ERIC Document Reproduction Service No. ED 307 577).

Spache, G. (1953). A new readability formula for primary-grade reading materials. *The Elementary School Journal, 53*, 410–413.

Suggate, S. (2009). School entry age and reading achievement in the 2006 Programme for International Student Achievement (PISA). *International Journal of Educational Research, 48*, 151–161.

Williamson, G. (2008). A text readability continuum for postsecondary readiness. *Journal of Advanced Academics, 19*, 4, 602–632.

Zeno, S.M., Ivens, S., Millard, R., & Duvvuri, R. (1995). *The educator's word frequency guide.* New York: Touchstone Applied Science Associates.

12

THE ROLE OF LITERATURE AND LITERARY REASONING IN ENGLISH LANGUAGE ARTS AND ENGLISH CLASSROOMS

Judith A. Langer

Editor's Note: In this chapter, Langer notes a disturbing shift from the centrality of literature in the English curriculum to a focus on literacy as a kind of autonomous process necessary for success in job and college. She points out the irony that other countries have recognized American school graduates as more creative, and so they are seeking to enrich their curricula at the same time that our students are being discouraged from creative responses.

KSG

Since literature became a school subject in the 19th century, it has played a central role in the K-12 English and English Language Arts (ELA) curriculum. What it would stress as important content and knowledge has changed from era to era, based on larger cultural forces that were pertinent to the times (Applebee, 1974). However, the centrality of literature in the English and ELA curriculum has historically remained constant. For example, starting with the *New England Primer* and extending through the McGuffy Readers, there was a widespread stress on moral and ethical traditions, and this affected the choice of literature to be read in the schools. In the 19th century, during an era of "faculty psychology," there was a stress on literature as a source of mental discipline, with a focus on literary history in English classes, with much to be memorized. During and after WW1, literature was seen as a source of patriotism and civic virtue, and this became a time when American Studies became a part of the curriculum. These kinds of change continued over time, with the more recent 20th century pedagogical foci reflecting the growing representation of diversity, and the inclusion of cultural and ethnic studies.

Since the early 21st century, a new phase has been creeping in, with college and career readiness as a focus in English (and all subject classes). From my perspective, the way this move is being conceptualized strikes at the very heart of literature as the central focus of the English curriculum, and is a major departure from the earlier shifts. There has been a turning away from the centrality of literature in the English and English language arts curriculum as a source of intellectual, moral, civic and/or ethical development, and a focus on English and ELA coursework as preparation for a set of more general literacy skills considered necessary to do well in college and the job world.

Literacy has long been considered important in the English curriculum: reading, writing and deep understanding and interpretation as well as the skills and strategies that enable them have always been taught across the changing times and across the school years. But literature has always been considered the central part of the curriculum, with literature as the vehicle through which to apply or to learn literacy. However, an essential change is taking place now, with the core central focus of English itself changing from literature to literacy.

For example, the curriculum is stressing more and more non-fiction as well as more content area reading material across the grades, with less and less literature expected to be read in English and ELA classes as the grade level increases. Also, the National Assessment of Educational Progress (NAEP) includes fewer literature selections as checks on comprehension, with more and more content reading passages being included as the grades increase. Further, the Common Core Standards do not specify what students should read or learn and know about literature, but instead focus on the complexity of the texts themselves.

This direction should be of concern not only to English and ELA scholars and practitioners, but to all who are concerned about student learning, not merely because students' developmental knowledge of literature is important, or because the content and cultural knowledge inherent in literature are important, but also because the reading of literature involves cognitive dimensions that are a critical component of intellectual development; dimensions that therefore make an important contribution to college and career readiness. It is this contribution that is being severely diminished, and in danger of being eradicated.

From my perspective, the ways in which we think when we read literature, and how this kind of thinking contrasts with and also works productively with how we think with informational material, is so important that it's been a central part of my research and scholarship for the past 25 plus years (see Langer 1986; 1990; 1992a; 1992b; 1994; 1995; 1995/2011; 2002; 2011a; 2011b). I don't claim to be the first one to have made this connection. Jerome Bruner (1986; 1990) and Suzanne Langer (1942/1967), each in their own way, argue that the well-developed intellect involves two different but complementary ways of viewing reality. So do James Britton (1970) and Louise Rosenblatt (1978). They each make slightly different arguments, but agree that there are these distinct ways of making sense, and that the well-developed mind does them both. There are other interesting bodies of work that are more work-related and point to these same complementary ways of making sense.

Julian Orr (1987a; 1987b), for example, studied what computer service workers do when they are called in to fix highly complex computers. He says they try to operate the computer, push buttons and call on some well-learned routines to make a diagnosis. But when they are stuck and cannot come up with a solution, they try to think of situations where similar or related problems might have existed. They then take turns telling "stories" about those situations, using storytelling as a way to spur them to think of possibilities that weren't coming to mind before. They create scenarios and search for possibilities in the storytelling mode.

In his book, *How Doctors Think* (2007), Jerome Groopman, a physician, describes how most doctors have been so well trained to follow diagnostic protocols that when the course of action that their protocol takes them to isn't helpful, they repeat the same steps time and again never putting those protocols aside to take a very different view of the problems. Thus many illnesses are never properly diagnosed or treated, alternative approaches to reasoning. Much of his book offers examples of successes. He counters the more limited approaches to non-traditional diagnostic problem-solving with descriptions of physicians who were more exploratory and open-ended in approaching their problems, and demonstrates how these quests led to heretofore unavailable diagnoses, in turn leading to different and more effective case-specific treatment.

We can also look at the research literature that focuses on creativity. Although conceptualized somewhat differently, it is relevant. Czikszentmihalyi (1996), for example, makes a distinction between creativity with a "Big C" and with a "small c." The Big C focuses on creativity as an act of genius (e.g., Koestler, 1964; Simonton, 1988; Wallace & Gruber, 1989), while the small c focuses on creativity as original acts that occur in everyday life. Halpern (1997) considers creativity to be marked by novel and appropriate responses to problems. (See Langer, 2011b for a further discussion of critical and creative thinking.)

Together, all this work resonates with my own (see Langer 1995/2011; 2011a). I make distinctions between ways in which we orient ourselves to make meaning, based on the primary reason we have for engaging in an activity in the first place: 1) to engage in a more information-getting, refining and concept-building experience like we usually do when we read to gain information, or 2) to engage in a more open-ended search like we usually do when we read literature. One is more focused, like hunting, and the other is more open and exploratory, like searching and gathering. The purposes of these orientations are different. We hunt when we want to gain particular information, particular kinds of information or when we want to build concepts (as when we search the web to learn more about hydrofracking). We search and gather when we want to collect ideas in a more exploratory and open-ended way (like the computer repairers or the exceptional doctors in Groopman's book). In both cases, as we strive to "make sense," we orient ourselves based on our purposes and direct our cognitive quests accordingly. Our cognitive problem-solving or search moves differ because our goals for the experience and our expectations about the kind of meaning we will come away with are different.

When our goal is to get information or build concepts, we expect to come away with some knowledge related to the topic we are investigating. By way of contrast, when our goal is to explore and discover, we expect to be filled with thoughts and images that we didn't imagine when we began the experience.

Maintaining a Point of Reference

When the purpose of the activity is primarily to gain concepts or information, the cognitive orientation involves "maintaining a point of reference." I use the word "point" because there is generally a particular kind of information we are after, at least in some broad sense. I use the word "reference" because we use this point as a guide to narrow in on what we think is relevant information and to filter out what we think is irrelevant. We try to narrow in on increasingly more specific meaning. When we maintain a point of reference, we usually have an idea of the content we are trying to gain information about; if not, from early on we try to establish a sense of that content, topic, author's point of view, bias, etc. Once decided, this sense of the whole becomes a steady reference point. As the experience progresses, we try to build upon, clarify, or modify our momentary understandings and check it to see how well it contributes to our understanding of the whole. As we move along, we try to remove ambiguities and build a web of understandings, all related to the information or ideas we are after. But we rarely change our overall sense of what the topic, the article, the book or documentary video is about—unless, of course, there is enough contradictory information to change our minds or enough of countervailing evidence that moves us to rethink it.

Exploring Horizons of Possibility

In contrast is the more open-ended search and gathering quest. I call it "exploring horizons of possibilities." I use the word "exploring" because we engage in the search activity explicitly for the open-ended nature of the experience. We let the experience lead us to meaning. When we are in a search and gather experience we ponder new ideas, calling on all we know, have experienced and can imagine to give us a fuller picture of the ideas and images that come to mind. I use the word "horizons" because as we ponder new possibilities, the overall shape of where our understandings might go (how the book may end or what the cause of the patient's problems might be) changes.

So, when exploring horizons of possibility, our thinking works on two planes simultaneously. It is as if you were rubbing your stomach and tapping your head at the same time. You might ask (from "Saraband," the last Ingmar Bergman film) "Why did she go back to see him after all those years? Will all the old patterns repeat themselves?" When you ponder your answers, the way you imagine how the story might end will change. You are exploring a relationship at the moment, but it also makes you look at its implications for the future of the movie—or the future of their time together. This double open-endedness comes from exploring possibilities. It is not an empty open-endedness, but one that is filled with a possibility of choice that is kept tentative—waiting for other possibilities to be considered. Each time, our search-and-gather acts lead us to consider different possibilities, our sense of the whole changes; it develops as our envisionments unfold. In my recent book, *Envisioning Knowledge* (2011a), I explore how Guttenberg created the printing press using both kinds of thinking. In a chapter I wrote for another book (2011b), I explore how Darwin used both kinds of thinking during his trips as he was creating his theory of the development of the species. Jerome Groopman and Julian Orr explain how these orientations are used on the job. In my two books *Envisioning Literature* (1995/2011) and *Envisioning Knowledge* (2011a), I explain how they are used at school and also how they interact with one another in ways that bring and extend understandings.

Educators in China and Japan have told me that in their countries they know how to make the best products, but the Americans come up with the new ideas. They want to add elements to their educational systems that will enable their teachers to help students become more creative. At the same time, the United States is diminishing this element in its educational systems.

What can be done to change these trends? First, educators and policy makers need to embrace the world-wide job-oriented focus on both critical and creative thinking. Across the world, universities are adopting mission goals related to innovation and creativity. Innovation and creativity have become expected ways of working throughout business and industry, and are becoming goals in more and more higher education. It involves not only enhancing students' abilities to integrate large amounts of information, evaluate its credibility and defend and argue for their choices, but students will also need to think flexibly, with agility and creativity. At the present time, even when students do have occasion and opportunity to think innovatively and creatively, most schools (including universities and many workplaces) have a tendency to ignore them. They set up a generational "barricade." By continuing in this manner, schools are failing to teach students to use those abilities in more and more substantive ways, around more complex information, ideas, and problems, which are at the heart of 21st century literacy and the 21st century workplace.

When I told my personal physician, who is a noted diagnostician, about Groopman's book and its relation to my work, he said, "Oh, I remember those classes. I kept thinking of other possible ways to look at the problem but was never given room to say what I thought. It was frustrating, but we didn't question it." My point is that education for all students of all ages needs to involve many experiences with both maintaining a point of reference and exploring horizons of possibility thinking across all the subject areas; both experiences, not one in favor of the other. Our goals toward school and success in the 21st century workplace demand this. However, we are presently in the process of increasing students' experiences with one and reducing their experiences with the other. My essential point is that literary activities and ways of thinking are an essential part of 21st century literacies, and for the preparation of college and career ready students. I worry that we are headed in the wrong direction, unwittingly limiting rather than expanding students' essential abilities needed for their, and our, success.

References

Applebee, A.N. (1974). *Tradition and reform in the teaching of English: A history*. Urbana, IL: National Council of Teachers of English.

Britton, J. (1970). *Language and learning*. London: Penguin.

Bruner, J. (1986). *Actual minds: Possible worlds*. Cambridge, MA: Harvard University Press.

Bruner, J. (1990). *Acts of meaning: Four lectures on mind and culture*. Cambridge, MA: Harvard University Press.

Czikszentmihalyi, M. (1996). *Creativity: Flow and the psychology of discovery and invention*. New York: HarperCollins.

Groopman, J. (2007). *How doctors think*. Boston, MA: Houghton Mifflin.

Halpern, D.F. (1997). *Critical thinking across the curriculum: A brief edition of thought and knowledge*. Mahwah, NJ: Lawrence Erlbaum.

Koestler, A. (1964). *The act of creation: The study of the conscious and unconscious in science and art*. New York: Dell.

Langer, J.A. (1986). *Children reading and writing: Structures and strategies*. Norwood, NJ: Ablex.

Langer, J.A. (1990). The process of understanding: Reading for literary and informational purposes. *Research in the Teaching of English*, 24, 3, 229–260.

Langer, J.A. (1992a). Rethinking literature instruction. In J.A. Langer (Ed.). *Literature instruction: A focus on student response*. Urbana, IL: National Council of Teachers of English.

Langer, J.A. (1992b). Discussion as exploration: Literature and the horizon of possibilities. In G. Newell, & R. Durst (Eds.). *Exploring texts: The role of discussion and writing in the teaching and learning of literature*. Norwood, MA: Christopher Gordon Publishers.

Langer, J.A. (1994). A response-based approach to reading literature. *Language Arts*, 71, 3, 203–211.

Langer, J.A. (1995). Literature and learning to think. *Journal of Curriculum and Supervision*, 10, 3, 207–226.

Langer, J.A. (1995/2011). *Envisioning literature*, 2nd ed. New York: Teachers College Press. (Presently being translated into Finnish.)

Langer, J.A. (2002). *Effective literacy instruction: Building successful reading and writing programs*. Urbana, IL: National Council of Teachers of English.

Langer, J.A. (2011a). *Envisioning knowledge: Building literacy in the academic disciplines*. New York: Teachers College Press.

Langer, J.A. (2011b). The interplay of creative and critical thinking in instruction. In D. Dai (Ed.). *Design research on learning and thinking in educational settings: Enhancing intellectual growth and functioning*, New York: Teachers College Press, 65–82.

Langer, S. (1942/1967). *Mind: An essay on human feeling*. Cambridge, MA: Harvard University Press.

Orr, J. (1987a). Storytelling as cooperative diagnostic activity. Field Service Manager. *The Journal of the Association of Field Service Managers International*. June, 47–60.

Orr, J. (1987b). *Talking about machines*. Palo Alto, CA: Army Research Institute.

Rosenblatt, L. (1978). *The reader, the text and the poem*. Cambridge, MA: Harvard University Press.

Simonton, D.K. (1988). *A psychology of science: Scientific genius*. New York: Cambridge University Press.

Wallace, D.B., & Gruber, H.E. (1989). *Creative people at work: Twelve cognitive case studies*. New York: Oxford University Press.

13

WRITING TEACHERS

The Roles Exploration, Evaluation, and Time Play in Their Lives

Jane Hansen

Editor's Note: Unlike reading, writing has not been the focus of organized attacks. That may be because it is not easy to come up with simplistic ways of organizing writing instruction. What happens instead is that policy makers emphasize simplistic aspects of writing: spelling, grammar, and usage, along with rubrics that assume rapid judgments of writing samples. In this chapter, Jane Hansen explores the wisdom of sensitive writing teachers in supporting the creative process. She points to the importance of early drafts and of finding the language to express what the writer is learning. What comes through is that authentic written expression develops in the context of creative construction, where the teacher serves as a mentor and coach, rather than an administrator of rules and conventions.

KSG

Writers explore, evaluate, and discipline their use of time. As writers ourselves, we teachers of writing find the nerve to write ourselves into new territories, and teach in ways we were not taught. We learn the value of the draft. It is where we, and our students, explore—our ideas, the edges of our knowledge, and our ways with words—and this challenges our thinking. We use writing to expand and clarify what we are beginning to know.

As we entice ourselves forward, we evaluate both processes and products—our own and those of our students. We wonder if we should write a draft from a different point of view, and we teach our students to wonder about their work. They must learn what works and what could be more effectively written if they are to become independent writers. To engage in the many decisions required by self-evaluation leads us, and our students, to intentionally become better at our work.

The overall context in which this happens places a philosophical umbrella over our writers' classrooms. The insistence that all students possess the nerve to let their voices boom across space influences how writing teachers spend their time. We spend a great deal of classroom instructional time strengthening our writers' voices, and a great deal of our outside time reading. Importantly, we not only read our students' words, we also read the literature of professional writers. In so doing, we carefully construct one hat to wear, whether we are reading the work of a novice or award-winning author. All are authorities on their own compositions, and we come to learn.

Writing Teachers and Students as Explorers

Explorers pursue many different treks and trails. This diversity hallmarks a writing class and, at the same time, can worry teachers. After many years of placing value on *voice* within writing, and *diversity* within our culture, these two issues continue to elude us. Then, to complicate matters, the two of them come together for writers. In classrooms of writers, each tries to be different; no two writers want to sound like any other! To feel comfortable writing about ideas that matter to them, students must be in classrooms where their ways with words are sought and valued.

Teachers, in order to understand the power of creating their own paper voices, write. They do not need to be published, but they need to write enough to know the art of what they are teaching. They need to know the angst and joy. They need to know what they do in order to create a draft, and what they do in order to move that draft along. As writers, teachers reflect on what they do to engage their writers in authentic experiences. And writing teachers study other writers so they know of various ways to go about the process of writing—processes actually used by "real" writers.

Writing Teachers Explore the Possibilities of Being Writers

Writing teachers are of many minds about being writers: "I'm scared of writing," "I can't write well enough," "I don't know what to write about." Our field is full of writing teachers who don't write, even though the importance of writing teachers being writers has been stressed at least as far as Murray (1968). There are, fortunately, increasing numbers of teacher-writers.

Recently, a third-grade teacher I know started to plan a unit on poetry, and it didn't occur to him to write. In our conversation, I learned that he had never written a line of poetry. I wondered aloud about that, and he said, "I don't know what to write about." So, he read 13 poems—all about different things—and started to write poetry. And so did his students.

In the classes that many of us teach at universities, we not only engage teachers in the act of writing, we engage them in the act of writing about what they did when they created a piece of writing, and this, at first, is hard. Teachers don't know what to write when we tell them to write a cover letter about the writing process they used to create that particular piece of writing. That request can be so foreign that teachers don't hear it, and write something like this in their cover letter: *I am presenting this to you as my class members for feedback to help me in the process.* Someone else may write: *I wrote this as a way to look forward to what I will experience when I go back to Texas.*

Soon, however, as we write in class, confer with them, they share for response, and they read our writing and cover letters, they do know what it means to write about, talk about, and intentionally use different writing processes, depending on what they are writing. Soon they write as much as 12 such lines: *This is the piece I started. . . . That first draft actually looked nothing like this. It didn't incorporate the song. . . . My second draft was a redraft of the first one . . . but, as I was writing it I realized that what I really wanted to express was . . . so I started over for my third. . . .*

When each of the pre- and in-service teachers becomes aware of the varied writing processes she uses, depending on whether she is writing poetry, an essay, or nonfiction about cardinals, she starts to expect variance within her students. Further, when we read each other's cover letters and talk in class about the differences among the writing processes each of us uses, we think about the variance among our students. If only one thing becomes clear, it is: There is no such thing as *the* writing process. Writers use various processes. They know about many and choose the ones that will work for them in a particular situation.

This tremendously affects what we do as teacher-writers. We use our own writing, that of professional writers, and the writing of the students, to teach the various options open to writers. In so doing, we learn: The wider we open the *territory to explore,* the greater the number of students who embrace writing.

Students Explore the Possibilities of Being Writers

Moffett (1968) started to set the stage for writers as explorers. Writers are not only to engage as writers in as many different discourses, genres, topics, and curriculum areas as possible, they are to keep themselves in their work. Contrary to writing only in English class, only within classic essays, and only in the third person, writers are to be upfront about who they are in relation to several ideas. To not write from a distant perspective keeps writing alive, keeps writers engaged, and keeps writing authentic.

The continuation of the idea of student writers as explorers, different from planners who outline their route before they begin, we move ahead only two short years (Macrorie, 1970). Students who engage in writing that is truthfully meaningful to them, who draft quickly, and who receive spontaneous, supportive response from peers, are on the path toward becoming writers.

Emig (1971) broke the field of writing instruction wide open with her research of 12th-grade writers. Her work remains the most cited in this field, and focuses us on the importance of honoring the composing process of young writers who are engaged, want their writing to be good, and work to make it so. To follow formulaic advice is not their bent.

Soon, the idea that the teacher should not step in as often as could be the case started to become more common—at least in the writings of academicians. Elbow (1973), praising Macrorie (1970) for his support, brought the teacherless writing class to the forefront. To clarify, he did not entirely think of a class with no teacher, but he decries the dominant instructional process used at his time, and to this day—40 years hence. One reason for the persistence of the old model: It promises structure and control and that's just what you yearn for when you're having trouble with writing (p. 72):

> And, even though that is what writers think they need, that is not what will help student-writers figure out the messy, alternative, diverse options they may consider when they draft and move forward the drafts they deem promising. Writers need to explore.

Lindfors (1980) showed this in relation to how children learn to talk. The better teachers understand the approximations of children the more likely they are to respond to young writers in ways that help them become confident. Language is language, and nearly every utterance is somehow new. For the speaker/writer to not fear her audience, she must know her listener will seek to understand. Otherwise, she will choose to remain silent.

Many teachers, however, interfere. We provide organization structures or other formulas and, thus, distort our students' notion of the creative exploration that language/writing require. Until we fully realize the reality of disorientation, the importance of writers/learners/lifers generating options and making decisions, we run the risk of turning them into nonwriters.

Whether today's students write in Manga format about cell division or in poetry about slavery, these writers explore in the presence of their peers, and benefit from interactions with them. The students look for difference, thrive on diversity, and find it interesting to see and hear what each other is in the process of creating. Many processes mark the classroom at any one time, all happening in classes where the student-writers, including young children, borrow and challenge each other's treks (Dyson, 1989).

The stance toward exploration keeps the energy high. Given the forays into new thoughts, territories, and processes, the value placed on "this is the first time" I've tried this (Mermelstein, 2007), keeps the writers engaged. Their writing time is one busy place, with lots of activity, lots of talk, and lots of writing going on.

Writing Teachers Use Evaluation to Guide Their Instruction

It can sound ordinary to use evaluation to guide instruction, but the typical place for evaluation, in many books about teaching, is in chapters at the end of the book. On the contrary, in writing instruction, evaluation precedes instruction. Further, it is evaluation of the writer more so than the writing. And, teachers perform a significant portion of this evaluation in the presence of the child, in the midst of the child's act of writing. To phrase it another way, the teacher, rather than turning to the next page in a language arts text, or studying test scores, turns to the next child on her list of students, and walks toward him for a conference. It is in the midst of these conferences, a few each day, that the teacher learns from her writers, teaches, feels the pulse of the class, and decides what may be wise to teach that particular child, or teach in an upcoming class lesson.

Over time, the teacher leads writers to study their own works and that of others to gain ideas for their own intentional progress. While they conduct their own all-class shares, she continues to reshape instruction based on what she hears, listens, and observes as they learn from and teach one another.

Writing Teachers Evaluate Writers at Work

When the teacher pulls a chair up beside a student-writer for a conference, the student knows the teacher has come to learn (Graves, 1983). The teacher is playing the role of a reader—readers read to learn. We learn from authors—authors are the *autho*rities on their own work, and we readers are interested.

In the classroom, the teacher seeks to learn, from each writer, what the writer is writing about and/or doing as a writer. The student-writer, in turn, realizes the genuine value the teacher places on him and his paper voice, "This teacher actually wants to understand what is distinctive about my thinking, my words."

Always, the teacher finds out whether the student is drafting, revising, or editing. While students draft, a conference may be very short, just a minute for the teacher to update herself on what the child is writing about, and the teacher leaves the student to resume his draft. Maybe the student was stuck, and the teacher asked a couple of questions to learn more about the worms, or whatever the little authority was writing about. The teacher asks genuine questions. Writing is not a game. The teacher honestly wants to know how deep the earthworms tunnel. When the writer knows what to write or what to research, the teacher is on to another student, leaving the engaged writer to work.

Maybe the writer at whose elbow the teacher stops is revising. A major task of the teacher is to find out what the one thing is the writer wants to say in this draft-to-become-a-piece-of-writing. It could be the student's focus is not apparent in the lead. When the student has a task, as with the student who is drafting, the teacher leaves the writer at work.

Teachers who forget to find out where the student is in his composing process sometimes interrupt a writer's generative process by pointing out a misspelled word. Or, while a child is revising, the teacher suggests the child elaborate on a certain scene, without realizing that the scene is not important to the point of the narrative. Or, while a child is editing for publication, the teacher may not assure the child that the brochure he is creating will actually appear, in multiple copies, in the school nurse's office.

The teacher keeps ongoing records of every writer she teaches. If they engaged in a teaching point, the teacher chooses something to record designed to have a lasting effect—something to help this child become a better writer.

This teacher is also considering which of these lessons could benefit other students in the class. It is from these conferences that she makes many of her decisions about what to teach (Anderson, 2000; Calkins, et al., 2005). Maybe the teacher uses one child's text with new headings as a lesson for the class. Or, the teacher invites the writer to use what he learned about headings as an upcoming mini-lesson for the class. These noticeable acts of evaluation continue to show the writers the value the teacher, and others, place on them and their writing.

Writing Teachers Teach Their Writers to Evaluate

The importance of teaching students to evaluate derives from a parallel practice among our profession—that of the teacher as reflective practitioner (Schön, 1983), or the slightly more recent notion of the teacher as researcher, honed by Gallas (2003). The teacher reflects, studies her own work in order to understand herself and her students. In so doing, she gains insights into her work, and plans for possible changes and growth.

Such teachers, in turn, teach their students to find value in: Their own writing, themselves as writers, their classmates, their classmates' work, and the work of professional writers. Student writers need to hear specific statements of value about their work. And they need to answer questions that show others they know even more about their topic than is on the page.

Before long the student can see himself as a writer and, by definition, writers always want to become better. No writer sees himself as stagnant into the foreseeable future. Writers make plans. And they evaluate their own growth.

The first-grade children in Kendra's classroom place their drafts on a document camera, read them to their awestruck classmates, and request response. Very carefully trained, these young writers lead the response to their work with statements and requests such as, "I want to add dialogue to my draft. Who should talk?" The classmates respond, "The boy!" "Well, I think the mother." And, "Dialogue is for both of 'em to talk!"

All of the above depend to a great extent on the writing teachers' uses of time. They provide regular, predictable, frequent time for their writers to share writing and reading for supportive response, to participate in conferences, to set goals and plans for their intentional growth, and to write and read.

Writing Teachers' Uses of Time

Writing teachers preserve, in their ultra-busy classrooms, time for their students to write, read like writers, talk, illustrate (with a broad definition, given the options available in our 21st century), and learn to project their ever-strengthening voices. It is the evolution of the person within that serves as the hallmark of strong writing instruction. All students' heads contain ideas; all ideas can find their way to paper.

It is much too common for students to be heard saying, "I don't have anything to write about." "I don't like to write." Or, worst of all, "I can't write." Those students are, in effect, saying, "I don't have anything to think about." "I don't like to think." Or, maybe worst of all, "I can't think."

Some of our students do find themselves with uncomfortable thoughts, and need to find themselves in a space where someone will hear their ideas. Fortunately, they can find themselves in classrooms where their teachers do create spaces in which students can explore and clarify their dreams (Ladson-Billings, 1994). These teachers place value on their writers' selves, and teach their writers to see value in their own thoughts and those of others.

Another precious feature of time is the amount of attention writing teachers devote to reading. They preserve, in their busy lives, time to read like writers, to read in the genres they write, to read, intentionally, in genres they do not write, to read the writing of their students, and to read about the teaching of writing.

Writing Teachers Live Amidst Strong Voices

The importance of student-writers' strong voices is not a new finding in writing instruction (Atwell, 1987), neither has it been abandoned (Tatum, 2010).

Heath (1983) may have opened the eyes of our profession to the dissimilarities we all knew in some ways. Her study of students in three different communities, all of whom attended one school and dwelt together in classrooms, showed us the differences in their roots and daily uses of language. She taught us to seek the differences, value them, and learn about them. To not try to erase them. To, instead, honor many ways with words.

Also during the 1980s, Taylor (1988) documented the rich, literate lives of inner-city children and, in contrast, the lack of agency they felt in school when their teachers assigned tasks the students saw as meaningless. Similarly, Rose

(1989) wrote about his own traumatizing experiences as a student who was seen by others as obviously different and, by inference, less talented.

James Gee (1990) emphasizes the importance of cultural settings, and Rief (1992), a middle school teacher capitalizes on his work. In a school not seen, typically, as diverse, she writes about the begetting of diversity, invitations across the curriculum, and infusion of the arts that release possibilities for her students' many voices.

Probably the greatest hindrance to students' success in schools is poverty. Solley (2005) underscores the importance of instruction of the highest quality that verifies, for students of poverty, several facts: they come to school with a great deal of knowledge, with many worthwhile ideas, and we can support their efforts to turn their tentative selves into strong paper voices

At a time when the United States is gaining large numbers of immigrants, Pransky (2008) writes about the intricate nature of understanding students different from us, and Fay and Whaley (2004), teachers in a school full of English Language Learners, show how the teachers in their school enable the writing of their students. Similarly, in her work with English Language Learners, Fu (2009) shows the importance of honoring writers' first language, and setting the students up for writing on their first day in this country. They are new, different, and hesitant. Right away, therefore, it is necessary for them to know their thoughts, words, and/or images count. Others are interested in them. Welcome!

Another sector of students sometimes overlooked are the very youngest ones. Horn and Giacobbe (2007), in their study of kindergarten writers, show the importance of talk and drawing to assist their entry into the world of writing, and others have shown the importance of writers' engagement as early as pre-kindergarten (Hansen, et al., 2010).

As writing teachers, we read our students' work—their strong voices on paper. To strengthen the shaky voices that come to us requires the hands-off approach advocated years ago, and still met with question.

At the same time, we know, as a profession, that many students are not only unengaged, our students, regardless of whether they are four or 14, come with full heads. Our task is to listen and to support their every effort to place their thoughts on paper. When they are strong, and can carry the additional idea of, "I'd like to do something with this draft so it is ready for publication," we offer supportive options for improvements. The going public of the paper voice reinforces the circle, strengthens this once-weak link, and the web of value strengthens.

Writing Teachers Spend Time Amidst the Words They Read

Writing teachers realize the role literature plays in their own growth as writers and teachers. They live amidst the words of professionals, their colleagues, and their students. Teachers notice ideas, formats, and ways with words they may try in their own work. We read as writers; we not only appreciate the character changes in a novel, the directions in a cookbook, the opinions in a blog, and the images in a poem—we take ideas from a blog for our poetry, a line from an editorial for a memo to our department head, and a line from a song for a short story.

We preserve time for the writers in our classes to read—to read like writers (Ray, 1999; Ray with Cleaveland, 2004). Writing teachers start to notice similarities between the reading processes we have used and taught for ages and the writing processes we now teach. As readers, we predict what will come next and as writers, we ask ourselves: What will my readers want to know next? As readers we infer, and student-writers learn to consider the inferences their readers will draw; these writers learn to include lots of information, but to leave out some for the reader to infer.

All of this depends on the writers actually writing for readers. Students write for themselves, for each other, and for a multitude of other writers, as we now open the world of writing to our students. Students write to community leaders, to students in other countries, and to others in their school.

Their teacher will be one reader, and she will read it as a reader who reads lots of materials with the eyes of a reader. This teacher has set up a classroom in which her students write real writing for real audiences, and she is right there, supporting them as they craft their message so their many readers will think it is great!

The teacher-reader also reads students' works with a fine-toothed comb. She artfully appreciates the forward motion of her writers (Shagoury, 2009). Over the years, she has acquired the great skills of readers of student writing: we read to see what writers understand from the worlds of content, what they know how to do as writers, and where they see themselves going. Gone are threats, red pens, squelching of voices, all of the weapons that we suffered as readers in days gone by. Instead, we appreciate our encounters with students' words—and they know we look forward to reading their words.

Closing Thoughts

Writing teachers admire the varied drafts and visions of the writers in their classes. The drafting process elicits many options, open to more formal decisions when and if these writers decide to turn them into final drafts.

In order to make revision decisions, young writers need the evaluation knowledge their informed teachers provide during individual conferences, and at various times during the periods of time when they write. Students learn to focus their writing, realize what's important, and create their paper voices.

In his book on the teaching of writing, Ralph Fletcher (2011), presents himself as a mentor author He shows teachers what he does, and invites them to be mentor authors in their classrooms.

References

Anderson, C. (2000). *How's it going? A practical guide to conferring with student writers.* Portsmouth, NH: Heinemann.

Atwell, N. (1987). *In the middle: Writing, reading, and learning with adolescents.* Portsmouth, NH: Heinemann.

Calkins, L., Hartman, A., & White, Z. (2005). *One to one: The art of conferring with young writers.* Portsmouth, NH: Heinemann.

Dyson, A.H. (1989). *Multiple worlds of child writers: Friends learning to write.* New York: Teachers College Press.

Elbow, P. (1973). *Writing without teachers.* London: Oxford University Press.

Emig, J. (1971). *The composing processes of twelfth graders.* Urbana, IL: National Council of Teachers of English.

Fay, K., & Whaley, S. (2004). *Becoming one community: Reading and writing with English language learners* (elementary). Portland, ME: Stenhouse.

Fletcher, R. (2011). *Mentor author, mentor texts: Short texts, craft notes, and practical classroom uses.* Portsmouth, NH: Heinemann.

Fu, D. (2009). *Writing between languages: How English Language Learners make the transition to fluency, grades 4–12.* Portsmouth, NH: Heinemann.

Gallas, K. (2003). *Imagination and literacy: A teacher's search for the heart of learning.* New York: Teachers College Press.

Gee, J. (1990). *Sociolinguistics and literacies: Ideology in discourses.* London: Falmer Press.

Graves, D. (1983). *Writing: Teachers and children at work.* Portsmouth, NH: Heinemann.

Hansen, J., Davis, R., Evertson, J., Freeman, T., Suskind, D., & Tower, H. (2010). *The PreK-2 writing classroom: Growing confident writers.* New York: Scholastic.

Heath, S.B. (1983). *Ways with words: Language, life, and work in communities and classrooms.* Cambridge: Cambridge University Press.

Horn, M., & Giacobbe, M. (2007). *Talking, drawing, writing: Lessons for our youngest writers* (K-1). Portland, ME: Stenhouse.

Ladson-Billings, G. (1994). *The dreamkeepers: Successful teachers of African American children.* San Francisco, CA: Jossey-Bass.

Lindfors, J. (1980). *Children's language and learning.* Englewood Cliffs, NJ: Prentice-Hall.

Macrorie, K. (1970). *Telling writing.* Rochelle Park, NJ: Hayden Book Company.

Mermelstein, L. (2007). *Don't forget to share: The crucial last step in the writing workshop.* Portsmouth, NH: Heinemann.

Moffett, J. (1968). *Teaching the universe of discourse.* Portsmouth, NH: Boynton/Cook.

Murray, D. (1968). *A writer teaches writing: A practical method of teaching composition.* Boston, MA: Houghton Mifflin.

Pransky, K. (2008). *Beneath the surface: The hidden realities of teaching culturally and linguistically diverse young learners K-6.* Portsmouth, NH: Heinemann.

Ray, K.W. (1999). *Wondrous words: Writers and writing in the elementary classroom.* Urbana, IL: National Council of Teachers of English.

Ray, K.W. with Cleaveland, L.B. (2004). *About the authors: Writing workshop with our youngest writers* (Grades K–1). Portsmouth, NH: Heinemann.

Rief, L. (1992). *Seeking diversity: Language arts with adolescents.* Portsmouth, NH: Heinemann.

Rose, M. (1989). *Lives on the boundary: The struggles and achievements of America's underprepared.* New York: Free Press.

Schön, D. (1983). *The reflective practitioner: How professionals think in action.* New York: Basic Books.

Shagoury, R. (2009). *Raising writers: Understanding and nurturing young children's writing development*. Boston, MA: Pearson.

Solley, B. (2005). *When poverty's children write: Celebrating strengths, transforming lives* (Grades K–5). Portsmouth, NH: Heinemann.

Tatum, A. (2010). *Reading and writing for resiliency DVD*. Portsmouth, NH: Heinemann.

Taylor, D. (1988). *Growing up literate: Learning from inner-city families*. Portsmouth, NH: Heinemann.

14

WHAT DO CHILDREN NEED TO SUCCEED IN EARLY LITERACY— AND BEYOND?

William H. Teale, Jessica L. Hoffman, and Kathleen A. Paciga

Editor's Note: Beginning reading instruction has alternatively had at its center literature, traditional phonics, and a set of mislabeled "scientifically-based" skills. This chapter traces the relation of these trends to children's learning, teachers' instruction, and educational policy goals present in U.S. literacy instruction from pre K-Grade 3, discussing policy forces that influence an "achievement gap" in how schools serve all children.

KSG

The literacy achievement gap refers to the disparity in academic performance between different groups—different, for example, in income, cultural background, or gender. In the United States, the literacy achievement gap means that, as a group, children from poverty backgrounds consistently score lower in reading and writing than children from middle- and high-income backgrounds and that a similar gap exists between African American and Latino students and their higher scoring Caucasian peers. The presence of this gap is illustrated with scores from the National Assessment of Educational Progress (NAEP), "Nation's Report Card" (Perie, et al., 2005), as summarized in Table 14.1. Because disproportionately high percentages of low-income, African American, and Latino children are found in most urban environments, the achievement gap is a particularly acute issue for urban schools. In fact, NAEP studies of fourth and eighth grade reading achievement in 11 urban districts conducted in 2007, 2009, and 2011 show that most of the existing gaps are significantly larger for urban students than for the overall student population (Table 14.1).

TABLE 14.1 Magnitude of the Achievement Gap, Report in Differences of NAEP Scale Scores

	African American / White gap		Latino / White gap		Poverty / Non-poverty gap	
	National	Urban	National	Urban	National	Urban
Grade 4						
2011	26	30*	25	29*	28	29
2009	25	32*	25	31*	26	28
2007	28	32*	26	32*	27	29
Grade 8						
2011	25	28	22	24	23	23
2009	27	29	24	27	24	24
2007	27	31*	25	28	24	23

* Statistically significant (higher) difference from National score

Addressing the Literacy Achievement Gap

Volumes have been written about reducing or eliminating the achievement gap, especially at the secondary school level, where differences are most pronounced and related to college entry and career readiness. What we argue for in this chapter is the need to address the literacy achievement gap at a much younger period in development—during the early childhood years, pre-K through grade 3. Our contention is that strong literacy curriculum during these years will do much to prevent the gap that continues as children proceed through school.

An ambitious, federal-level early education initiative related to the literacy achievement gap occurred from 2002 through 2008 in the United States. It was called Reading First (RF), a nationwide professional development and implementation effort guided by the findings of the *National Reading Panel* (National Institute of Child Health and Human Development, 2000) and implemented under the auspices of the No Child Left Behind (NCLB) legislation of 2001. It was designed to enhance beginning reading instruction, raise reading achievement for all students, and provide targeted support for the teaching of reading to the most economically challenged schools. RF was underwritten with considerable federal funding; more than US$4 billion were spent to improve reading instruction in the primary grades (K–3, students from 5–9 years old). The monies were aimed at helping schools with high percentages of children from families with incomes below the poverty line (see www.ed.gov/programs/readingfirst/index.html) and primarily funded teacher professional development, instructional materials, and literacy assessment programs. RF focused on "putting proven methods of early reading instruction in classrooms . . . to ensure that all children learn to read well by the end of third grade" (from www.ed.gov/programs/readingfirst/index. html), centering on having primary-grade teachers implement the "big 5"— phonological awareness, phonics, vocabulary, fluency, and comprehension—in teaching reading.

Ultimately, RF imploded because of improprieties with respect to conflict of interest among government officials and university consultants (Dillon, 2006). A government report indicated it had wasted $6 billion dollars with no benefit (Gamse, et al., 2008), but there were also those who argued that it had positive effects on early literacy achievements (e.g. Spellings, 2007).

The Curriculum Gap—What Is It, Why Is It, and Why Does It Matter?

The RF investment in improving early literacy instruction was certainly welcome, and the authors of this chapter continue to believe firmly that the so called "big five" foundational pillars are components of a quality beginning reading program. But, as we noted, in 2007 a disturbing trend also resulted from the impact of RF on early literacy instruction in urban classrooms in the United States. We referred to this trend as the curriculum gap, the absence or insufficiency of attention to certain curriculum elements critical for continued success in reading and writing. Our visits to urban primary-grade classrooms and our conversations with curriculum directors, reading specialists, and literacy coaches indicated three significant dimensions to the curriculum gap:

- Comprehension instruction.
- Instruction focused on developing children's knowledge of the world in general and of core concepts in content domains like science and social studies.
- Writing instruction.

At that time, this gap could be traced to the professional development teachers received and the student assessment instruments typically used as part of RF. Although based on the "big five" foundational pillars, the RF message that large numbers of K–3 teachers in urban schools took from their participation in RF and associated assessments of adequate yearly progress (AYP) was that reading instruction in the early grades is fundamentally about children learning phonological awareness, how to decode, and how to read words accurately and fluently.

Since that time, early literacy practices have changed and not changed. The instructional orientation described above still features centrally in the educational landscape in the Obama educational platform. And, largely because it acquired such a foothold as part of RF during the Bush era, DIBELS (or DIBELS-like) testing is now essentially second nature to most K–2 teachers in urban schools. Other writers have commented at length on the limiting influences of such assessments on curriculum, instruction, and school experience (e.g., Meier & Wood, 2004; Pearson, 2006); and we shall not reiterate the details of those arguments here. What is important to point out, however, is that the impact of these assessments has been so profound that vast numbers of primary-grade teachers have come to view early literacy instruction as focused on a limited set of foundational literacy skills. In that sense, such assessment processes contribute directly to the curriculum gap addressed here.

Comprehension Instruction Gap

Sustained and strategic attention to comprehension is still absent in far too many primary-grade urban classrooms. We suspect this is largely because the litany many primary teachers have taken to heart goes something like the following:

- Reading words accurately and fluently is the key to comprehension.
- Lots of practice with grade-level text is the key to developing fluent word recognition.
- The conceptual load in K–3 grade-level texts is simple.
- Therefore, as long as one teaches word-recognition skills, comprehension will pretty much take care of itself.

There is quite a bit of truth in the first three points. But the final point is problematic, and using all four of these tenets as the guiding principles for a beginning reading program means that teachers get the message that comprehension instruction is something that can (or even should) be put off until later grades. For two main reasons, we believe such a perspective is, in the long term, a recipe for reading disaster—especially for urban children.

First, although it is a fact that an unacceptably large number of primary-grade children in urban schools historically have failed to master two of the foundational skills of reading—phonics and fluency—they are by no means all that is necessary to help these young children become successful readers. During the primary grades it is also critically important to teach children appropriate comprehension strategies and skills that enable them to understand texts that are more complex than those made of everyday words they already know and conversations they routinely hear.

Second, focusing merely on accurate and fluent word recognition makes the content and quality of what children read less important for teachers to consider in selecting and evaluating the texts that children will interact with. Teachers and children in the United States are fortunate to have a rich body of children's literature available, but that literature gets little more than lip service where the emphasis is on short-term reading achievement goals coupled with the relative lack of attention to long-term goals. When we think long term, one of the most important questions to be asked is, "What is going to make young children be readers, now and when they are teenagers and adults?" The answer to that question lies solidly in the realm of ideas, of content—the stories and information in the pages of books and magazines and on the screens of computers and iPads. Successful readers do not result merely from having young children practice reading texts that have transparent, innocuous, or sometimes rather inane ideas.

Good texts are key to creating good readers. And for the many urban children who do not find much support in their home or community environments for interacting with extended written texts, the school is an especially important source of their developing comprehension, argumentation, and critical thinking abilities.

Background/Domain Knowledge Gap

All states in the United States have learning standards for social studies and science in each of the primary grades, and the Common Core State Standards have recognized the important link between literacy and disciplinary learning, as evidenced by their emphasis on "Literacy in History/Social Studies, Science, and Technical Subjects" (see www.corestandards.org/, Appendix A). Also, almost every teacher we work with is well aware of the connection between background knowledge and reading comprehension. Yet, when we examine what happens in primary-grade classroom instruction, we come to the conclusion that in many instances the connection between disciplinary knowledge and early literacy achievement is not viewed as a priority.

A study completed by the Center on Education Policy (CEP, 2007) is very telling on this point. The CEP surveyed 349 school districts and conducted additional in-depth district- and school-level interviews in 13 school districts. Results showed that about 62 percent of districts overall and 77 percent of urban districts had increased time for English language arts instruction considerably since 2002; *and* that to enable this increase, 44 percent of districts substantially reduced instructional time in other subject areas. Moreover, the reduction in instruction in other content areas was even greater in districts that had at least one school identified as needing improvement under NCLB and in urban districts. For example, more than half of the districts with at least one identified school reduced instructional time in social studies by an average of 90 minutes per week; and 43 percent of such districts cut science instruction by an average of 94 minutes per week (CEP, 2007, p. 7).

What this means is that many primary-grade children in urban schools are being shortchanged on domain specific knowledge. "So what?" some would argue—those children are getting a better foundation in literacy. It could appear that way, and it may even show up that way in those mandated K–3 assessments: Scores on tests of phonics skills, word recognition, and word reading speed and accuracy may well rise a bit in the short run. But what happens in fourth or seventh or tenth grade when what it takes to be a good reader depends even more on vocabulary knowledge, domain knowledge, and the ability to comprehend a variety of genres of text at a deep level? Our observations indicate that the initial "bump" at best fades away by fifth or sixth grade and at worst translates into an even larger achievement gap. Why? Because what are being treated *in practice* as the foundational skills of reading represent only a part of what children need to learn during the primary grades and continue to be good readers in upper elementary school, middle school, and high school. In other words, we may well be losing more than we are gaining by increasing attention to reading instruction, *if* it is being done at the expense of instruction in content areas such as science and social studies.

Writing Instruction Gap

Another legacy of the six-year influence of RF was that urban primary-grade classrooms increasingly focused on just that—*reading*. Beginning in 2000, Chicago Public Schools (CPS), for example, implemented a Reading Framework that equally emphasized instruction in word knowledge, fluency, comprehension, and writing at all grade levels. By 2007 the district's program evaluation data from primary-grade classrooms indicated such a lack of instructional attention to writing that CPS focused its entire district-wide literacy professional development on writing for an entire school year.

Such a pattern happened in a number of urban districts. Instead of capitalizing on the well-documented connections between reading and writing (Shanahan, 2005), the elements of reading instruction took over a number of "literacy blocks." Writing is an excellent way to foster phonological awareness skills (Schickedanz & Casberge, 2009; Snow, et al., 1998) and awareness of the functions and uses of literacy (Vukelich & Christie, 2009), as well as being important for its own sake as a significant part of early literacy learning (Schickedanz & Casberge, 2009; Van Sluys, 2011). As the Common Core State Standards become implemented, the presence of writing in the curricula of the primary grades will likely increase since the standards explicitly describe text types that primary-grade children benefit from composing, and the two consortia approved to develop aligned assessments plan to assess achievement of writing standards at all levels.

The Curriculum Gap and Urban Schools—What Is to Be Done?

The first years of school are critical to children's development as capable and lifelong readers and writers. This period is the time for learning foundational literacy skills and dispositions. But it is essential—especially for children who depend heavily on the school as a place for their early literacy learning—that the curriculum encompasses all aspects of the foundation in order to promote long-term growth in literacy. A focus on phonological awareness/decoding, word recognition, and fluency instruction is central to early literacy development. However, as we have attempted to show, other foundational aspects of literacy are also essential but often missing from or only attended to in passing in daily instruction in urban K-3 classrooms, thus creating a severe curriculum gap. Lack of sustained instructional attention to comprehension, disciplinary knowledge, and writing in the early grades is rather like expecting children to grow up to be healthy teenagers with a childhood diet of meat and potatoes but no fruits or vegetables.

The curriculum gap must be bridged if we hope to ameliorate the achievement gap. This necessitates rethinking early literacy programs so that they systematically attend to helping children develop comprehension and writing skills as well as letter knowledge, letter–sound correspondence, and word recognition skills. It also necessitates rethinking how much and in what way subjects like social studies and science are taught in the primary grades. Such instructional changes likewise imply reform of early literacy assessment programs, so that what is counted in terms of early literacy development is what really counts. In essence, we encourage primary-grade educators to think comprehensively about what constitutes a good beginning in reading and writing, because a good ending is far more likely when there is a good beginning.

Acknowledgment

This chapter is based on Teale, W.H., Paciga, K.A., & Hoffman, J.L. (2008). Beginning reading instruction in urban schools: The curriculum gap ensures a continuing achievement gap, *The Reading Teacher, 61*, 4, 344–348.

References

Center for Education Policy (CEP). (2007). *Choices, changes, and challenges: Curriculum and instruction in the NCLB era.* Washington, DC: Author.

Dillon, S. (2006). Report says education officials violated rules. *New York Times,* September 23. Retrieved July 30, 2007, from www.nytimes.com/2006/09/23/education/23education.html

Gamse, B.C., Bloom, H.S., Kemple, J.J., Jacob, R.T. (2008). *Reading First Impact Study: Interim Report* (NCEE 2008–4016). Washington, DC: National Center for Education Evaluation and Regional Assistance, Institute of Education Sciences, U.S. Department of Education. Retrieved from http://ies.ed.gov/ncee/pdf/20084016.pdf

Meier, D., & Wood, G. (2004). *Many children left behind: How the No Child Left Behind Act is damaging our children and our schools.* Boston, MA: Beacon Press.

National Institute of Child Health and Human Development. (2000). *Report of the National Reading Panel. Teaching children to read: An evidence-based assessment of the scientific research literature on reading and its implications for reading instruction.* (NIH Publication No. 00–4769). Washington, DC: U.S. Government Printing Office.

Pearson, P.D. (2006). Foreword. In K.S. Goodman (Ed.). *The truth about DIBELS.* (pp. v–xix). Portsmouth, NH: Heinemann.

Perie, M., Grigg, W., and Donahue, P. (2005). *The Nation's Report Card: Reading 2005* (NCES 2006–451). Washington, DC: U.S. Department of Education, National Center for Education Statistics, U.S. Government Printing Office. Retrieved from www.nces.ed.gov/nationsreportcard/pdf/main2005/2006451.pdf

Schickedanz, J., & Casberge, R. (2009). *Writing in preschool,* 2nd ed. Newark, DE: International Reading Association.

Shanahan, T. (2005). Relations among oral language, reading, and writing development. In C. MacArthur, S. Graham, & J. Fitzgerald (Eds.). *Handbook of writing research* (pp. 171–185). New York: Guilford.

Snow, C.E., Burns, M.S., & Griffin, P. (Eds.). (1998). *Preventing reading difficulties in young children.* Washington, DC: National Academy Press.

Spellings, M. (2007). *Reading First: Student achievement, teacher empowerment, national success.* April. Retrieved July 30, 2007, from www.ed.gov/nclb/methods/reading/readingfirst. html, http://ies.ed.gov/ncee/pdf/20084016.pdf

Van Sluys, K. (2011). *Becoming writers in the elementary classroom.* Urbana, IL: National Council of Teachers of English.

Vukelich, C., & Christie, J. (2009). *Building a foundation for preschool literacy,* 2nd ed. Newark, DE: International Reading Association.

15

THE "IMPACT" OF CHANGING CONCEPTIONS OF LANGUAGE ON CURRICULUM AND INSTRUCTION OF LITERACY AND THE LANGUAGE ARTS

David Bloome and Melissa Wilson

Editor's Note: Consider government authorities that have written laws and mandates based on a simplistic, narrow, and decontextualized view of written language instruction, a view that is limited to questions about whether analytic or synthetic phonics should be the basis of beginning reading and writing instruction as discussed in the chapters by Dombey, Ellis, Fijalkow, and others. Would the child whose writing is considered in this chapter be appreciated as a developing writer who is using his awareness of the functions and systems of language? Or would his spelling and grammar be corrected?

Would he even have had the time and opportunity to have produced such examples if the curriculum defines written language as an autonomous skill that prioritizes the ability to sound out nonsense digraphs in three seconds? Would this child have a hug from his apologetic teacher for imposing her grief on him? Or would he be humiliated by failing a phonics test the first week in his new school?

This chapter presents a history of the scholarship on language development that is now devalued and marginalized by many governmental decision makers. It shows the remarkable knowledge that should be available to teachers if they were to become skilled "kidwatchers." How fortunate is the child who is learning to read and write with the support of kidwatchers who use their knowledge as professionals to understand, encourage, and value the child's progress? And how unfortunate that there is little support for activities such as the "Impact" conferences hosted by Yetta Goodman as President of the National Council of Teachers of English, and by Dorothy Strickland, President of the International Reading Association in 1979 and the 1980s.

KSG

Lamarr's First Grade Writing

At the beginning of the school year, Lamarr's (pseudonym) mother had told his teachers that she had been the victim of violent domestic abuse during the previous year. She had left the abusive relationship and entered a program that provided her and her children with shelter, counseling, and skills to find a job and housing. Lamarr had been enrolled in a new school as part of this process; he was repeating first grade after tests showed that he was not reading on grade level.

His teacher asked him and his classmates to respond to the question "Why is it important to learn how to read?" His response is shown in Figure 15.1. He wrote, "It is npornt [important] to read because if you don't read you won't go to colich [college] and you will be a bum on the stret [street]."

The picture that accompanies Lamarr's writing shows a figure holding a rectangular shape with the number six on it ("a six pack") standing by an empty trashcan on the street showing us a sad face.

In the spring of that school year, Lamarr was working with his Reading Recovery teacher, Miss G. (they had worked together every day for half an hour since

FIGURE 15.1 "Why Is It Important to Learn How to Read?"—Lamarr's Response

the semester break in January). Near the end of the lesson, she received a long distance call on her cell phone from her brother in Chicago, which she answered. This is not something she would have normally done while she was working, but her father was having a pacemaker replaced and she suspected her brother was calling to let her know that her father was out of surgery. In fact, he called to tell her that their father had died.

When Miss G. heard this unexpected news, she burst into tears, indeed, into wails of shock and pain that could be heard in the classroom next door. Teachers quickly hurried over to find out what had happened; one teacher stayed to comfort Miss G. while the other took Lamarr to join the music class. Miss G. went home but returned later that day for the afternoon session.

That evening, Miss G. realized that she had probably scared Lamarr rather badly. She thought that, because of his experiences with domestic abuse, he might associate crying women with his own terrible and horrifying memories. As she would not be at school the next day, she called Lamarr's regular classroom teacher at home that evening and asked that she explain to Lamarr the next morning when he came in what had happened and give him a big hug from her.

Lamarr's teacher delivered Miss G.'s message to Lamarr and gave him a hug when he arrived in the classroom the next morning. As the teacher was doing various chores to start the day, and as the students were continuing work on their research reports, Lamarr wrote a sympathy note to his Reading Recovery teacher (Figure 15.2).

Perhaps to keep his teachers happy, he drew the picture about his research topic (bees). In Figure 15.2 we can see a drawing of a boy (labeled with his initial) holding a net standing under a tree with a wasp-style hive hanging from a tree. There was a bee (labeled bee) flying away from the figure with the net and two ducks (also labeled) swimming in a pond by his feet.

How might we, as researchers and educators, understand these writing events involving Lamarr?

In this chapter, we briefly consider the impact of conceptions of language on curriculum and instruction of literacy and the language arts. We are concerned with both the official and explicit curriculum and instructional processes and with the so-called "hidden" ones including what is known, how it is known, and most importantly what it means to be a human being in the world. As Williams (1977, p. 21) writes, "A definition of language is always, implicitly or explicitly, a definition of human beings in the world."

We begin with a discussion of the "Impact" conferences of the late 1970s through the 1990s (see Goodman, et al., 1980; Jaggar & Smith-Burke, 1985). Then, we examine how recent discussions of language since the "Impact" conferences might yet again redefine curriculum and instruction for literacy and language arts education. In this second section we focus on two directions for defining language: the first is grounded in the ethnography of communication and related theories of language and social processes; while the second is grounded in definitions of language derived from the Bakhtin Circle and the philosophy of

FIGURE 15.2 Lamarr's Sympathy Note to His Reading Recovery Teacher

Martin Buber. We will use the writing events involving Lamarr above to illustrate issues across the theories.

Before we begin, two caveats are needed. First, there are many definitions of language; in this chapter we are only addressing a small number of them as there is not space here for discussion of a broader range. Second, differing definitions of language provide different interpretations of language events, such as the writing events described above. This might lead people to view curriculum and instruction of literacy and the language arts as a relativist endeavor; "it all depends on the framing." In order to hold a relativist view, one must view definitions of language as neutral with regard to the social, cultural, political, and economic consequences for people across diverse configurations and groups; and similarly so the rationalities underlying the conduct of social science. However, as Clifford and Marcus (1986), Flyvbjerg, et al. (2012), Luke (1988), and Street (1995b; 2003), among others, argue, there is no neutrality. Acknowledged or not, researchers of language and literacy are inherently involved in discussing what it means to be human; and given the use of "science" representations in social policy (Moss, 2012), mass media (Flyvbjerg, 2012), and in framing daily life (DeCerteau, 1984; Lefebvre, 2009), it is a discoursing with consequences.

The "Impact" Conferences

There is a history to considering the impact of conceptions of language on curriculum and instruction, most prominently the "Impact" conferences sponsored by NCTE (National Council of Teachers) and IRA (International Reading Association) from the late 1970s through the early 1990s. Those conferences brought together linguists, sociolinguists, scholars of child language development, and psycholinguists, with educational researchers, educators, and scholars of reading, writing, and literacy. Together they asked, "What might be the impact of newly evolving theories of and research on language and on child language development on curriculum and instruction in reading and the language arts?"

The answer to that question began with axioms that criss-crossed diverse approaches to linguistics (e.g., theoretical linguistics, cf., Chomsky, 1957; systemic linguistics, cf., Halliday, 1993):

- all children are language learners;
- all languages equally provide ways of expressing meaning and exploring the world; and
- language learning requires active engagement with the world through the use of language.

These axioms define, in part, what it means to be human. As Goodman (1979, p. 153) wrote, "To be born human is to be born with a potential for thinking, for knowing, for understanding, for interacting, for communicating, for developing language."

Designs for curriculum and instruction, whether in early childhood or adolescent years, whether in the language arts or in subject matter disciplines, needed to acknowledge that "language" was located within the child (the child as inherently a language learner) as well as out in the world. These curricular and instructional theories offered an alternative to dominant theories of curriculum and instruction that focused on the incremental accumulation of discrete reading and writing skills. Learning to read and write was viewed as a language development process and parallels were drawn between the development and learning of spoken language and the development of written language (Goodman & Goodman, 1979). These curricular and instructional theories also offered an alternative to implied definitions of human beings as merely sets of stimulus-response-reinforcement shaping and of some human beings as inherently deficit in language learning because of race, culture, or socio-economic class.

One aspect of the Impact conferences was "kidwatching": paying close attention to what children do with language, and trying to make sense of it based on theories of language and language development (Goodman, et al., 1980; Goodman, 1985). For example, consider Figure 15.1, which shows a child writer who knows what sentences are, has a concept of punctuation conventions (e.g., that periods end sentences, sentences begin with upper case letter), uses word order to signal syntactic relationships among words and phrases, uses complex verb tenses, and connects the meaning of the text to a visual representation. Spelling patterns reveal efforts to sound out words (e.g., "n" for "im" in "important," and "lich" for "lege" in "college") while not yet fully mastering all of the rules governing representations of vowel sounds. The child also appears to know that the purpose of writing is to communicate meaning. If what is seen in Figure 15.1 is part of an evolving pattern for this child across time, teachers would be able to track the child's progress in developing written language concepts noting the grapho-phonemic, syntactic, and semantic principles the child has acquired thus far, and what language strengths can be employed as a basis for instruction. What can be seen in Figure 15.1 is a child who is making sense of the explicit and implicit structure and nature of written language as a means to express meaning by using his inherent competence in language development. A curriculum derivative of the Impact conferences is the continued provision of opportunities to explore language, so that the child can further explore and acquire the patterns, principles, and concepts of language, both spoken and written.

Kidwatching, the close observation of the child as a language learner, was a key ontological tool of the theories of language promulgated through the Impact conferences. While derivative of the application of theories of language to practice, in fact, kidwatching entails a paradigmatic shift in the relationship of theory and practice and the relationship of researchers and teachers with regard to theorizing reading and writing curriculum and instruction. Kidwatching implicitly pushed for the interplay of extant theories of language with close analysis of particular,[1] concrete language events that emphasize local knowledge. Rather than a top-down dynamic view of theory *into* practice, kidwatchers viewed theory *and* practice as reciprocally informing and mutually defining.

Kidwatching placed a premium on knowledge and theorizing in and of the particularity of children's use of language structures and related psycholinguistic processes. In order to craft context-sensitive learning opportunities that would actively engage students, teachers needed to be knowledgeable about how children acquired language and how they used language for learning. Teachers needed to be keenly observant of what children were doing with language, and to view themselves as theorists constructing a praxis.

Although perhaps not well recognized at the time, the underlying shift in the relationship of theory and practice offered a paradigmatic shift in what constituted knowledge for curriculum and instruction. Although curriculum theorists such as Dewey (1902) had offered conceptions of curriculum that emphasized both the child and the curriculum, here was an underlying epistemology for language and literacy education that linked what was to be learned with how learning occurred with how knowledge of language and learning were generated in the abstract and in the particular. That is, the knowledge defining curriculum and instruction derived not just from theories from "above" (from abstract theories of language generated at a distance by university-based scholars and similar sources) but also from theories grounded in the particular language events of particular classrooms and communities and in the actions people (teachers and students) took to act within and on those events. The dialectic process inherent in kidwatching also called for changes in the relationship of researchers located at universities and teachers. Curriculum and instruction had been defined by renowned scholars and educators and handed down to teachers to implement (often through a basal reader or the scope-sequence of a reading program); theory was the province of scholars, and teachers were relegated to apply theory to practice. Kidwatching placed as much value on "theorizing up" from the particulars of naturally occurring language events as it did on "theorizing down" from extant theories and research. Teachers were to be considered collaborators in theory-making.

In summary, the Impact conferences defined the child as a language learner and as a user of language for learning and generated conceptions of teaching, learning, and curriculum based on that conception of being human.

Definitions of Language Derived from the Ethnography of Communication

The theories of language that informed the Impact conferences focused on formalisms (i.e., idealized language structures) and on the child. Acknowledgment of social and cultural contexts focused on language variation (Goodman & Buck, 1973) and systems of social semiotics (Halliday, 1978). Grounded in cultural and linguistic anthropology, the ethnography of communication (also known as sociolinguistic ethnography) rejected the distinction between language as a set of idealized structures and speaking, supplanting the concept of linguistic competence with the concept of communicative competence (Hymes, 1974). The unit of analysis was the speech event: a contextualized, embodied communicative interaction of people acting and reacting to each other. This unit of analysis implies a definition of being human as being inseparably part of social interactions with others. Metaphorically, it is as Yeats (1968) wrote: "O body swayed to music / O brightening glance / How can we know the dancer from the dance?"

The application of the ethnography of communication to the study of literacy and language arts in education has covered a broad range of educational events and settings (classrooms, tutorials, families, apprenticeships). An early emphasis was placed on cultural variations in how students used spoken and written language in classroom literacy events, how educators responded to those variations, and how attending to and building on culturally derived ways of using spoken and written language might provide students with access to the literacy practices of academic communities (Au, 1980; Erickson & Mohatt, 1982; Heath, 1982; Lee, 2007; Philips, 1983; Scollon & Scollon, 1981; Street, 1995a). Emphasis was also placed on redefining teaching and learning as a language-in-context process (Green, 1983), in which students played roles as cultural beings and members of multiple cultural communities, who were socialized into multiple academic communities, each with its own ways of using written language (Yeager, et al., 1998). The social construction of what counts, *in situ,* as reading, writing, literacy, knowledge, learning, teaching, and academic achievement, as well as the *in situ* social construction of social identities including gender, race, class, struggling reader, precocious reader, writer, etc., supplanted presumed decontextualized and universalistic cognitive and linguistic processes as the locus for reading and literacy research.

Under the broad banner of discourse studies (Bloome, et al., 2009; Martin-Jones, et al., 2008; Rex, et al., 2010), educational researchers began to explore how people used language, literacy, and other semiotic systems to structure (and restructure) social systems and power relations, to impose and maintain cultural ideologies; as well as how people adapted extant ways of using language and literacy to challenge, deconstruct, and reconstruct who they were socially, what it meant to be human, and the social systems and structures that supported existing definitions and practices.

From the preceding discussion, several axioms emerge pertaining to curriculum and instruction:

- People act and react to each other, primarily through language and related semiotic systems.
- The use of language reflects and is influenced by the social situations and social contexts of use; the social situations and social contexts in which people find themselves reflect and are influenced by language use.
- There is no separation between people and the social and cultural events of which they are a part; the unit of analysis therefore is the embodied social event.
- Literacy encompasses a diverse set of social and cultural events and practices involving written language (in non-trivial ways).

Consider Lamarr's composition in Figure 15.1. Given a definition of language derived from the ethnography of communication and related theories of language and social processes, the questions to ask are not about whether Lamarr has acquired the concept of word, phonemic awareness, or particular syntactic structures as decontextualized skills. Nor is it to ask whether he has constructed a coherent message using his knowledge of the social semiotic system of written English. Rather, the more telling questions are: what social events and contexts provided opportunities for Lamarr to acquire the literacy practices represented in Figure 15.1, literacy practices of a particular kind of moral rationality within a particular social genre? What social events, contexts, and structures are indexed by the implied "if, then" rationality in his writing, and in his use of the binary opposition of "go to colich [sic]" versus being "a bum on the stret [sic]"? What were the events that provided Lamarr with the communicative competence to know how to use written language appropriately in this situation ("appropriate" referring to the register of his writing, the meaning and significance of his writing, and his social identity indexed by his writing)?

Decontextualized processes and skills flowing from other definitions of language (e.g., decontextualized knowledge of grapho-phonemic relationships, orthography, grammatical structures, etc.) emerge as varied, inseparable parts of a literacy practice (a way of using written language in a particular set of situations) no less socially constructed than any other aspect of a literacy practice. The best questions to ask about these processes center around how they are manifested as part of the literacy events in which Lamarr has participated. That is, how is "doing learning" (McDermott, 1997) socially constructed through teachers' and students' uses of language?

Figure 15.2 is also complex, given the previous definition of language. From the events immediately surrounding the production of Figure 15.2, it is reasonable to infer a connection between those events and the written text. Lamarr appears to have acquired a shared literacy practice for expressing condolences and sympathy. That he has juxtaposed his condolences with a picture seems likely to have been responsive to the classroom task; we may infer that he is demonstrating communicative competence in addressing both the classroom academic context as well as the context of personal relationships with Miss G. Given the cooperative principle of assumed relevance (Grice, 1989), the last sentence of Lamarr's composition can be viewed as also addressing his personal relationship with Miss G.; it is a comforting move. One available interpretation is that he is trying to make Miss G. feel better by documenting that her student, Lamarr himself, is "reading beter [sic]"; that is, that she has succeeded in reaching him.

Language Definitions of Language Derived from the Bakhtin Circle

The Bakhtin Circle refers to a series of scholars including Mikhail Bakhtin, V.I. Volosinov, and P.N. Medvedev, among others, who generated theories of language and literary analysis that focused on the dialogic and heteroglossic aspects of language. In part, dialogic refers to the relationship of one sign and another. Volosinov (1929/1973, p. 10) writes, "A sign does not simply exist as a part of reality—it reflects and refracts another reality." Dialogic also refers to the relationship of people to each other, "[A] word is a two-sided act. It is determined equally by whose word it is and for whom it is meant" (p. 86). Taken together, the dialogic thus provides a conception of being human as defined by social relationships and textual relationships, and is therefore inherently historical. As Bakhtin (1935/1981, pp. 276–277) writes:

The living utterance, having taken meaning and shape at a particular historical moment in a socially specific environment, cannot fail to brush up
against thousands of living dialogic threads, woven by socio-ideological
consciousness around the given object of an utterance; it cannot fail to become an active participant in social dialogue. After all, the utterance arises
out of this dialogue as a continuation of it and as a rejoinder to it—it does
not approach the object from the sidelines.

Friedman (2001) claims that Bakhtin was knowledgeable about and influenced
by the philosophies of Martin Buber on dialogue. Bakhtin is reported to have said
that Buber was the "the greatest philosopher of the twentieth century" (quoted in
Friedman, 2001, p. 25). Elsewhere, Bakhtin is quoted as saying, "I am very much
indebted to [Buber]" (Kaganskaya, p. 141, cited in Friedman, 2001). Buber's (1970)
philosophy of dialogue emphasizes an essential twofold nature of being human:

The world is twofold for man in accordance with his twofold attitude.
    The attitude of man is twofold in accordance with the two basic words
he can speak.
    The basic words are not single words but word pairs.
    One basic word is the word pair I-You.
    The other basic word is the word pair I-It; but this basic word is not
changed when He or She takes the place of It.
    Thus, the I of man is also twofold.
    For the I of the basic word I-You is different from that in the basic word
I-It.

The curricular and instructional implications of the Bakhtin Circle's and Buber's
discussion of dialogue is not an emphasis on a particular form of talk or writing
but rather on social relationships (including the relationship a person has to her/
himself) that are intertwined with and reflected (and refracted) in textual relationships. More simply stated, curriculum and instruction are always about what it
means to be a human being in the world; engaged and dialogic or alienated and
objectified.
    Returning to Lamarr's writing, both compositions reveal his relationships to
people who are close to him. Both are contextualized and reflect his family's
(his mother and himself) experiences with domestic abuse. His status as a struggling reader reflects a particular educational context that organizes people along
a continuum of a particular kind of reading practice. The connection between his
status as a struggling reader and the domestic abuse reflects a cultural ideology and
definition of personhood (i.e., students' educational progress is affected by family
experiences). The register in which Figure 15.1 is written—the use of the second
person, the formal register, the moral precept—reflects ideologies that Lamarr has
previously heard and taken on himself. The binary opposition of going to college

versus being a bum on the street reflects a naturalized ideology that has a powerful effect on what Lamarr, his teachers, and others value and on what they do. His spelling mistakes reflect a history of the standardization of English orthography and they reflect an approach to deriving spelling ("sound it out"). (Compare his effort to reproduce standard spellings to the writing practices people use in texting and tweeting which violate standard spelling frequently without negative sanction.) The relationship in Figure 15.1 would seem more so an I–It relationship; reading and college are things to acquire, and the self acquires a particular social capital depending upon which side of the binary one lands.

Figure 15.2 appears to involve two representations. The picture shows Lamarr outside capturing bees with a net; he presents himself as part of nature. The picture could reflect an I–It relationship with nature (capturing bees) or an I–You relationship where he is part of and interacting with nature (i.e., in dialogue with nature, cf., Buber, 1970). The verbal text, although occasionally formulistic ("I hop you feel beter.") reflects an emotional closeness Lamarr has with Miss G., a caring and loving relationship characterizable as an I–You relationship. It is that relationship that contextualizes the subsequent sentence ("my mom said I am reading beter!") and transforms it into the I–You relationship. As such, it refracts the ideology of schooling as decontextualized reading achievement, making it part of an I–You social relationship. It is through the verbal text that Lamarr engages in an I–You relationship with his teacher and with himself.

The theories of language discussed in this section also suggest a series of axioms for curriculum and instruction:

- The essential relationship that people have with each other, with themselves, and with nature is a dialogic and heteroglossic one.
- That dialogic relationship involves processes of reflecting and refracting what has been said, written, represented, and constructed previously through language.
- The dialogic relationship people have with each other, with themselves, and with the material world (including nature), can be characterized at times as I–It and at times as I–You.

Final Comments

The Impact conferences from the 1970s through early 1990s redefined curriculum and instruction by foregrounding definitions of language and literacy that conceptualized students as inherently active language learners who were naturally disposed to making meaning with and through language. More recent definitions of language grounded in the ethnography of communication and related social theories of language emphasize the inseparability of people from the social events and social contexts of which they are a part. Linguistic competence is supplanted by communicative competence, and literacy is redefined as diverse sets of social practices involving written language. Curriculum and instruction become a social process of engagement in those social events and social practices involving written language that define particular communities and consequently oneself. Recent discussions of language derived from the Bakhtin Circle and from Buber's philosophies have emphasized heteroglossia and dialogue not as form or genre, but as an historical, social process that contextualizes people, their relationships to each other and to themselves, and the texts they consume and produce. To return to the earlier quote from Williams (1977), what is at stake for curriculum and instruction is a definition of language about what it means to learn to be human beings in the world with others.

Note

1. We are using "particular" as used by Becker (1988).

References

Au, K. (1980). Participation structures in a reading lesson with Hawaiian children. *Anthropology and Education Quarterly*, 11, 2, 91–115.

Bakhtin, M. (1935/1981 trans.). Discourse in the novel. In M. Holquist (Ed.). *The dialogic imagination*. Austin, TX: University of Texas Press.

Becker, A. (1988). Language in particular: A lecture. In D. Tannen (Ed.). *Linguistics in context*. (pp. 17–35). Norwood, NJ: Ablex.

Bloome, D., Carter, S., Christian, B., Otto, S., Shuart-Faris, N., Madrid, S., & Smith, M. with Goldman, S., & Macbeth, D. (2009). *On discourse analysis: Studies in language and literacy*. New York: Teachers College Press.

Buber, M. (1970). *I and thou*. (W. Kaufman, trans.). New York: Touchstone.

Chomsky, N. (1957). *Syntactic structures*. The Hague: Mouton de Gruyter.

Clifford, J., & Marcus, G. (Eds.) (1986). *Writing culture: The poetics and politics of ethnography*. Berkeley, CA: University of California Press.

DeCerteau, M. (1984). *The practice of everyday life*. Berkeley, CA: University of California Press.

Dewey, J. (1902). *The child and the curriculum*. Chicago, IL: University of Chicago Press.

Erickson, F., & Mohatt, G. (1982). Cultural organization of participation structures in two classrooms of Indian students. In G. Spindler (Ed.). *Doing the ethnography of schooling: Educational anthropology in action*. (pp. 132–175). Prospect Hts., IL: Waveland Press, Inc.

Flyvbjerg, B. (2012). Why mass media matter and how to work with them: Phronesis and megaprojects. In B. Flyvbjerg, T. Landman, & S. Schram, (Eds.) *Real social science: Applied phronesis*. (pp. 95–121). New York: Cambridge University Press.

Flyvbjerg, B., Landman, T., & Schram, S. (2012). Introduction: New directions in social science. In B. Flyvbjerg, T. Landman, & S. Schram, (Eds.) *Real social science: Applied phronesis*. (pp. 1–14). New York: Cambridge University Press.

Friedman, M. (2001). Martin Buber and Mikhail Bakhtin: The dialogue of voices and the word that is spoken. *Religion & Literature*, 33, 3, 25–36.

Goodman, K. (1979). Language development: Issues, insights, and implementation. In Y. Goodman, M. Haussler, & D. Strickland (Eds.) (1980). *Oral and written language development research: Impact on the schools. Proceedings from the 1979 and 1980 IMPACT conferences sponsored by the International Reading Association and the National Council of Teachers of English.* (pp. 153–159). Newark, DE: International Reading Association.

Goodman, K., & Buck, C. (1973). Dialect barriers to reading comprehension revisited. *The Reading Teacher*, 27, 1, 6–12.

Goodman, K., & Goodman, Y. (1979). Learning to read is natural. In L.B. Resnick & P.A. Weaver (Eds.) *Theory and practice of early reading.* (pp. 137–154). Hillsdale, NJ: Erlbaum.

Goodman, Y. (1985). Kidwatching: Observing children in the classroom. In A. Jaggar & M.T. Smith-Burke (Eds.) *Observing the language learner.* (pp. 9–18). Newark, DE: International Reading Association.

Goodman, Y., Haussler, M., & Strickland, D. (Eds.) (1980). *Oral and written language development research: Impact on the schools. Proceedings from the 1979 and 1980 IMPACT conferences sponsored by the International Reading Association and the National Council of Teachers of English.* Newark, DE: International Reading Association.

Green, J. (1983). Exploring classroom discourse: Linguistic perspectives on teaching-learning processes. *Educational Psychologist*, 18, 3, 180–199.

Grice, H.P. (1989). *Studies in the way of words.* Cambridge, MA: Harvard University Press.

Halliday, M.A.K. (1978). *Language as social semiotic.* London: Edward Arnold.

Halliday, M.A.K. (1993). Towards a language-based theory of learning. *Linguistics and Education*, 5, 2, 93–116.

Heath, S. (1982). What no bedtime story means: Narrative skills at home and at school. *Language in Society*, 11, 1, 49–76.

Hymes, D. (1974). *The foundations of sociolinguistics: Sociolinguistic ethnography.* Philadelphia, PA: University of Pennsylvania Press.

Jaggar, A., & Smith-Burke, M.T. (Eds.) (1985). *Observing the language learner.* Newark, DE: International Reading Association, and Urbana, IL: National Council of Teachers of English.

Lee, C. (2007). *Culture, literacy, and learning: Taking bloom in the midst of the whirlwind.* New York: Teachers College Press.

Lefebvre, H. (2009). *Everyday life in the modern world.* New Brunswick, NJ: Transaction Press.

Luke, A. (1988). The non-neutrality of literacy instruction: A critical introduction. *Australian Journal of Reading*, 11, 2, 79–83.

McDermott, R. (1977). Social relations as contexts for learning in school. *Harvard Educational Review*, 47, 2, 198–213.

Martin-Jones, M., de Mejia, A-M., & Hornberger, N. (2008). *Discourse and education: Encyclopedia of Language and Education (Vol. 3).* New York: Springer.

Moss, G. (2012). Literacy policy and English/literacy practice: Researching the interaction between different knowledge fields. *English Teaching: Practice and Critique*, 11, 1, 104–120.

Philips, S. (1983). *Invisible culture: Communication in classroom and community on the Warm Springs Indian Reservation.* New York: Longman.

Rex, L.A., Bunn, M., Davila, B.A., Dickinson, H.A., Ford, A.C., Gerben, C., Orzulak, M.J.M., & Thomson, H. (2010). A review of discourse analysis in literacy research: Equitable access. *Reading Research Quarterly*, 45, 94–115.

Scollon, R., & Scollon, S. (1981). *Narrative/literacy and face in interethnic communication.* Norwood, NJ: Ablex Publishing Corporation.

Street, B. (1995a). Academic literacies. In D. Baker, C. Fox, & J. Clay (Eds.). *Challenging ways of knowing in maths, science and English.* Brighton: Falmer Press.

Street, B. (1995b). *Social literacies: Critical approaches to literacy in development, ethnography and education.* London: Longman.

Street, B. (2003). What's "new" in New Literacy Studies? Critical approaches to literacy in theory and practice. *Current Issues in Comparative Education,* 5, 2: 77–91.

Volosinov, V. (1929/1973 trans.). *Marxism and the philosophy of language.* (trans. L. Matejka & I. Titunik). Cambridge, MA: Harvard University Press.

Williams, R. (1977). *Marxism and literature.* Oxford: Oxford University Press.

Yeager, B., Floriani, A., & Green, J. (1998). Learning to see learning in the classroom. In A. Egan-Robertson & D. Bloome (Eds.). *Students as researchers of culture and language in their own communities.* Cresskill, NJ: Hampton Press.

Yeats, W.B. (1968). Among schoolchildren. In A. Norman Jeffares (Ed.). *W.B. Yeats: Selected Poetry: 127–130.* London: Macmillan.

COMMENTS

Nu! . . . So! . . . Where Do We Go From Here?

Yetta M. Goodman

This book began with discussion among members of the Reading Hall of Fame about their frustration over how political agendas have taken over government literacy policies while a strong base of knowledge about literacy is being ignored or marginalized. The writers in this book have devoted their professional lives to producing this knowledge. It is sad and perhaps tragic that learners are being denied the benefits of the best knowledge available. Clearly it is not enough to produce knowledge if it is ignored by decision makers.

So in my comments I want to talk about what we, the researchers and literacy educators, need to do together with parents, teachers, and concerned citizens to change what has happened to literacy education.

In this book, some authors address the central question—"whose knowledge counts?"—directly, while others draw on their scholarship to share the results of their years of engagement with literacy teaching, and learning. Together, we who have devoted ourselves to understanding literacy need to be advocates for access to sensible informed literacy programs for all students.

The authors have varying perspectives, but they have in common concern for comprehension, the complexity of the literacy processes, the interrelationships among reading and writing, the text and the reader, and understandings about the social and cultural aspects in studies of literacy and learning literacy. Other areas of general agreement include the central role of teachers in curriculum development (Flippo, 2012) and the important role readers and writers have in their own learning as a result of rich literacy opportunities.

Professional education is not the only field of research that is concerned about the place of knowledge in the decision making of nations. Philip Yam, managing editor of *Scientific American*, in his September 22, 2012 blog, voices his concerns from the field of climate science:

Groups that advocate scientific reasoning, such as CSICOP and the Skeptical Society, have long tried to combat paranormal and pseudoscience beliefs and claims. But the fight has been a slog. When I interviewed CSICOP founder Paul Kurtz in 1996, he said that "we thought that if you just provide information, people would reject" paranormal thinking. Clearly, that hasn't worked. "The problem is more massive and complicated than we imagined," he lamented. Climate scientists face a similar challenge.

It obviously takes more than knowledge, research, and evidence for decision making to influence governmental policies. It takes political sophistication and actions. Each concerned educator, parent, and citizen and our professional and civic organizations need to take visible stands on issues such as high stakes testing and teacher evaluation. And professionals need to see our expertise, abilities and educational leadership to communicate beyond our professional communities to parents, teachers and the public and demand that governmental and policy groups act on the basis of the best knowledge.

We must all support classroom teachers to act as informed professionals to use their expertise to make instructional decisions on behalf of their students, and to support them in resisting harmful mandates. Those with knowledge need to inform parents as they advocate for their children about the misuse of standardized tests, and about methods and materials that are developmentally inappropriate and unsupported by the best knowledge. We need to help parents support teachers who know how to involve their students in authentic literacy experiences as they inquire in excited ways about their learning. We can partner with parents to influence politicians concerning decisions about curriculum and testing. We also need to support groups within professional organizations who are working to advance professional knowledge.

I have selected several issues raised in the chapters that are concerned with *the knowledge that counts*. As we collaborate we can challenge policy makers to consider knowledge over political agendas in their decision making.

Issue 1: Economic Inequality and Access to Education

We need to raise the issues of worldwide poverty in the development of educational reform, especially at a time when poverty, at least in the U.S., is being downplayed as a national educational problem. David Berliner (2012, p. 7) cautions that:

> Ignoring the powerful and causal role of inequality and poverty on so many social outcomes that we value . . . , particularly school achievement, is easily as shameful as having educators use poverty as an excuse to limit what they do to help the students and families that their schools serve.

Berliner explores the role that "inequality in wealth and poverty play in determining many of the social outcomes that we value for our youth . . . America's youth score remarkably high if they are in schools where less than 10 percent of the children were eligible for free and reduced lunch" (pp. 2, 5). And "some American students do well" even in schools that have poverty rates up to 49.9 percent of economically poor children (p. 6).

Emilia Ferreiro (2003, p. 16) sees poverty as a global issue in her essays on literacy:

> Poor countries have not overcome illiteracy, while rich countries have discovered "functional illiteracy." . . . There are countries that have illiterate people because they don't provide a minimum of basic schooling to all inhabitants, and countries that have functional illiterates because, despite guaranteeing the minimum of schooling, they haven't produced readers in the full sense of the word.

A recent television program reported on the positive results of a New York University/Bellevue Hospital study about their Reach Out & Read program promoting literacy as a component of primary pediatric care (www.reachoutandreadnyc. org). The medical and psychiatric care of economically poor children and families would benefit from *knowledge that counts* if we reached out to them with our expertise, time, and effort. And decision makers must attend to the agreements and collaborations among professionals from various disciplines working to alleviate the effects of poverty.

Issue 2: Intergenerational and Family Literacy

Tom Sticht asserts that effective adult literacy programs integrating with early childhood programs would break the pattern of intergenerational literacy histories (Sticht, et al., 1992). Denny Taylor (1997) highlights the roles of family literacy in the literacy development of children throughout the world. Helping parents and family members value themselves as children's first literacy teachers provides avenues for parents and teachers to collaborate in successful literacy learning experiences for their children (Endrizzi, 2008).

When I work with tutors in Literacy Volunteers of Tucson, we discuss the possibilities of using children's literature in English and the native language of their adult students to read to and with their children. It is surprising to them that such experiences enhance the reading growth of both the adults and their children and at the same time expand the concept of literacy as a social, cultural phenomenon to new levels of understanding. The professional literacy community should be leading the way to bring the knowledge we have about children's literacy learning to parent and community groups, and to encourage related literacy programs (family, adult, intergenerational and early literacy development) with related academic units to discuss collaborations that would support literacy reforms in schools and universities, especially when decisions are being made about disseminating meagre literacy research monies.

Issue 3: Support for Teachers

Research by teacher education experts such as Linda Darling-Hammond make clear that well educated, knowledgeable and experienced teachers are *the essential elements* that make a difference in the academic achievement of students and in the development of a rich curriculum that engages students with diverse interests and backgrounds (Darling-Hammond & Young, 2002). Literacy researchers need to collaborate more fully and effectively to support teachers as informed professionals who make use of the *knowledge that counts* for the development of an inquiry oriented and relevant literacy curriculum.

Researchers who have spent years studying classrooms report eloquently about the importance of teacher knowledge, and how much they learned as a result of their involvement with classroom professionals (Short & Harste, 1996). The research of classroom literacy learning documents the success of powerful educational environments in which teachers and students come together to negotiate curriculum to motivate students and engage them in their own learning (Calfee & Perfumo, 1996). We need to be champions for articulate and knowledgeable classroom teachers and school administrators, whose input should be more highly valued than politicians and business leaders in making decisions that impact and control the environments in which teachers and students work and learn.

We need to make successful classrooms visible to parents and community members. The use of digital technologies for disseminating the stories of classrooms and classroom teachers can take great teaching and exciting learning experiences from classroom settings to the wider public.

Issue 4: Abusive Testing

We need to establish the concept among politicians, business leaders and the general public that, although standardized testing measures provide information for comparisons among countries, states and other political units, they do not provide the information that teachers need to develop innovative curriculum and that parents need to value their children's literacy growth. Because of the ease with which standardized, high stakes tests can be completed and results made available, politicians continue to rely on such measures.

Issue 5: A Rich and Challenging Curriculum

Again, there is general agreement that in-depth and qualitative descriptions of students and classrooms provide research that highlights the influences of a rich literacy curriculum on students that can be used to plan specific instruction for individual students and provide the social opportunities for classroom discussions and interactions that also influence literacy growth.

The Washington Post recently reported the lack of attention by politicians in Chicago and New York to letters and petitions written by professors, teachers, and researchers raising questions about the research efficacy of a teacher evaluation system based on student test scores (Strauss, 2012). Many teacher accountability measures are based on misconceptions about literacy development, and lead to methods for assessing teacher accountability that can harm students.

It all comes down to the literacy research community organizing itself to highlight the knowledge that counts in significant ways for those who are in powerful decision-making venues, and ensure that knowledgeable professionals are involved directly in the decision making. The knowledge represented in this book makes clear the richness of the research and teaching in literacy. We need to work collaboratively to expand that knowledge to wider circles of stake holders, to deal with the situations eloquently portrayed by Emelia Ferriero (2003, p. 56):

> The real challenge is that of growing inequality, for the chasm that separates the illiterate from the literate has grown ever wider. Some have no news-papers, books or libraries, while others are flying with hypertext, email and virtual pages of nonexistent books. Will we be capable of coming up with policies on access to books that can be something to reverse this grow-ing inequality? Or will we let ourselves get carried away by the vortex of competitiveness and profitability, even though the very idea of participatory democracy perishes in the process.

References

Berliner, D. (2013). Sorting out the effects of inequality and poverty, teachers and schooling on America's youth. In Nichols, S.L. (Ed.) (2013). *Educational policy and the socialization of youth for the 21st century*. New York: Teachers College Press.

Calfee, R., & Perfumo, P. (1996). *Writing portfolio in the classroom: Policy and practice, promise and peril*. Mahway, NJ: Lawrence Erlbaum Associates.

Darling-Hammond, L., & Young, P. (2002). Defining "highly qualified teachers": What does "scientifically-based research" actually tell us? *Educational Researcher*, 31, 9: 13–25.

Endrizzi, C. (2008). *Becoming teammates: Teachers and families as literacy partners*. Urbana, IL: National Council of Teachers of English.

Ferreiro, E. (2003). *Past and present of the verbs to read and to write*. M. Fried (trans.). Toronto, Canada: Groundwood Books.

Flippo, R. (2012). *Reading researchers in search of common ground: The expert study revisited.* New York: Taylor & Francis.

Short K., & Harste, J. (1996). *Creating classrooms for authors and inquirers.* Portsmouth, NH: Heinemann.

Sticht, T., Beeler, M., & McDonald, B. (Eds.) (1992). *The intergenerational transfer of cognitive skills* (2 vols). Norwood, NJ: Ablex.

Strauss, V. (2012). Researchers blast Chicago teacher evaluation reform. *Washington Post*, March 28.

Taylor, D. (Ed.) (1997). *Many families, many literacies.* Portsmouth, NH: Heinemann.

Yam, P. (2012). Fox news distorts climate science; In other news, the Pope is Catholic. September 22. Available at: www.scientificamerican.com

LIST OF CONTRIBUTORS

Kathryn H. Au, SchoolRise LLC, Honolulu, Hawaii, United States

Rudine Sims Bishop, The Ohio State University, Columbus, Ohio, United States

David Bloome, The Ohio State University, Columbus, Ohio, United States

Robert C. Calfee, Stanford University, Stanford, California, United States

Henrietta Dombey, University of Brighton, Brighton, United Kingdom

Sue Ellis, University of Strathclyde, Glasgow, Scotland, United Kingdom

Jacques Fijalkow, Université de Toulouse-le-Mirail, Toulouse, France

Kenneth S. Goodman, University of Arizona, Tucson, Arizona, United States

Yetta M. Goodman, University of Arizona, Tucson, Arizona, United States

Jane Hansen, University of Virginia, Charlottesville, Virginia, United States

Elfrieda H. Hiebert, TextProject and University of California, Santa Cruz, California, United States

Jessica L. Hoffman, Miami University, Miami, Ohio, United States

Judith A. Langer, State University of New York at Albany, Albany, New York, United States

Kathleen A. Paciga, Purdue University at Calumet, Hammond, Indiana, United States

Taffy E. Raphael, University of Illinois at Chicago, Chicago, Illinois, United States

Patrick Shannon, Pennsylvania State University, University Park, Pennsylvania, United States

Kathy G. Short, University of Arizona, Tucson, Arizona, United States

Joel Spring, Queens College and Graduate Center, City University of New York, New York, United States

William H. Teale, University of Illinois at Chicago Circle, Chicago, Illinois, United States

Renate Valtin, Humboldt University, Berlin, Germany

Katie Van Sluys, DePaul University, Chicago, Illinois, United States

Melissa Wilson, Columbus Area Writing Project, The Ohio State University, Columbus, Ohio, United States

INDEX

Note: 'T' after a page number indicates a table.

Löffler, I. 101, 102
Luke, A. 70, 75, 190
Lundberg, I. 96, 100
Lyon, R. 3, 9

Macrorie, K. 170, 171
Mandelbaum, P. 120
Manhattan Institute 26
Manzo, K.K. 8, 29
Marcus, G. 190
Marsh, G. 101
Martin-Jones, M. 194
Martschinke, S. 96
Marx, P. 97, 104
Maurois, P. 49
May, P. 97
Mayer, A. 95, 96
McDermott, R. 195
McGuiness, D. 9
McQuillian, J. 152
media: literacy research interpreted by
    87–8; negative focus of, on public
    schools 26–8, 114
medical research 82, 87
Medwell, J. 69, 70
Meier, D. 181
Meltzer, M. 116
memory 116
Mermelstein, L. 171
Meyer-Schepers, U. 102
Miller, G. 26, 29–30
Mineo, R.J. 101
minorities: and literacy achievement gap
    179; and literacy education in Africa
    180t
Moffett, J. 170
Mohatt, G. 193
Moss, G. 82, 190
movement conservatism. *See* conservative
    movement
Mullis, I. 145, 152
multiculturalism 141, 174–5
multinational corporations 22–3, 90
Murata, K. 150
Murray, C. 42
Murray, D. 169

NAEP. *See* National Assessment of
    Educational Progress (NAEP)
National Academy of Science 7
National Assessment of Educational
    Progress (NAEP) 132, 162, 179
National Council for Teachers of English 14

National Institute of Child Health and
    Human Development (NICHD) 3
National Reading Panel (NRP):
    challenges to 7; as part of conservative
    movement to privatize education
    28; Pressley on 7–8; as proponent of
    Reading First (RF) program 1–2
National Reading Panel (NRP) Report:
    focus on phonemic awareness in
    11; focus on phonics in 3–4, 9–11;
    lack of science in 8; phonics and
    reading comprehension in 4; on
    Reading First (RF) program 6;
    recommendations of 3–4
Nation's Report Card 179, 180t
NCLB. *See* No Child Left Behind Act
    (NCLB) (2002)
Nelson, J. 146, 154
neoconservatism 48
neoliberalism 48
Newmann, F.M. 129, 134
New York Times 139
NICHD. *See* National Institute of Child
    Health and Human Development
    (NICHD)
Nisbett, R. 41
No Child Left Behind Act (NCLB)
    (2002): as attack on literacy education
    24–5; and evidence-based research 80;
    as federalization of literacy research
    1; overview of 141; Ravitch as
    opponent of 22
Norman, K.A. 9
NRP. *See* National Reading Panel
    (NRP)
Nutt, D. 83

Obama, Barack 26–7
Okwumo, S. 97
Olson, D.R. 99
Openshaw, R. 82
Orr, J. 163, 165
Orshansky, M. 38
Owocki, G. 6

PA. *See* phonemic and phonological
    awareness (PA)
Palacio, R.J. 123
Park, L.S. 120, 123
Paterson, K. 125
Payne, C. 44
Payne, R. 42
Pearson, P.D. 8, 69, 148, 154, 181